Love and Lies

Also by Clancy Martin

Love and Lies

AN ESSAY ON

TRUTHFULNESS, DECEIT,

AND THE GROWTH AND CARE

OF EROTIC LOVE

Clancy Martin

FARRAR, STRAUS AND GIROUX   NEW YORK

Farrar, Straus and Giroux
18 West 18th Street, New York 10011

Portions of this book have previously appeared, in different form, in *The Chronicle of Higher Education*, *The Faster Times*, *Guernica*, *Gulf Coast*, *Humana Mente*, *Lincoln Center Theater Review*, *The New Yorker*, *NOON*, and *The Paris Review Daily*, and as part of the Great Courses lecture series Moral Decision Making: How to Approach Everyday Ethics.

Grateful acknowledgment is made for permission to reprint the following material:
An excerpt from *Being and Nothingness*, by Jean-Paul Sartre, translated by Hazel Barnes (New York: Philosophical Library, 1956). Reprinted by agreement with Kensington Publishing Corp. All Rights Reserved.
"Disparu," from *Red Shoes* by Honor Moore. Copyright © 2005 by Honor Moore. Used by permission of W. W. Norton & Company, Inc.
An excerpt from "Thoughts on Conjugal Love" by Eric Schwitzgebel, courtesy of Eric Schwitzgebel.

Library of Congress Cataloging-in-Publication Data
Martin, Clancy W.
    Love and lies : an essay on truthfulness, deceit, and the growth and care of erotic love / Clancy Martin. — First edition.
        pages   cm
    ISBN 978-0-374-28106-9 (cloth) — ISBN 978-1-4299-4594-3 (ebook)
    1. Deception.   2. Self-deception.   3. Truthfulness and falsehood.
    4. Love.   I. Title.

BJ1421 .M28 2015
177'.3—dc23

                                                                              2014023447

Designed by Abby Kagan

www.fsgbooks.com
www.twitter.com/fsgbooks • www.facebook.com/fsgbooks

10   9   8   7   6   5   4   3   2   1

For my parents:

Anna Victoria Moody

John William Martin (1940–1997)

Lie to me
I promise, I'll believe
Lie to me
But please don't leave.
      —Sheryl Crow

Contents

Love and Lies

Prologue: Why I Wrote This Book

My wife, Amie, and I were lying in bed that morning, being lazy and reading. It was a Monday morning, so we both should have been up working, but we weren't ready for the weekend to be over. We were in Iowa City—my wife was at the Writers' Workshop—and spring had arrived at last. It was lovely with the tulips and the swollen river and the very sudden arrival of such a late spring. I had just finished a book, and she was in the middle of hers. "Okay, I'm getting up," I said, and she said, "No, let's stay in bed a little longer," and dug another book out of the big tin steamer—a kind of old sailor's trunk—that she keeps at the end of the bed. She gave me the book. It was William Maxwell's *So Long, See You Tomorrow*. I knew about his reputation as an editor but, I am a bit embarrassed to admit, had never read any of his writing. I didn't want to read the book because I did not know its name and something about the title bothered me. Also, I sometimes have the stupid, arrogant idea that if I have not heard of a book, it's probably not very good.

The book opens with the account of a shooting. Then Maxwell's narrator goes back to his own childhood, which was very much like my own—bookish, the middle of three brothers, raised by his own parent and a stepparent he could never accept. His narrator seemed to understand that feeling of confusion that characterized my own childhood. I was drawn into the book; I had that exhilarating feeling—the best feeling we can get, perhaps, from reading—of encountering a long-lost friend, someone whom I would never meet (Maxwell died in 2000, at the age of ninety-two), but who saw the world through eyes similar to my own, who felt some of the things I had felt; I had that feeling of being not so alone in the world as I was before I opened the book. Then I came to this passage:

> What we, or at any rate what I, refer to confidently as memory—meaning a moment, a scene, a fact that has been subjected to a fixative and thereby rescued from oblivion—is really a form of storytelling that goes on continually in the mind and often changes with the telling. Too many conflicting emotional interests are involved for life ever to be wholly acceptable, and possibly it is the work of the storyteller to rearrange things so that they conform to this end. In any case, in talking about the past we lie with every breath we draw.

"Listen to this," I said to my wife, and read it to her.

"Well, maybe you guys lie about the past," she said, "but not me." She is a very intelligent, very funny person, my wife.

There are many books, like Maxwell's *So Long, See You Tomorrow*, or Marguerite Duras's *The Lover*, or Stendhal's *Love*, that may in a more artistic way capture what I try to say in a more analytical way here in this little book of my own. One way of restating my own thesis would be to say, with Maxwell: "In talking about love we lie with every breath we draw." But obviously for Maxwell and me talking about the past and talking about love are also how we get to the truth of things. Talking about the past, like talking about love, is not so much lying as it is trying to tell a story that must be told and cannot be told any other way—telling the truth, but telling it slant, as Emily Dickinson famously recommends. Perhaps the truth we are trying to get at could be told in many different ways, none of which would be nakedly factual. In any case, what we mean by "telling the truth" is itself much more complicated than we normally pretend it to be, particularly when we're talking about the past and about love.

Furthermore, for most of us, we can't talk about love without also talking about our pasts. In this prologue and throughout this book, I will be talking about my past in order both to illustrate how I came to be fascinated with the interconnections of love and lying and to provide concrete examples of the arguments I make: to provide grist for the philosophical mill. Consequently, this book is part memoir, part self-psychoanalytic analysis, part philosophical argument, and, because many of the most fascinating lovers are in literature, part literary criticism. Here and there a little science also finds its way in, because much of the most interesting recent research on deception is being done in experiments and laboratories.

When I was twelve or so, my mother found some *Penthouse* magazines under my bed. When she confronted me with them, I lied, and said: "Dad gave them to me." I had recently returned from his home in Miami—we lived in Calgary, Alberta—and it was a plausible fib.

When my mother called my father to confront him, he said, "Clancy has some difficulty when it comes to the truth."

"Well, at least he comes by it honestly," my mother said, and hung up on him.

My father was a great storyteller. So is my mother, and for a long time I believed both of their stories were true, even when they disagreed. It was perhaps for this reason that it was natural to me when, later in life, I encountered the philosophers Søren Kierkegaard and Friedrich Nietzsche, both of whom argue that truth is a matter of one's perspective, that not only will different people see the truth differently but also the truth itself may vary from person to person. This way of thinking about truth doesn't work very well with statements like "$7 + 5 = 12$"; it looks as though we'd all better agree about the truth of that claim, if we understand the claim at all. But it works much better with statements like "We were meant to be together, son" or "Your father and I were never happy" or "I'll never love another woman" or "The marriage could never work" or "That was the best year we ever had." Statements that we genuinely care about, in short, are the ones in which their truth looks as if it were involved with the perspective of the narrator. "Subjectivity is truth," Kierkegaard provocatively wrote, under a pseudonym (thus showing that he was speaking from a particular perspective); what I sometimes think he intended by this was "Subjectivity is *meaning*." My perspective, my truth, is inextricably bound up with what I find to be meaningful.

When I say, for example, that it's true that I love my daughters or that I love my wife, I couldn't attempt to specify the truth conditions that govern that claim. I can't point to the truth of it in the way that I can point to the truth that "The apple is on the table." Furthermore, the fact that I love them seems to be an importantly different kind of fact from the fact that the apple is on the table. That the apple is on the table is fundamentally a matter of indifference to me. It's the sort of fact that is easily demonstrated to be true, but I don't care that much about it, even if I'm hungry. That I love my children and my wife is the kind of fact that is of the utmost importance to me. But it's also the sort of fact that is private to me, though naturally I hope they know it too. And it would be difficult, perhaps impossible to "prove" that I love them in the way I could prove that the apple is on the table. The truth or fact of my love is subjective; the truth or fact of the

apple's being on the table is objective. The crucial difference between the two sorts of facts is that my love for my wife and children is part of the world of those truths that matter most to me,
that give my life meaning, that define who I am and how I in-
habit the world. And I am involved with those facts or truths in
an active way, in which I am not particularly involved with the
fact about the apple. If I die today, my love for my wife and my
children goes with me, but that darned apple stays right where it
is. This requirement of my active participation with the truth of
my love is part of why it is meaningful to me; it is also part of why
that kind of truth—the truth of my love—is much more complex,
slippery, and interesting than the usual sort of truth or fact.

Here's a story from early in my first marriage (I've been married three times) that will help illustrate just how complicated
and tricky these sorts of subjective truths are. Again, I want to
emphasize that these subjective truths are the most important
sorts of truths for us.

It was a spring afternoon in Nazaré, a little fishing town on
the Portuguese coast. I was vacationing with my first wife. We'd
been married for about a year and were living in Copenhagen. I
was trying to write a dissertation on Kierkegaard's *The Concept
of Irony* but was in fact just going to the Royal Library every day
and turning the delicate pages of two-hundred-year-old manu-
scripts that, despite my years of studying Danish, I couldn't really
read. I took notes for a book that would never be written. But
we'd decided to get away, and Portugal was cheap then, and it was
a sunny break from the dreary weather of Denmark in March.

We'd taken a funicular—a little, meticulously crafted mahogany car on narrow train tracks and cables, with old cracked-
leather seats and windows that louvered open—up the side of the
mountain to a peak. We stood near the edge of the cliff, holding
hands, and watched the waves breaking against the rocks hundreds

of feet below. Then the funicular man gestured, we saw the sky—enormous black thunderheads were coming in swiftly from the sea—and all of us, a dozen or so, maybe fewer, crowded back into the funicular for the ride down. The storm broke. The little car rocked in the rain; we closed the windows. We laughed and cried out as the lightning struck. At the bottom we all ran down the cobblestoned, high-curbed seaport streets for our little hotels or guesthouses—it was out of season, and the one big hotel was closed—and my wife and I accidentally passed our house.

"Let's get something to eat!" I shouted—we both were soaking wet, and the pouring warm rain, heavy as standing in the shower, was rushing down the streets higher than our ankles—and we ran, still holding hands, down almost to the beach, where we saw a light under an awning and a tiny restaurant crowded with Portuguese. It was not much larger than a large hotel room, and they squeezed us in on one of the benches and brought us bread and red wine. Almost everyone was wet, but it was warm from the bodies. They brought us huge bowls of fish stew. The main fish in the stew was entire; it still had its head, tail, and eyes. The room was smoky from cooking and lit with candles. We couldn't understand what people were saying or laughing about. The stew was too fishy for me, but I ate it, and I looked up at my wife, thinking, "This is the most romantic moment in my life. It will never be more romantic than this." Her face was twisted into that sad frown she used to make, and when she saw me looking into her eyes, she started to cry. "I don't want this stew. I want to go home," she said. I waved the woman over—she was cooking in plain sight—and paid our check. She was worried that we didn't like the stew, and I gulped down my wine and tried to explain that we were just wet and tired.

This event meant more to me than a simple miscommunication between a young husband and wife, and helps illustrate what

Kierkegaard means by the claim that "Subjectivity is truth" or I mean by "Subjectivity is meaning." My experience of that rainstorm in Portugal was that it was one of the most intensely romantic experiences of my life, until I abruptly realized that my wife was experiencing it entirely differently. In his *Discourse on the Passion of Love* Pascal puts the same point nicely: "A true or false pleasure can equally fill the mind. For what matters it that this pleasure is false, if we are persuaded that it is true?"

Both experiences, both the romance and the disappointment that followed it, had their unique truthfulness. I still nostalgically remember that rocking funicular and that run down the flooding cobblestoned streets. When I talk to my ex-wife about it now, she also remembers it as a beautiful moment in our early marriage (she has entirely forgotten the fish stew incident). And I also will never forget how intensely close I felt to my wife, until I suddenly, vertiginously understood how far apart, at that moment, our experience actually was. Then the whole event took on a new meaning. None of the "facts" of the afternoon had changed, but the way it mattered to me, the meaning of it all, its "truth," was fundamentally altered.

That sounds solipsistic, and it should: we can never get all the way inside each other's heads, no matter how much we love each other. Interestingly, much of the story I tell here will illustrate that love is simply the long journey we make from our early identification with another human being (usually a parent, commonly our mothers) to the recognition that we are fundamentally separate from others and our subsequent creative attempts to return to that state of union. To love is to try to transcend the boundaries of our own minds. It seems like an impossible project, and yet we manage to accomplish it over and over again. How we do it, and that it requires not only truthfulness but also deception and self-deception, are the subject of this book. In fact, every time you lie, like every time you love, you are engaged in a kind of projection of your own mind into another's.

But let me be honest, there's more to my interest in love and deception than my philosophical fascination with the subject. I've long had a practical interest in deception because I spent seven years of my life as a professional liar.

Ever since I was a kid, I'd struggled with telling the truth. But the jewelry business was my graduate school in the dark arts of confabulation, prevarication, secrecy, and misdirection.

Here's that story. A few months after the trip to Portugal, I decided to drop out of graduate school and join my older brother as partner in his luxury jewelry store. When I did it, I decided to burn all my bridges. I didn't fill out any forms. I didn't have the ordinary courtesy even to contact my two dissertation directors, Robert C. Solomon and Louis H. Mackey. I simply vanished.

I told myself that it was a conscious strategy, to prevent myself from going back, but I also knew the truth: that I was simply too ashamed to tell them that I had gone into business for the money. Like many of our deceptions—both of ourselves and of others—mine was motivated by cowardice: "Tell the people what they want to hear," or if you can't do that, simply don't tell them anything at all.

A few years later my next-door neighbor (my first wife and I had just moved in) caught me in the driveway and asked, "Hey, Clancy. Did you go to grad school at the University of Texas?"

"I did, that's right." I was already uncomfortable. I opened the door of my convertible. The Texas summer sun frowned cruelly down on me.

"I'm an editor of Bob Solomon's. He told me to say hello."

Busted. This was Solomon's way of calling me on my bullshit.

It was his personal and philosophical motto, adopted from Sartre: "No excuses!" Take responsibility for your actions. Above all, avoid bad faith. Look at yourself in the mirror and accept—if possible, embrace—the person that you are.

But I was on my way to the jewelry store, and Bob Solomon, at that point in my life, was the least of my problems. I had him stored neatly in the mental safety-deposit box of "people I had not lied to but had betrayed in a related way."

I often think, now, of that decision to leave graduate school to go into the jewelry business. Being a professor, I have since learned, plays to my strengths: curiosity, the love of reading and writing, storytelling. Selling jewelry, by contrast, played to all my weaknesses, because the jewelry business depends on the art of creating illusions. The vast majority of jewelry has no inherent value; the salesperson must create the perception of value. It is, in this way and in many others, a business that encourages deception. I used deception to take the easy way out of selling. I was too eager to please my customers. When we were in trouble with the bank, there was always some lie I could invent to sell my way into a quick deal and easy cash from one of my regulars. I was miserable most of the time, but I told myself that this was how business was done.

The jewelry business—like many other businesses, especially those that depend on selling—lends itself to lies. (I should add that my brothers, both in the jewelry business today, are two of the most scrupulously honest people I know.) It's hard to make money selling used Rolexes as what they are, but if you clean one up and make it look new, suddenly there's a little profit in the deal. Grading diamonds is in many ways a matter of opinion, and the better a diamond looks to you when you're grading it, the more money it's worth—as long as you can convince your customer that it's the grade you're selling it as. Here's an easy, effective way to do that: first lie to yourself about what grade the diamond is;

then you can sincerely tell your customer "the truth" about what it's worth.

As I would tell my salespeople, if you want to be an expert deceiver, master the art of self-deception. People will believe you when they see that you yourself are deeply convinced. It sounds difficult to do, but in fact it's easy; we are already experts at lying to ourselves. We believe just what we want to believe. And the customer will help in this process because she or he wants the diamond—where else can I get such a good deal on such a high-quality stone?—to be a certain size and quality. The customer wants to believe just as much as the salesperson does. At the same time, he or she does not want to pay the price that the actual diamond, were it what you claimed it to be, would cost. The transaction is a collaboration of lies and self-deceptions.

Pretend you are selling a piece of jewelry, a useless thing, small, easily lost, that is also grossly expensive. I, your customer, wander into the store. Pretend to be polishing the showcases. Watch to see what is catching my eye. Stand back; let me prowl a bit. I will come back to a piece or two; something will draw me. You wait for and then seize the moment when you recognize the spark of allure—all great selling is a form of seduction. Now make your approach. Take a bracelet from the showcase that is near, but not too near, the piece I am interested in. Admire it; polish it with a gold cloth; comment quietly, appraisingly on it. You're still ignoring me, your customer. Now, almost as though talking to yourself, take the piece I like from the showcase: "Now this is a piece of jewelry. I love this piece." Suddenly you see me there. "Isn't this a beautiful thing? The average person wouldn't even notice this. But if you're in the business, if you really know what to look for, a piece like this is why people wear fine jewelry. This is what a connoisseur looks for." If it's a gold rope chain, a stainless steel Rolex, or something else very common and mundane, you'll have to finesse the line a bit.

From there it's easy. Use a mixture of the several kinds of lies Aristotle identified in *Nicomachean Ethics*: a good blend of subtle flattery, understatement, humorous boastfulness, playful storytelling, and gentle irony will establish that "you're one of us, and I'm one of you." We are alike; we are friends; we can trust each other.

The problem is, once lying to your customer as a way of doing business becomes habitual, it reaches like a weed into other areas of your business and then into your personal life. Soon the instrument of pleasing people becomes the goal of pleasing people. For example, who *wouldn't* want to buy a high-quality one-carat diamond for just three thousand dollars? (Such a diamond would cost forty-five hundred to ten thousand, retail, depending on where you bought it.) But you can't make a profit selling that diamond for three thousand dollars; you can't even buy one wholesale for that amount. Since the customer can't tell the difference anyway, why not make your profit and please the customer by simply misrepresenting the merchandise? "But that's deceptive trade! There are laws against that!" There's a body of federal law, in fact: the Uniform Deceptive Trade Practices Act. Texas awards triple damages plus attorney's fees to the successful plaintiff. "Aren't you worried about criminal—or at least civil—consequences? And how do you look at yourself in the mirror before you go to bed at night?"

During my bleakest days in business, when I felt like taking a Zen monk's vow of silence so that not a single lie would escape my lips, I often took a long lunch and drove to a campus—Southern Methodist University, Texas Christian University, the University of Texas at Arlington—to see the college kids outside, reading books or holding hands or kissing in the sunshine or hurrying to class, and to reassure myself that there was a place where life made sense, where people were happy and thinking about something other than profit, where people still believed that truth mattered and were even in pursuit of it. (Yes, I was a bit naive about academic life.)

I was in the luxury jewelry business for nearly seven years, and though I don't believe in the existence of a soul, exactly, I came to understand what people mean when they say you are losing your soul. The lies I told in my business life migrated. Soon I was lying to my wife. The habit of telling people what they wanted to hear became the easiest way to navigate my way through any day. They don't call it the cold, hard truth without reason: flattering falsehoods are like a big, expensive comforter.

It seemed that I could do what I wanted without ever suffering the consequences of my actions, as long as I created the appearance that people wanted to see. It took intellectual effort. I grew skinnier. I needed more and more cocaine to keep all my lies straight. And then, one morning, I realized that I had been standing in the "executive bathroom" (reserved for my brother and me) at the marble sink before a large gilt Venetian mirror every morning for days, with my Glock in my mouth. I still remember the oily taste of that barrel. Before I confronted the fact that I was trying to kill myself, I had probably put that gun in my mouth, oh, I don't know, twenty, thirty times. I said, "Enough."

I called my old mentor Robert C. Solomon. That was in May 2000.

I was relieved when he didn't answer his phone. I left a message. "I'm sorry, Dr. Solomon. I'd like to come back to graduate school." Words to that effect, but at much greater length. I think the beep cut me off.

When he called back, I was too frightened to pick up. I listened to his voice mail message. He said, "Clancy, this is not a good time to make yourself difficult to get hold of."

I called again. He let me off easy. (He was one of the most generous people I've ever known.) I caught him up with the past seven years of my life. He told me to call him Bob, not Dr. Solomon: "We're past that." Then he said, "So, why do you want to come back?"

"I want to finish what I started, Bob."

"That's a lousy reason. Try again."

"I need to make a living that's not in business. I hate being a businessman, Bob."

"So be a lawyer. Be a doctor. You'll make a lot more money than in philosophy. It's not easy to get a job as a professor these days, Clancy."

"It's the one thing I really enjoyed. Philosophy was the only thing that ever truly interested me. And I have some things I want to figure out."

"Now you're talking. Like what? What are you thinking about?"

"Lying."

He was quiet for a few seconds.

"Lying is interesting. Deception? Or self-deception? Or, I'm guessing, both?"

"Exactly. Both. How they work together."

With the help of a couple of other professors who remembered me fondly, in the fall semester of 2000 Bob Solomon brought me back to the philosophy doctoral program at Austin, and I started work on a dissertation titled "Nietzsche on Deception."

I went to work on deception not because I wanted to learn how to lie better—I had mastered that twisted skill, as far as I was concerned—but because I wanted to cure myself of being a liar. What had begun as a morally pernicious technique had become a character-defining vice. I had to save myself. I needed to understand the knots I had tied myself into before I could begin to untangle them.

It seems like an odd solution now. But in fact it's an old idea: the Delphic injunction "Know thyself" is an epistemological duty with moral muscle, intended for a therapeutic purpose. Throughout the history of philosophy, until quite recently, it was thought that the practice of philosophy should have a powerful impact on the philosopher's life, even, ideally, on the lives of others. So I studied deception and self-deception, how they collaborate with each other, why they are so common, what harms they might do, and when, in fact, they may be both useful and necessary. The more work I did on the subject, the more I realized that deception was much more complicated than I had initially supposed. I also learned that it was much more common than I had thought—in short, that everyone practiced lying and other forms of deception and often for morally legitimate reasons. I was never so naive or narcissistic that I supposed I was the only liar out there in the world plying my false wares. But I hadn't realized how pervasive deception was, and I hadn't thought about how necessary and valuable it can be. I also hadn't realized how closely interwoven deception of others is with deception of oneself.

Because deception of others and self-deception so often collaborate, and because we will be working with these concepts throughout the book, let me quickly distinguish the two. This is a rough distinction, which we will refine as we proceed. When I deceive someone else, I persuade some other person that something I believe to be false is true. When I deceive myself, I persuade myself that something I believe to be false is true. The former act—deception of others—is relatively easy because I can hide the contents of my head from the person I am trying to deceive. The latter act—self-deception—ought to be impossible, as we normally suppose that we can't hide our own thoughts from ourselves. But the truth of the matter is that we are experts at hiding our thoughts from ourselves, and we are probably even better at deceiving ourselves than we are at deceiving other people. Perhaps that shouldn't come as a surprise, since we know ourselves better than we know other people, and so we know which buttons to push and levers to pull to get ourselves to believe what we want to believe, regardless of its truthfulness.

Briefly consider the example that, in many different ways, will occupy us for the rest of this book: falling in love. Who hasn't asked, when falling in love, "But am I making all this up?" When we are falling in love with someone, we engage in so many and such a variety of misrepresentations, evasions, creative manipulations, and often straightforward lies. ("How many people have you slept with?") Not to mention the self-deceptions, both in how we see the person we are falling in love with and about ourselves. As Erving Goffman famously argues in *The Presentation of Self in Everyday Life*, we are always "presenting ourselves," playing a part, acting a role, selling ourselves: and how much more so when love is at stake. Chris Rock gets it exactly right in his joke "When you meet someone new, you aren't meeting that person; you're meeting his agent."

Here's another way of thinking about the complexities of deception, especially in love: try making a list of all the people you love to whom you've never told a lie. Maybe that's not fair to ask; it's not so easy to make a list of people you've never lied to, period, much less the same list focused on people you love. So try making a list of—or merely stop and think a moment about—the people you lie to most often. It's an uncomfortable question: Whom do I lie to the most? For the majority of us, we lie most to the people we love most. Why that might be the case is fascinating. Because for thousands of years, at least since Plato taught in the *Symposium* that love is a ladder that leads us to the truth, our culture has supposed that intimacy and truthfulness go hand in hand. Of course in many instances they do. And yet while we are holding the beloved by one truthful hand, we're using the other hand, fingers crossed, to hold on with deception.

Once while I was delivering a lecture on this subject to a large, mixed crowd at a university, a woman who must have been in her late seventies or early eighties raised her hand and said: "So I take it you think we lie a lot to our relatives?"

"Yes, I do," I said.

"But my sister is the only person on earth I always tell the truth to," she said.

"And how do you get along with your sister?" I asked her.

"Oh, I hate that bitch," she said. Everyone laughed, and she smiled too, but she wasn't joking.

So in part this book is my attempt to summarize much of what I've spent the last thirteen years learning, as an academic, about deception. More important, it's what I've spent the past forty-five years learning about how deception works in love, which I take to be, for most of us, one of the highest values in life. This book is about my truth, my perspective, my meaning, my life. It is my attempt to make sense of my own life within the context of whom and how I have loved, the ways in which truth and deception have played into those loves, and why, at the end of the day, I believe so deeply in the value of love. I rarely talk about my children in this book or why and how we love our kids because, well, they are my kids. I do discuss why part of loving our children includes lying to them and also why we should accept that they will—indeed, often should—lie to us.

"A man's life of any worth is a continual allegory," Keats writes. The worth of all of our lives seems to be in the people we love and try to love—and try to love well or love better—and that allegory is worth a good-natured investigation. I should add that none of this will work—the reading or the writing, the loving of ourselves or of others—if we don't try to keep our sense of humor. As Baudelaire observes, a bit humorlessly, sounding very much like a Buddhist, and thinking of his own life explicitly as an allegory ("in this allegory," he writes): "Lord give me strength and courage to behold my body and my heart without disgust!"

Imagine a samurai who was the worst warrior ever to carry a sword. This samurai was so bad that he couldn't take his sword from its sheath without accidentally slicing himself or someone he cared about. So he decided to write a book titled *How to Be a Samurai.*

Why did I write this book? I guess, at age forty-six, standing at a crossroads in my life—this book began when I was married to my second wife, continued through a yearlong affair and a two-year divorce, and now has been completed two years into my third marriage—I am trying to figure out how I've loved and how to do it better. More brutally put—and more honestly?—I am trying to behold my body and my heart without disgust. Along the way I hope to familiarize myself and you, my reader, with what I think we both already know: how intimately deception and self-deception have informed our conceptions of love from childhood forward. I think the greatest threat to a mature and enduring conception of erotic love—the reason, in short, that I think we still ought to marry or engage in long-term monogamous romantic partnerships—is the popular, thoughtless idea that genuine love depends upon absolute truthfulness (with either the beloved or oneself). It is this cultural myth, which comes with our Greco-Judeo-Christian heritage, that makes for so many unhappy love affairs and disastrous divorces. Curiously, then, I am arguing in defense of lies in the service of the truth. Let's be honest about our lying. Then we will be better able to love.

The story I tell develops in five stages. In the first chapter I give the reader a bit of the history of philosophical thinking about lying and deception in order to provide us with some of the tools we will use in the subsequent discussion. In the second chapter I examine how we learn to lie and to love as children; our first attempts at loving are inextricably interwoven, I show, with our first attempts at lying. In the third chapter I look at our first great direct encounter with perhaps the most powerful psychological force in human psychological life—self-deception—and how it influences our early attempts at romantic love (so-called first love). In chapter 4 I examine the wildly complex phenomenon of deception in erotic love. Finally, in the fifth and final chapter, I show how self-deception and deception of each other in marital love, when practiced by thoughtful experts, can make enduring romantic love possible.

1. A Brief Introduction to the Morality of Deception

These six things doth the Lord hate: yea, seven are an abomination unto him:
A proud look, a lying tongue, and hands that shed innocent blood,
An heart that deviseth wicked imaginations, feet that be swift in running to mischief, a false witness that speaketh lies, and he that soweth discord among brethren.
                                        —Proverbs 6:16–19

Everything is deception: the question is whether to seek the least amount of deception, or the mean, or to seek out the highest.   —Franz Kafka, *The Zürau Aphorisms*

THE PREVALENCE OF DECEIT

The younger a child is when she starts to lie, the more likely she is to succeed and the more intelligent she is likely to be. In studies in which children have been observed in social interactions, four-year-olds lied at least once every two hours, while six-year-olds lied at least once every ninety minutes. Children who lie frequently are generally more intelligent than their peers, and the capacity to lie convincingly is a reliable predictor of social and financial success among adults. More intelligent adults lie more often and more skillfully. Conservative estimates show that people lie at least once a day. Other recent psychological studies have shown that Ivy League university students (perhaps not the most truthful sample of the population) lie as many as forty times per day, and the most successful college students lie about their GPAs more often than their less successful peers—despite the fact that the liars consistently have higher GPAs than the truth tellers. When confronted with their deception, the high GPA liars reported that they did not consider themselves to be lying so much as "reporting a future truth." (When asked about their current GPAs, apparently they tended to reply with the GPA they expected themselves to have in the not-too-distant future.) In yet another study, two strangers were asked to have a conversation for ten minutes; on average, each person in the conversation told three lies in that much time. To make things messier still, other recent research has shown that most times we are telling a lie we don't realize that we are doing so, probably because it is to our evolutionary advantage if we think we are telling the truth when lying (think how much more successful you are at bluffing if you don't know that you're bluffing).

Nevertheless, most of us have been taught since we were children that it is always wrong to lie. We mistakenly think that "Lying is always wrong" is written in the Ten Commandments. Honesty is in fact addressed in the ninth commandment, but it only recommends the much more modest and reasonable claim that we "do not bear false witness against our neighbors." If we are honest with ourselves, we recognize that we all tell lies—probably more often than we'd like to admit—and that, more interestingly, often we do so for good reasons.

First we should notice that there is a difference between what we actually do and what we ought to do. Suppose that most of us do eat oysters. It doesn't follow from that fact that we *ought* to eat oysters. This is the difference, often insisted upon in moral philosophy (but also as often attacked) between facts and values. In Aristotle's time, nearly all Athenian citizens owned slaves; again, it does not follow from that fact that they ought to have owned slaves.

So even if we agree that it is true that most of us do lie quite frequently, it doesn't follow from that fact that we ought to lie as often as we do. Contemporary psychology, economics, and evolutionary biology have collectively destroyed the old Judeo-Christian cultural conviction that most of us don't lie most of the time. But whether or not deception is *morally* wrong remains a compelling question.

It's interesting that we lie so often and easily, because as a rule other moral prohibitions are not so commonly, comfortably, and recognizably flouted. We all agree that it's usually wrong to steal, and most of us follow this moral rule; stealing is an exceptional event in the average human life. We all agree that it's wrong to take another human life, except, perhaps, under extraordinary conditions like war or self-defense, and most of us happily never have and never will kill another human being.

So one question is: Given the general consensus that lying is wrong, why is it so commonly practiced? Another question is: Are there circumstances in which it is appropriate to lie? Because if there are, then we might be operating under a kind of collective hypocrisy about deception in everyday life, and collective hypocrisies are at least worth examining more closely. Indeed, as a rule, we think that collective hypocrisies are morally dangerous and should be vigorously exposed.

It is with this cognitive dissonance in mind—the conflict between how commonly we lie and the fact that we generally profess that it is wrong to do so—that I often ask my students: "Is there anyone in here who has never told a lie?" With younger students, there are usually several hands, and I let the other students do the work of showing the ways in which their fellow students must have lied—to such questions as, for example, How are you today? Or, Do you like my new haircut? Or, Did you make it to all your classes today? Or, Why was your paper late? But I was particularly fascinated when on one occasion I asked mid-career business professionals in an MBA class the same question. Usually my adult students won't take the bait. In this instance a fifty-something man raised his hand and said: "In all my life I've never told a single lie." Another student about the same age immediately replied: "Well, congratulations, you just told one." Nevertheless, the first student, who was an accountant, insisted that he had never told a lie, even for the sake of politeness, not even as a child to his parents. He was happy to admit that everyone else lied quite often. He just happened to be the exception to the rule.

For all I or anyone else in the classroom knew, he was telling the truth. But I think we all suspected the same thing: that this was a man who was particularly deeply entrenched in a self-deceptive self-image that, for whatever complex psychological reasons, simply couldn't accept the possibility that he had ever told a lie. The reason I mention this case is that it struck me, as it clearly struck many other people in the room, as disturbing. The dogmatic insistence that one has never told a lie in his or her life is obviously false. As Mark Twain remarked, "A man is never more truthful than when he acknowledges himself as a liar." But the fact that this particular statement, "I've never told a lie," is blatantly false, indeed, self-contradictory—so much so that we suspect it might even be a sign of a kind of mental or psychological imbalance in the person who protests it—shows that we are more realistic about ourselves as liars than we pretend to be. This fact about us as liars—that we know we lie, but we don't like to admit it—will be important for our thinking in the pages ahead.

We should also remember the importance of truthfulness. In the movie *Liar, Liar*, the character played by Jim Carrey, an incorrigible liar, who lies for a living, finds himself suddenly incapable of lying, and we all quickly realize that it is impossible to engage in everyday life without lying, at least now and then. At the same time, over the course of the movie, the hero realizes that there are certain goods, like trust and intimacy, that are available only if we try to be honest most of the time.

In the ethics of our everyday lives, most absolute moral prohibitions—such as "Never kill a human being"—don't come up, because we don't find ourselves in those kinds of situations. But an absolute moral prohibition such as "Never tell a lie," whether it's offered by the German philosopher Immanuel Kant, the insect philosopher Jiminy Cricket, or the young George Washington after he (fictionally) chopped down the cherry tree is the sort of claim we need to examine more closely, because we want to do the right thing, for the right reasons, as often as we can.

So I want to take a closer look at the popular notion that lying is wrong. In this chapter, before we get to the tough subject of lying and love, I'll first discuss several philosophers who argue that it is okay to lie at least some of the time. Then I will turn to several philosophers who argue that it is always wrong, or almost always wrong, ever to lie. Finally, I will discuss a few philosophers who argue that when and why it is right or wrong to lie depends upon a variety of considerations and careful thinking about the kinds of situations we find ourselves in.

SOMETIMES WE OUGHT TO LIE

Plato was the first philosopher in the Western tradition who argued that sometimes we must tell lies, and for good reasons. He argues in his book on the ideal society *Republic* that the leader must tell "a noble lie" (*gennaion pseudos* in the Greek; sometimes loosely translated as "noble and generous fiction") to the populace so that citizens will be content with their roles in life. Plato's idea that sometimes the government must lie to the populace for its own well-being has since become a relatively standard view in political theory, even in democracies where transparency and truthfulness in government are prized. It is obvious that the government cannot always tell the citizenry "the truth, the whole truth, and nothing but the truth" when at war (because strategy would be compromised—"Loose lips sink ships") or during terrorist threats (because then it could be very difficult to observe and catch terrorists). We can easily think of many similar examples.

Plato's "noble lie" is justified on the philosophical principle known as paternalism, from the Latin word *pater*, "father." The familiar idea is that just as in the case of seat belt laws, sometimes a government, ruler, or parent may know what is better for us than we ourselves know. Sometimes if we knew the truth, this line goes, we would be made miserable by it, frightened by it, discouraged by it or would act in ways destructive to ourselves or others or both.

In the example given by Plato, citizens of his imaginary ideal state will be told that they were originally made of different metals—bronze, silver, gold—which suit them for different roles within the society. Tradesmen will be happy as tradesmen because they will believe the lie that they were naturally made for that role; similarly, warriors will believe that they were made to be warriors. A caste system that benefits the entire society can be harmoniously established on the basis of a simple lie that puts the minds of the citizenry at ease.

Plato's ideal state sounds a bit too much like Aldous Huxley's dystopian brave new world for our contemporary, democratic, class-conscious ears. But paternalistic defenses of lying are none-theless vigorous and familiar. One of the most common and plausible justifications of a paternalist defense for lying comes from the lies we tell to children. We lie about Santa Claus in or-der to make Christmas a happier time for children and to teach them about the spirit of giving (also, perhaps, to control their behavior; how many times have I lied: "Santa's watching! Now get to bed!"); think about how many billions of dollars are spent every year in supporting this lie. Many people, both inside and outside the medical community, think that a lie to a dying child— such as "No, honey, we don't know for certain that you are going to die"—is generally justified (the medical profession is all over the map on this question, I should add; there is good evidence both for telling the truth to dying children and for lying to them). Many doctors argue that the right to lie to their patients is neces-sary to the best practice of the profession. And most of us who are parents have lied to our own children many, many times in order to preserve their peace of mind, either about family mat-ters or about the way things are in the world. If a five-year-old asks a penetrating question about a matter she is not yet ready to understand, such as rape or murder or war or whether a plane is more likely to crash during heavy turbulence, most parents will not tell the unvarnished truth. We may not always out and out lie, but we will certainly say something that is not entirely honest and accurate.

Deceiving, prevaricating, exaggerating, storytelling, lying by omission: there are many different ways to lie, but all of them involve the desire to convince the person who is listening to the liar that she, the listener, believes something different from what the liar believes to be true. This is why Montaigne, who was generally opposed to lying, said: "The truth has only one face, but a lie has a hundred thousand." The liar can invent so many things that are different from the truth he knows, especially when speaking to a child, or someone with less knowledge than the liar.

Here's an interesting philosophical puzzle: For something to be a lie, must it be false? Normally we assume that a lie is not true. But consider this case: a man who always lies stands at a crossroads. You approach him and ask him for directions. He tells you to take the road to the left, lying to you about which road to take, as he always does. But it turns out that this man who always lies is also very bad at directions, and so, while lying, he sends you down the right road. Has he lied to you or not?

One solution to this puzzle is to argue that all that is required to lie is the intention to deceive. This is an appealing view because it frees the liar from the large epistemological burden she would otherwise bear to know the truth before lying. If I must *know* the truth before lying to you because to lie to you, I must tell you something that is false, then I may often be required to do an awful lot of work to discover what the truth actually is. Often we think we know the truth when we do not. Take the example of an ancient Greek astronomer who sincerely believed that the sun revolves around the earth. If we required that the astronomer know the truth about solar and planetary motion before having the capacity to lie about it, we see that he would find himself incapable of lying. But surely he has the capacity—within his particular context—both to report the truth as best he understands it and, consequently, to mislead.

But just to illustrate how vexing this puzzle actually is, if all that is required to deceive is the intention to deceive, then in some sense one can never fail to deceive, because we are completely in control of our intentions. To fail to deceive would, on this account, simply mean that the liar was not believed. However, if you approached the liar at the crossroads, and he intended to deceive you but, because he is bad at directions, pointed you down the right road, and yet you did not believe him, you would find yourself going down the wrong road . . . and perversely, the intention of the liar at the crossroads to mislead you would be successful. These philosophical tangles of what exactly constitutes a lie are not trivial for our purposes because part of the reason we deceive so commonly and with such a clean conscience about it is precisely the fact that deception, as Montaigne points out, is so complex and difficult to understand, even for the practiced liar. As we proceed, we shall also find—I gestured at this with my discussion of truth and subjectivity in the prologue— that contra Montaigne, truthful communication is also much more complex than it initially appears to be.

Here's another quick, personal example of how complicated it is to sort out what counts as a lie. I was recently driving to Iowa City, where my wife is a graduate student, when a friend called and asked if I could drive him to the store (his car was in the shop, and he was stuck at home). I said, "I wish I could, but I'm driving to Iowa City." Now, as it happens, I was on the outskirts of Kansas City, where I live, and only a dozen or so miles from my friend's house. I had spoken the literal truth—I was indeed driving to Iowa City—but when I asked my wife what she thought of the statement, she said: "Well, I think you did the right thing, but you should also admit to yourself that you lied to him." Her point was that the naked truth would have hurt his feelings ("I'm in a hurry, and I'm not going to make you a priority"), so yes, the deception was well intended, but my "literal truth" was nonetheless an example of deception. But the same sword cuts the opposite way: sometimes a literal falsehood may disguise a deeper truth.

Let's return to the phenomenon of paternalism as a justification for lying. The English philosopher John Stuart Mill argued that it is permissible to lie when the good consequences of lying outweigh the bad consequences of lying, but we must always remember that one of the bad consequences of lying is that it tends to corrode our trust in communication and each other over time. As a general rule of thumb, therefore, lying does more harm than good, but in particular circumstances a lie might generate more good than harm. Mill appeals to what we call soft paternalism, which in the context of deception is the idea that if you had all the facts and were in a position to make the decision on the basis of the truth, you would decide to do what the lie encouraged you to do.

Let's say I'm guarding a bridge that will collapse if more than a dozen or so people try to cross it at once, and because of an emergency a huge crowd of people are in a hurry to cross. I know that if I say, "Only a few people can cross this bridge at a time, or it will collapse," many people will rush the bridge, trying to be the first to cross, and the bridge will in fact collapse. If, however, I lie and say, "Only one person can cross this bridge at a time, or it will definitely collapse," I know that only one person at a time will dare try to cross the bridge, and everyone will be able to cross safely.

Now, because of the noise, the urgency, the smoke, the chaos, I am unable to explain to everyone the whole situation, so I tell the lie. This is justified, Mill argues, because *if you were in a position to understand the truth, you would act according to the lie.* You would say, "Yes, I see the wisdom of one person's crossing the bridge at a time," and wait your turn in line. It is only the circumstances that require the lie—circumstances that constrain what you and others can be told. This is different from Plato's "noble lie," because, according to Plato, we should be told the lie specifically because we cannot handle the truth—and if we knew the truth, we might act very differently than Plato's ruler wants us to act.

The difference in Plato's and Mill's approaches in part reflects a suspicion that emerged in the intervening two thousand years that we don't know ourselves as well as we suppose we do. Plato's citizens have to be told a bald-faced lie, because if they knew the truth, they would want something that did not benefit the populace as a whole (even if it might help them personally). For Mill, by contrast, we must at times be lied to because we often simply aren't in a position to judge what is in our own particular best interest. Plato imagines that the citizens of his fictional Republic are more rational and self-aware than Mill recognizes actual people to be. This is not to say that Plato thinks people are so rational that they need not be lied to at all; the perfectly rational citizen, in Plato's view, would not need to be deceived because he or she would understand that society requires different people to occupy different roles within society. Plato insists that the people must be lied to for their own good. But the qualification Mill puts on his paternalism is interesting, for our purposes, because it incorporates the modern suspicion, already widespread in the nineteenth century, that we are often irrational, and so we may need to hold and be told false beliefs in order to promote our own flourishing.

Another philosopher who argues that it is sometimes permissible to lie is Dietrich Bonhoeffer, who died in a Nazi concentration camp for, among other things, refusing to lie about his beliefs. Bonhoeffer argued for a concept he called "the living truth." According to Bonhoeffer, we often mean something different from the literal truth of what we say, and we are often understood to mean something different from the literal truth of what we say.

So, for example, if I ask my wife, "Do you think I'm getting fat?" and she says, "No, honey, you haven't gained a pound," we both know that literally she's telling a lie: it's January, and I always gain about five or ten pounds over the holidays. But "the living truth" of what she's telling me is that she thinks I look fine, and I don't need to worry about my weight. This is also, she knows, the real reason I'm asking the question: I am in fact asking her to lie to me, though I wouldn't want her to lie even more and say, "You look too thin! You need to put on a few pounds! Let's order pizza tonight!"

Many of the stories we tell each other, or the stories in the Bible, Bonhoeffer argues, are not literally true; they are often in fact literally false. Nevertheless, they may communicate a "living truth" that could not be communicated in a better way.

To return to the story of Santa Claus: explaining that giving is a good, virtuous, kind thing is going to make only so much headway with a four-year-old. But telling a story about a good-natured, funny fellow who picks one day a year to give gifts to everyone, after spending the whole year making them—that falsehood teaches the four-year-old a living truth about generosity that the child otherwise might not understand. Bonhoeffer's notion of the living truth introduces the idea that sometimes the successful communication of a particular way of understanding the world or interpreting a situation—of communicating, to refer to our earlier discussion, a subjective truth or meaning—may require that we use fictional or false discourse.

The connection between the difficulty of communicating subjective truth and Bonhoeffer's notion of the living truth is not coincidental: Kierkegaard, who introduced the notion of subjective truth into our discussion, was Bonhoeffer's single most important philosophical influence. Bonhoeffer's idea of the living truth derives from Kierkegaard's notion of indirect communication, and though we don't want to be distracted by the intricate philosophical nuances of Kierkegaard's view, the basic idea is that an underlying truth can sometimes be conveyed only by a literal falsehood. This is why, both Kierkegaard and Bonhoeffer thought, so many of our most important truths are communicated in myths, fables, stories, and other forms of discourse that are strictly speaking false.

Bonhoeffer expands the idea of "the living truth" into realms of discourse and meaning where the truth is at best unknown. For example, when we make our marital vows—to love each other "until death do us part"—we are not really in a position to make any such promise. Half of all marriages end in divorce; many other marriages that last until death are unhappy ones. And yet the vow contains a "living truth" about the nature of love, the intensity of our particular love for each other, and our intention to try our best to maintain that love. When I say, "I will love you until I die," I may well have a nagging question in my mind about whether or not that is likely or even possible. Some cynic might reasonably protest: "Come on! You're in no position to make a promise like that!" But the point, Bonhoeffer would insist, is that I am communicating a living truth about my intentions and about what I hope will be the case, as well as about how I am feeling at that particular time. The literal truth of my words may be suspect, but the living truth of what I am saying, Bonhoeffer argues, is secure.

Of course we can readily see that a notion like "the living truth" can also get us into all sorts of trouble. It's all too easy to tell a lie and then protest, "But what I was really trying to say was that I loved you!" If a nine-year-old is suddenly embarrassed by a friend in the schoolyard when she protests that Santa Claus is real and all her friends mock her for continuing to believe that childhood lie, she won't be easily consoled by her parents' long-winded explanation of Bonhoeffer's idea of the living truth or Kierkegaard's notion of indirect communication. The living truth may be used to manipulate the beliefs of others—in fact that's what it is designed to do—and we generally worry, and for good reasons, that the manipulation of the beliefs of others is at least morally suspect, if not simply morally blameworthy. Paternalism of this kind—if we assume that we know what's best for someone else to believe—is sometimes presumptuous and always risky (when and why does paternalism end?).

Now we'll turn to some arguments that it is always (or almost always) wrong to lie.

ONE SHOULD NEVER LIE

There's a ferocious knocking on your door. It's past midnight. You stumble downstairs, open it a crack, and a bloody man screams: "She's after me! Please save me! She's going to kill me!" He's large and strong but young, and you can see he's in terrible trouble. You open the door and tell him to hide in the closet upstairs. A few minutes later, while you try to explain the situation to your spouse, who is already calling the police, you hear a polite rapping. Back to the door. An old woman stands on the porch, an ax in her hands, and she asks: "Excuse me, is there a man hiding in your house? Because I plan to murder him."

Do you lie?

No, you cannot, the eighteenth-century German philosopher Immanuel Kant says. It is always wrong to lie, even to the murderer at your door, even in the attempt to save a human life. There may well be other things that, morally speaking, you ought to do:

close the door; resist the murderer; try to help the poor man escape through a window. But absolutely under no circumstances can you lie to the murderer.

This is one of the most famously controversial and contested claims in the history of the literature on deception—indeed, in the history of moral philosophy. How on earth does Kant defend it? And why would he want to do so?

We don't want to attempt to learn the intricacies of Kant's moral philosophy—he is probably the most influential, and the most complicated, of all the moral philosophers—but we have to learn a little bit about Kant's ethics before we can understand why he is so strict in his prohibition of lying.

For Kant, to act morally requires that one act freely. He summarizes this in one of the great slogans of moral philosophy: "Ought implies can." That is, if we say that a person ought to do something—that she is morally required to do something—it follows from this that she is free to do it (or not do it). If I duct-tape you to a lawn chair and start to throw house cats into your swimming pool—sorry, there are lots of odd examples when you begin with the problem of the murderer at the door—it doesn't make sense for me or anyone else to insist that you ought to save the drowning cats. Why not? Because you are in fact incapable of doing so; it's silly to say you ought to do it when you can't do it. If, however, you are simply lounging by the pool with a margarita in your hand when I start my cat-tossing act, then we will say, "Hey, you ought to do something about it," whether by stopping me or by saving the cats.

So to be moral, we must be free. But to be free is to make choices based on our beliefs. We don't think freedom is merely acting out randomly; we think freedom is fundamentally the ability to choose. Furthermore, for my choices to be free, they must be based on reasons that I have arrived at freely. If you have coerced me into believing something, through controlling my thoughts with drugs or some kind of diabolical technology, we would not say that I am acting freely on the basis of those beliefs.

An example: I freely get out of bed most mornings to go to the office to write and lecture. Why? Because I correctly believe it is something I both enjoy and need to do. But let's suppose you gave me a drug that made me believe that my kitchen was in fact my office, and my living room my classroom. Then, when I get up in the morning to type at my sink and lecture to my bookshelves, I am not really freely doing what I would choose to be doing. You are controlling my beliefs and interfering with my freedom. You are making me do what you want me to do and manipulating what I can do, no more and no less than when I duct-taped you to your lawn chair.

But what is it that I do when I lie to you? I control your beliefs, or attempt to control your beliefs, in precisely the same way as you controlled mine when you gave me the drug that kept me in my apartment. And insofar as you are controlling me, you are preventing me from being free. But if I am not free, I can no longer do what I ought to do. I can no longer exercise the power of morality. When you lie to me, no matter what you lie to me about, you enslave me.

In arguing against the laws permitting slavery in the European colonies, as well as against forced prostitution and other immoral practices, Kant writes: "Always treat every human being, whether in your own person or the person of any other, never merely as a means, but also always as an end in themselves." When you treat someone as a means, you are using that person, you are controlling him or her, and so you are preventing that person from participating in the moral sphere. There is nothing worse we can do, Kant argues, than prevent a person from exercising his or her morality. (Indeed, what could be more immoral than denying someone else the right to morality?) When we treat others as "ends in themselves," we are respecting them as free human beings, moral creatures like us.

Accordingly, when you tell the ax-wielding old lady on your doorstep that there is no man hiding in your house, you are preventing her from even having the choice to do the right thing. True, you might send her away, but she wouldn't leave freely. And suppose, Kant says, that as you send her away, she sees the burly young man who has been hiding in your attic climbing down the gutters outside? Now you have been a cause of her discovering him, because you controlled her beliefs. You cannot control the world, Kant argues—it is full of surprises—but you can control your own intentions and make your own choices, and you can respect the right of every other human being to do the same. When you lie to the old woman, you interfere with the very possibility of her making the right choice. Now this does not prevent you, should she make the wrong choice, of trying to stop her. Kant is not suggesting that we all should be allowed to do whatever we like or whatever we choose. He is simply pointing out that to control someone else's beliefs by lying to that person is to immorally interfere with the very possibility of that person's making a moral choice.

There's another reason it's always wrong to lie, according to Kant. To act morally, he thinks, is to act rationally; reason inclines us toward the good, in the most ordinary, commonplace sense. This is an idea Kant found in Socrates, and it was further developed by Plato and Aristotle, but the simple idea is that when we act reasonably, we will naturally choose what is good for us rather than what is bad for us. A moral life, at the end of the day, will on this account be the culmination of a whole series of rational choices about what is good for you and those around you.

These good choices need not be about abstract ethical problems but can include very ordinary, everyday decisions. A reasonable person will choose a bed that suits his needs over one that does not; that bed is the bed that is "good" for him. If you go into Home Depot and reasonably ask for a hammer that is excellent at pounding and pulling nails, you will wind up buying a good hammer, the right hammer for you. If, however, you irrationally ask for a hammer that is made of cheap plastic and will break at the first whack, you will wind up buying a lousy (though perhaps very cheap) hammer. Similarly, to find the good action, Kant thinks, we will use reason to seek the best beliefs and principles to guide us in that action.

Now, bear with me. To be rational is to be consistent. The basic principle of logic is noncontradiction: our basic ideas, if true, must not contradict one another. A thing must be either a hammer or not a hammer; it can never be both a hammer and not a hammer. Think about lying, Kant says: Is it a consistent and rational thing to do or an inconsistent and irrational thing to do?

Well, to lie is to pretend that one is telling the truth. If I said to you, "Now I'm going to lie to you," and then told a lie, it wouldn't work. In order successfully to lie, I must feign truthfulness. But that's self-contradictory; lying works only if you suppose that I am speaking truthfully. If we always told the truth, we would not contradict ourselves (though the world might be a bit difficult to get along in); if, however, we always lied, it would be impossible to communicate at all—and thus impossible to lie. Lying contradicts itself; it is therefore irrational and, Kant argues, contrary to the good.

We can never lie, therefore, not even to the murderous old woman at the door, because we are coercing her out of her very morality, and we are acting in a fundamentally irrational—and thus immoral—way. We are coercing her and contradicting ourselves.

Kant's odd but powerful arguments can be traced back to another, much older philosopher who also believed it was (at least almost) always wrong to lie: Socrates, the fourth-century ancient Greek. The ancient Greeks consulted oracles when they were confused about the right thing to do, and on an archway above the oracle at Delphi, the most renowned of the ancient Greek oracles, were carved the words *gnothi seauton*, "know thyself." Socrates understood this maxim as not merely an epistemological but also, and more important, as a moral imperative. Socrates advocated the famous, controversial thesis that "Knowledge is virtue, and vice is ignorance." No human being, he thought, would willingly choose to do harm to himself, and so long as we are free to choose the good, it is only through a deficiency of thinking about it that we would do the wrong or harmful thing.

Socrates argued that a rational person will easily see, if he thinks it through, what will be in his best interest: cultivating friends; eating simple, healthy foods; having enough money, but not too much; acting in a pious and law-abiding fashion; treating others with respect. All these things are simple truths that are recognizable to a sound reason, which is also willing to inspect itself and recognize where it has defects (thus, "Know thyself"). But given this way of thinking, one can see that among the worst things would be bad information—falsehood—and worse even than bad information is the deliberate spreading of falsehood, or lying. Because no one person can know everything, we have to rely upon one another for the truth: on carpenters for the truth about good shelves and beds; on sailors for good information about ships; on butchers and farmers for good information about food; on priests for good information about the wants and needs of the gods. So long as we report the truth to one another, and we all consult people who we believe have reason to know the truth—if we stick to the experts—we shall ourselves be able to live good, happy lives. But if those people should lie to us or if we lie to the people who rely upon us, we are undermining our collective ability to live good lives. (Socrates was notorious for exposing the ignorance of self-proclaimed experts.)

For the ancient Greeks and Socrates, to live a good life is to live a moral life, to be a moral person. They did not separate the good life of a person from the good or bad actions of a person in the way that we sometimes tend to do today. So to lie to someone is to interfere with the possibility of that person's being happy. And it's just as important not to lie to ourselves. We must not pretend to know things we don't or fail to investigate our own beliefs in order to make certain that we have the right sorts of beliefs that will lead to good, rational lives. To lie is not merely to interfere with goodness: it will also undermine the very possibility of happiness.

One final, quick note on another thinker who argues that it is almost always wrong to lie, the feminist and poet Adrienne Rich. Rich argues that it is wrong to lie, especially in contexts of trust, because we build our entire worldviews around the beliefs that we suppose are truly reported to us by the people we love. To find out that one has been lied to by an intimate, Rich says, is to feel as if we were going crazy. She also says that lying is terrible for the liar because "the liar leads an existence of unutterable loneliness": by hiding her beliefs, her mind from the people around her, the liar makes it difficult or impossible for intimacy to be established between her and others. In a breathtaking statement of why we should at least try to tell the truth to each other, Rich writes:

> It isn't that to have an honorable relationship with you, I have to understand everything, or tell you everything at once, or that I can know, beforehand, everything I need to tell you. It means that most of the time I am eager, longing for the possibility of telling you. That these possibilities may seem frightening, but

not destructive, to me. That I feel strong enough to hear your tentative, groping words. That we both know we are trying, all the time, to extend the possibilities of truth between us.

Socrates was never quite this earnest; he preferred a good ironical joke to strong statements of emotional feeling. But I think he nevertheless would have agreed. To love one another is to trust one another, and to trust one another is to try, at least most of the time, not to lie.

THE MORAL COMPLEXITY OF TRUTHFULNESS AND DECEPTION

The Tibetan Buddhist lama, philosopher, and filmmaker Dzongsar Jamyong Khyentse Rinpoche was once asked by a student: "Is it ever right to lie?" The Rinpoche said: "Well, suppose a murderer comes to your door, searching for his victim. Which would do less harm: to lie to the murderer and send him away, or to tell him the truth and help him accomplish his bloody goal?"

A principle of Buddhism is the practice of right speech, and in general right speech means truthfulness. But there are many circumstances, the Buddha teaches, in which right speech, which also means skillful speech, requires something other than the truth, including an out-and-out lie. For the Buddhist, there is a greater moral principle at stake—the principle of avoiding doing harm—that informs and even trumps the general moral virtue of telling the truth.

Similarly, in Confucianism the virtues of harmony and filial piety may require the moral person to tell a lie or at least to avoid speaking the truth. To maintain harmony among many members of a group or even to maintain harmony among two friends, one cannot answer every question honestly. If a husband asks his wife, "Honey, does my butt look fat in these jeans?" the naked truth—so to speak—could certainly destroy harmony between the husband and the wife. Similarly, if a mother were to ask her son-in-law, "Do you want me to move out of the house and leave the two of you alone?" filial piety—respect for one's elders, especially when those elders are parents—requires the son-in-law to give the answer the mother-in-law is seeking, regardless of whether or not he is speaking the truth.

In the Western tradition the fourth-century ancient Greek Aristotle, the student of Plato, who was the student of Socrates, first introduces the idea that truthfulness is a virtue that depends upon circumstances. According to Aristotle, it is permissible for Socrates, the famous ironist, to dissemble by pretending to know less than he really does. Aristotle is the first among the Greek philosophers to call Socrates a liar, though many philosophers after him make the same surprising claim. The reason Socrates could ironically dissemble without doing something morally blameworthy, Aristotle argues, is that Socrates was dissembling with an educational purpose. (In the nineteenth century, Kierkegaard used the same example to illustrate his idea of indirect communication, and in the twentieth century, writing under the influence of Kierkegaard, Bonhoeffer used it to illustrate the idea of the living truth.) According to Aristotle, if Socrates admitted that he in fact had a lot of knowledge—rather than, as Aristotle says, lying by claiming he had none—then the persons around Socrates would not recognize that like Socrates, they too had to search for the truth. By pretending not to know, Aristotle says, Socrates encourages us to recognize that we too don't know what we think we know, and we have some work to do before claiming that we understand the truth. Truthfulness is almost always to be preferred, Aristotle insists, but sometimes lying is the only way you can get through to people. Aristotle also notes that at least certain kinds of lying, such as boasting, may be relatively harmless or even entertaining.

Most of us think of the fifteenth-century Renaissance philosopher Niccolò Machiavelli as one of the few figures in the history of Western thought who actually advocates lying. When we say Machiavellian, we almost think "deceptive" and rarely mean it as a compliment. But the fact of the matter was that Machiavelli believed that all modes of speech, and especially truth and deception, were entirely pragmatic in nature. A person—and especially a ruler—should consider the circumstances before deciding whether or not to tell the truth. In most circumstances, Machiavelli observes, the truth is the quickest and easiest way to deal with a problem. The truth is easy to remember, and lies often are not. The truth does not require creative energy; lies can be exhausting to invent and to maintain. The truth often "speaks for itself"; sometimes people can simply see that what you say is true, and no further argument is required. A lie, by contrast, often requires some salesmanship.

In fact Machiavelli warns leaders that if they want to hear the truth, which he thinks is invaluable for a successful leader to hear, he must make the people around him understand that they will not benefit from lying to him or suffer for being honest with him. He advises: "There is no other way to guard yourself against flattery than by making men understand that telling you the truth will not offend you."

All that said, Machiavelli is quick to add that should circumstances require it, there is nothing morally blameworthy about a lie, so long as it is the most practical and effective way to achieve the practical goals a person has given him or herself. For a leader, that goal is the maintenance of power and the welfare of the state, so he will lie to the populace—and even to his own advisers—whenever he needs to do so in order to guarantee both his own and the state's security. When the leader does in fact need to deceive, Machiavelli writes, "Men are so simple of mind, and so much dominated by their immediate needs, that a deceitful man will always find plenty who are ready to be deceived."

Machiavelli gives the discussion an interesting twist because he takes the moral content out of statements and places it on the uses and consequences of statements. What we say is in itself morally neutral, according to Machiavelli. Being true does not make a statement good; being false does not make a statement bad. What will determine the value of a statement and, therefore, whether or not it is moral to make that statement will depend upon its effects. In this way, Machiavelli is like John Stuart Mill, whom we discussed in the first section of this chapter: he is concerned about the good or bad consequences of what we say, rather than the statement or even the intention behind the statement. It is right to lie when it helps your cause, wrong to lie when it harms it. When in doubt, tell the truth, because it requires less effort and is less likely to cause you trouble down the road.

Like Machiavelli, popular culture has given the nineteenth-century German philosopher Friedrich Nietzsche a bit of a bad reputation, and here again we might expect that Nietzsche advocated lying. But in fact Nietzsche was a vigorous champion for the truth; he thought, like Socrates, that the most dangerous force in culture is our collective tendency to close our eyes to the truth. Nietzsche feared the coming effects of the increasingly anti-Semitic politics of Germany and the Aryan movement that came with it (Nietzsche's sister was married to a famous anti-Semite, and Nietzsche despised the man for it). The most dangerous lies, Nietzsche argues, are what he called blue-eyed lies (a jab against the Aryan movement), lies that we tell ourselves before we tell them to other people. Nietzsche argues that we all learn to lie by first lying to ourselves; he argues (and contemporary scientific research on the subject agrees) that we lie much more often to ourselves than we lie to other people. But the worst process, according to Nietzsche, is when we want something to be true that we know is false, convince ourselves of the truth of it so that we feel comfortable with the falsehood, and then proceed to tell that lie to other people.

So, for example, when the fervor over weapons of mass destruction was at its worst during the Second Iraq War, *The Economist* magazine ran a cover showing George W. Bush and Tony Blair, smiling, arm in arm, with the caption "Sincere Deceivers." What the editors of the magazine meant to convey was that Bush and Blair were not consciously lying because they had already convinced themselves of the truth of what they wanted to believe, even though all the evidence suggested that the truth was something else.

This is not to say that Nietzsche thought self-deception was blameworthy; on the contrary, he was a vigorous advocate for the strategic value of self-deception. What he argues against is what we might call naive self-deception—self-deception practiced by people who do not understand the trick they are playing on themselves; self-deception of the variety that simply selects beliefs unreflectively. Sophisticated self-deception, on Nietzsche's account, will require that the self-deceiver actually uses her manipulation of her own beliefs strategically to accomplish goals that would otherwise, with the wrong set of beliefs, be unattainable (this sounds complicated or even impossible, but we will look more carefully at how this works in the pages to come).

Despite the fact that he is suspicious of many kinds of lies, Nietzsche agrees with Machiavelli that many good things can be achieved only through deception. According to Nietzsche, one of the primary ways that life acquires meaning is through the power of art, and art relies heavily on deception in order to achieve its effects. "Art is the least dishonest lie," Gustave Flaubert observes, and Nietzsche, who early in his career claimed that only art could justify human existence, is entirely in agreement. Novels are literally false, but they can offer us great consolation during difficult times, make us feel less alone, and even teach us "truths" about human psychology and ourselves. Movies depend entirely upon illusion, but how many of us have learned about compassion for the less fortunate—and other forms of empathy—through film?

A difference between most forms of art and, say, the living truth communicated in the story about Santa Claus is that art can achieve its effects despite the fact that we recognize its falsehood. For Nietzsche, this is crucial to what makes art a model for the kind of truthfulness he finds most compelling: we can both recognize that a novel is literally false or fictional and nonetheless find a great deal of meaning in it. In fact, if you consider the intellectual works that have most influenced your own way of looking at the world—at least this is certainly true for me and many people I know—I suspect you'll find that novels, movies, and plays (all of them literally false) have had a far greater impact on your general attitude about life than the nonfiction works you have read and experienced. This fascinating kind of mental experience—when we know something to be false and yet experience it to be truthful or meaningful—will prove to be the model for the account of love I give throughout the book. In my account, as we shall see, marriage is like a terrific novel a couple is writing together; Nietzsche himself saw all human existence this way, understanding life as literature.

For Nietzsche, Odysseus is the exemplar of the character who understands lying, in both its bad and its good aspects. Odysseus lies very often (some say constantly), though he does it mostly for the entertainment of others. But he is also perfectly happy to deceive in order to get himself out of a jam by causing as little harm to others as he can. He often lies merely to give someone else a good surprise, as when he lies to his father, pretending to be someone other than his son, so that he can give him all the more pleasure when he reveals himself and his father realizes that after all those years, his son has at last returned safely home. We should note that according to the ancient Greeks, to lie to one's parents was the very worst kind of lie you could tell, so when Homer has Odysseus lie even to his own father, Homer is strongly endorsing the idea that a clever lie told with good intentions is not a morally blameworthy thing. Importantly, according to Nietzsche, Odysseus always lies with his eyes open—that is, he does not lie to himself when he lies to others. Odysseus is a master deceiver, but he is not self-deceptive.

In a famous scene from the film *Lawrence of Arabia*, T. E. Lawrence accuses the diplomat Mr. Dryden of telling lies to the Arabs because he led them to believe that they were fighting for a free Arabia. Dryden responds strongly to Lawrence: "If we've been telling lies, you've been telling half-lies. A man who tells lies, like me, merely hides the truth. But a man who tells half-lies has forgotten where he put it."

Lies, other kinds of deception, and self-deception, Nietzsche thinks, all may often be necessary to achieve good ends; like Machiavelli, he did not think that either truthful statements or falsehoods have a morality attached to them. They are as good or as bad as the circumstances and the outcomes make them. Replying to an accusation he makes against himself that he may tell lies, even to himself, in his own philosophical work, Nietzsche writes:

> But even if this all were true and I were accused of it with good reason, what do *you* know, what *could* you know about the amount of self-preserving cunning, or reason and higher protection that is contained in such self-deception—and how

much falseness I still *require* so that I may keep permitting myself the luxury of *my* truthfulness? Enough, I am still alive; and
life has not been devised by morality: it *wants* deception, it *lives*
on deception.

Nietzsche is intellectually refreshing in a way so few thinkers
are precisely because he refuses to oversimplify and because he is
honest—honest enough to admit that he has to lie in order to create a truthfulness that captures the world as he understands it.

What Nietzsche did fear, however, were the psychological,
political, and social consequences of what Dryden calls half-lies,
the kinds of lies told by a person who refuses to honestly examine the truth before deciding whether or not a lie is appropriate.
These, according to Nietzsche, are both the most common and
the most blameworthy sorts of lies.

THE PARADOX OF SELF-DECEPTION

Not only do we lie to one another, but as we've already observed,
we are enormously accomplished at lying to ourselves. Evolutionary biologists speculate that even nonhuman animals self-deceive
because it is easier to frighten off a potential predator or intimi-
date a competitor if the member of a species "believes" the deceptive appearance that creature is trying to create. All species
bluff more successfully when the bluffing species "believes" its
own bluff.

Self-deception has often been described as a paradox because
it doesn't seem possible both to know that something is true and
to persuade oneself of the opposite (or vice versa). I can lie to
someone else because I can hide the truth of my belief from that
person, but to lie to myself, I have to hide from myself what I

know myself to believe. I have to know some proposition p and yet convince myself of the untruth of p, or of some other proposition that is at odds with p. If we didn't do it all the time, we'd be certain that it simply wasn't possible.

The so-called paradox of self-deception has not been solved, but among philosophers, psychologists, and evolutionary biologists something like a consensus has emerged that depends primarily on the notion that the mind has many parts, and you can hold one belief in one part of your mind while holding a different belief in another part of your mind. We can experience cognitive dissonance, or the experience of holding two contradictory beliefs as true, even at the same time. It looks as if there are many different ways we can lie to ourselves: with selective attention; in the manner we describe our beliefs to ourselves; in the way we remember and misremember events or "facts"; through the kinds of narratives we use to make sense of ourselves and our beliefs. We rationalize—that is, we use reason to select the facts that will provide for us the conclusion we already know we want to arrive at, and we ignore those facts that might tend to contradict that conclusion.

Often we suppose that self-deception is straightforwardly bad. The self-deceived alcoholic who tells himself that he will stop drinking tomorrow is not doing himself any favors. But the same example cuts the other way: one of the maxims in Alcoholics Anonymous is "I will take a drink tomorrow," a consciously chosen self-deception that works because, as the old saying goes, tomorrow never comes. We all self-select false beliefs; whether the process is good or bad depends upon the ends that those self-deceptions serve. What is particularly fascinating about human psychology and self-deception is that even when we know the belief we are choosing is false, the false belief may still help us achieve goals we otherwise couldn't accomplish. The alcoholic "knows" he won't really be taking a drink tomorrow, but the fact that he tells himself he will take that drink tomorrow is enormously helpful in enabling him to avoid taking the drink today.

William James explains how self-deception works, and why it is so powerful, with the story of a hiker contemplating the daunting task of leaping a mountain crevasse. The truth is that the hiker doesn't know whether or not he can make it; it looks like too great a jump. If forced to confess "the truth" of what he believes, James suggests, the hiker would have to admit that the leap is simply farther than he can possibly jump. But because he has no realistic choice other than to venture it, he lies to himself and tells himself that it can be done. If he tells himself he'll never make it, we all know what will happen. But if he insists, despite his justified doubts, that he can leap farther than he's ever leaped before, he at least—we all know this from personal experience—has a better chance of making the jump than he otherwise would.

Some self-deceptions are consciously chosen; many others are not. Much of what we suppose we know to be true may be self-serving lies we are telling ourselves: consider how adept we all are at rewriting our own pasts in order to make them more palatable. And this fact of course considerably complicates our ability to tell the truth to others. I can be completely sincere—in some sense, utterly truthful—while reporting a falsehood that part of me knows to be false. The better we are at thoughtless self-deception, the easier it becomes for us to think of ourselves as completely truthful people. By contrast, if we cultivate the habit of carefully scrutinizing our beliefs, we may find that being a truth teller is much harder than we previously supposed, as many of the beliefs we really want to believe are true are exposed as false.

William James tells another story to explain how self-deception works. He asks us to consider how many young men have convinced women to fall in love with them by protesting over and over: "But you simply must love me!" The self-deception here is complex: it requires that the young lover believe that the beloved can love him, and also that his protests can persuade her to love him; it perhaps even requires that he self-deceptively believe that she already does love him but has not yet recognized the fact. In any event, James argues, it works: through self-deceptively insisting that what is not the case must be the case, the young lover manages to transform his false belief into a true one. Suddenly the sought-after beloved does in fact return his love.

As with the hiker example, James is relying on two deep psychological forces to accomplish the successful self-deceptive act: the need to believe and the resources provided by the belief. This combination of need and resourcefulness in the operation of self-deception is useful for our purposes, because these are the same powers, according to Plato, that give birth to erotic love. In closing this discussion of what several philosophers have had to say about deception and self-deception, allow me to anticipate our subject in the chapters to come by briefly looking at the parallel between one of Plato's accounts of erotic love and William James's account of self-deception.

In *Symposium,* probably Western literature's most celebrated work on love—the *Kama Sutra* is the most celebrated work from Eastern literature—Plato has several characters discuss the nature of love during a drinking party, while they wait for Socrates, who is running late. When Socrates at last arrives, he approves the subject but admits that he himself doesn't know anything about love, a characteristic Socratic claim. But he adds that he was once taught about love by a woman named Diotima who, to him, seemed to be a reliable source on the subject. (That Socrates would refer to a woman in this context is fascinating, even shocking, given the chauvinistic and homoerotic world of ancient

Athens.) Diotima ultimately teaches Socrates that love is a ladder to the truth. But along the way she tells him a myth about how erotic love, or *eros*, came to be conceived. Eros, she warns him, is the child of "resourcefulness" (*Poros*) and "need" (*Penia*). Poros, she tells Socrates, had to get drunk before he would sleep with Penia, who deceived him into getting her pregnant while he was in a blackout. Thus eros, conceived in deception, is a combination of our resourcefulness and our need.

Now the idea that both self-deception and erotic love combine these two psychological forces, need and resourcefulness, does not itself advance an argument. Lots of different psychological situations involve both need and resourcefulness: to desire at all, we might argue, is both to need (or imagine a need) and to seek, imagine, or rely upon the resources to satisfy that need. The connection between James's account of self-deception and Diotima's account of eros is merely allusive. But what appeals to me about this comparison between self-deception and erotic love is that it is in the coupling of need and resourcefulness that both find their strength. Mere need alone will not sustain a self-deception for long; no matter how earnestly a parched wanderer in the desert lies to himself that an oasis is real, he will eventually die of thirst. Similarly, need alone will not create erotic love; unless there is some hope of that love's being requited, unless the lover believes he has some resources to accomplish the goal of being loved in return, he'll soon give up in despair. Still more to the point, we shall soon see that self-deception is not only a common strategy of lovers but among the most useful techniques they have at their disposal. Diotima recognizes, when she tells Socrates her useful myth, that it is deception and not the truth that brought love into the world.

2. Childhood

> One prefers that they know their lessons and lie, rather than remain ignorant and true.
>
> —Jean-Jacques Rousseau

> Not that you lied to me, but that I can no longer trust you, has shaken me. —Friedrich Nietzsche

LITE-BRITES AND MAGIC LANTERNS

When I was with my mother, I did not feel alone.

But whenever I was away from her, I suffered. On this particular occasion, I had devised a ruse to get a bit of attention after my bedtime. It must have been about eight o'clock at night, because it was dark outside, but I don't know what time of year it was, and this was in Calgary, Alberta, so if it was winter, it could have been earlier; in winter it gets dark early that far north. I was three years old. I went to my parents' bedroom to show my mother a Lite-Brite I had made.

A Lite-Brite, if you don't know the toy, has a lightbulb behind a plastic screen with many small holes. You cover the screen with a piece of black paper and then poke a small peg of brightly colored plastic through the paper; the light from the bulb shines through the pegs, creating a beautiful, glowing, gemlike effect. As you add pegs, you form pictures or patterns.

It was, in my opinion, the prettiest Lite-Brite I had ever made.

We were not allowed in our parents' bedroom, but I stood in the dark hallway, getting my nerve up, at last knocked on the door, and my mother opened it.

"Why aren't you asleep, honey?" she asked me. "You should be in bed."

I could hear my father moving about in the room, and I didn't want him to see me.

"I made a Lite-Brite," I told her. "Can you come look at it?"

"I'll see it in the morning," she said.

I heard my father calling out to her from behind the door. "Vic, we've got to get moving."

"You should be asleep already. I'll see your Lite-Brite in the morning, Clancy," she said. She looked over her shoulder back into the bedroom. It was brightly lit in there and inaccessible. In my memory the peeks I had into it were more colorful than other places in our house. It always looked like Christmas in their bedroom.

"But it will be day then. You won't be able to see it the same."

"We'll look at it in your closet then," she said.

My father called out again. "Go to bed now. You shouldn't even be up."

I went back to my room and tried the Lite-Brite in the closet—I remember how the cord just reached; I remember sliding it between the carpet and the closet door—and she was right: it was even better in the tiny dark space. There was just room enough for my mother to squeeze in there with me. I admired it for a few minutes. Then I unplugged it and went to bed.

In the morning I padded down the stairs—I seem to remember how my feet felt in my footed pajamas—and found my mother in the kitchen, cooking breakfast, in her robe. I pulled on her blue terry cloth bathrobe, eager to show her the Lite-Brite.

When she turned around, it wasn't my mother. It was our baby-sitter. My mother and father had left for Hawaii for two weeks. Why my babysitter was wearing my mother's bathrobe is anybody's guess. But it completed the deception.

The child psychiatrist Adam Phillips writes:

In the beginning every child is only a child. The child is not possessive of the mother because he already possesses her; he behaves—in fact, lives—as if he is entitled. Our first inklings, that is to say, are monogamous ones: of privilege and privacy, of ownership and belonging. The stuff of which monogamy will be made. Because everyone begins their life belonging to someone else—physically and emotionally inextricable from someone else—being separate, or having to share, leaves us in shock. For us, then, it is all or nothing; and so there is always potentially the feeling of being nothing that comes from not being at all.

This is as elegant and as accurate a description of separation anxiety as I have ever encountered. This will be one of our themes: that to be in love is to recollect separation anxiety. When I was a child, my separation anxiety was so intense that when separated from my mother—or even at the prospect of separation from my mother—I would fall into a psychological state that, with no exaggeration, is best described as psychotic and from the outside resembled something like a protracted epileptic seizure, with tears and screaming added in for good measure. From the inside, I remember, it was like drowning. It was a terrifying despair. It was like death must be. And, of course, throughout my adulthood I've had small tastes of it when my father died, when my mentor died, when I divorced, when I've been separated for any serious length of time from my children, during heartbreak.

Phillips tells us what separation anxiety is. Proust brilliantly shows us the agony of love's separation, first when little Marcel is in bed longing for his mother; in the opening pages he lies to Françoise to convince her to deliver a note to his mother, desperate as he is for his goodnight kiss—and again when the older Marcel learns that Albertine has left him, desperate as he is for a different sort of goodnight kiss. For me, it was like what Phillips describes: falling down into a black hole at the bottom of which is an obliteration that nevertheless does not destroy the feeling of abject loneliness, of abandonment, "the feeling of being nothing"—nothing that still feels that it is nothing.

How my mother dealt with my separation anxiety was, in the Lite-Brite instance, just to avoid it. It is the understandable, if shamefaced, motivation for so many of our lies. (Many of our lies are motivated by simple fear of telling the truth; both Nietzsche and Aristotle considered lying "base" or "cowardly," as opposed to the "nobility" of truth telling, for this very reason.) No doubt she deployed the familiar self-deceptive technique of trying as best she could to forget it. When I childishly tease her about it or tell her that I've used it as an example in a lecture, she winces and admits that she regrets it to this day. Now a parent myself, I think of what it must have been like for her sitting on the airplane, trying to be excited for my father's sake about their trip to Hawaii, and worrying for three thousand miles about what my reaction was going to be when I woke up. The lie probably ruined at least the first few days of her trip. "As well it should have!" the child in me wants to complain. Or perhaps she didn't worry about the lie at all and suffered only the anxiety that every parent does when separated from her or his children: a twofold suffering, made up of both your own missing them and your fear about the pain the child is suffering from missing you.

LOVE AND TRUST

We regret a lot of the lies we tell to the people we love, whether children or parents or romantic partners—especially when we are busted. (Or is that true? Sometimes successfully hiding the lie is more painful than having it exposed.) That doesn't mean we shouldn't acknowledge, at least to ourselves, the lies we have told and try to understand why we told them and especially why we might tell them again. My teenage daughter recently confronted me with a lie I had told her and said: "Dad, if you want me to trust you, I really need you to try hard to always be honest with me." Of course what she wants, though she may not understand this until she has children of her own, is to be lied to, or at least to be kept in the dark about, those things that she truly does not need to know and that might disturb or harm her and to be told the truth about those things the truth of which bear directly on her well-being, her confidence in relying on me, and our relationship more generally.

When I was a child, my separation anxiety was about trust; whenever my mother left me, I didn't trust—I couldn't even understand that—she would come back. And of course the reason the Lite-Brite lie has stayed with me in a way that no other lie my mother ever told me has was that the lie entailed not just her absence but her absence when I had trusted, as most children reasonably do, that when I went to sleep at night, the mother who was there at bedtime would still be there in the morning, especially when she had explicitly promised to be there.

Adrienne Rich writes, recalling very much what it feels like for the child: "When we discover that someone we trusted can be trusted no longer, it forces us to reexamine the universe, to question the whole instinct and concept of trust. For a while, we are thrust back onto some bleak, jutting ledge, in a dark pierced by sheets of fire, swept by sheets of rain, in a world before kinship, or naming, or tenderness exist; we are brought close to formlessness." You can't trust the surface words anymore; there are a hundred possible interpretations for every gesture or action, and all of them may be contrary to what you want to believe: that you are loved and can trust the person who has lied to you. A mother normally would come to see your Lite-Brite; now any time she hesitates before coming to watch you at play you wonder if it portends her disappearance. The child reduces his understanding of the beloved's actions to the simplest, most feared possibilities. He understands his mother as clumsy, careless; she's dangerously thick fingered with his love.

To trust is to grace the beloved with elegance. The child who trusts supposes that his mother understands him well enough to comprehend his anxiety and to act accordingly. The trusted mother acts as she does because her action expresses just what she means it to convey, and for the child's perspective, what she means to convey is her caring for him, her carefulness, her respect for the tenderness of his feelings. The child understands himself as a delicate, vulnerable creature who can too easily be injured by this powerful being who dominates his world.

WHEN CHILDREN LIE

There are two old psychologists' dogmas about children and lying, both now demonstrated to be false. The first is that children don't learn to lie until the age of four. This was thoroughly disproved only in the past twenty years or so; we now know that clear signs of deceptive behavior in typical children appear at latest by the time they are six months old (making a strong case, so it seems to me, that research psychologists weren't paying very close attention to their own kids until quite recently, and it perhaps comes as no surprise that much of the best contemporary research on the subject comes from a woman, Dr. Victoria Talwar). Anyone who has children and observes them closely will see that they learn to deceive before they learn to talk, and they start lying virtually as soon as they start talking. The case has sometimes been made that children don't understand the difference between truth and falsehood as well as adults do, but even if this were the case, we should pursue further, and ask whether adults know the difference between truth and falsehood as well as they pretend. Or are they simply more convinced of their own prejudices, self-deceptions, and errors?

The second dogma is that children learn to lie from outside the family; it's television or other kids ("the bad kid") or advertising or school that teaches them to lie. We now know that children learn to lie more or less entirely from observing their parents. A quick example that can stand for hundreds: you are driving up to preschool while talking on the phone and you see in the parking lot another parent you don't like. You tell your partner on the phone, your child strapped in her car seat behind you, "Oh, no, there's Don. I can't stand that idiot." Thirty seconds later while you're carrying your child in the doors, you bump into Don and, beaming, say, "Don, hey, how are you? We need to get the kids together soon!"

Now you might say that the parent in this situation isn't exactly lying to Don; he's engaged in another kind of deceptive activity, like Confucian politeness. But what the child sees of course is that on the one hand the parent has expressed a sincere belief to his other parent (I don't like this person) and then with the same apparent sincerity acted in a way that expresses a completely incompatible belief (effectively: "Don, I like you a lot!"). We shouldn't draw from this example the conclusion that the parent acted inappropriately; we have to engage in social deceptions of many different kinds all the time. Ordinary life would be impossible without them. But where we err is in daily providing our children with deceptions of this kind and nevertheless insisting on teaching them that "Lying is always wrong." We are simply underestimating how smart and observant our children are and, in doing so, are confusing them. The real but regrettable lesson being taught to the child here seems to be: "Lie as necessary, and then lie about the fact that you lie." Which lesson is of course, and very unfortunately, what so many of us actually practice in everyday life.

In my mother's Lite-Brite lie, motivated by her fear of my reaction, she was similarly inadvertently teaching me how to deal with my fears about separation—and their reaction to that separation—from the people I love. If you fear the separation and the other person's reaction to the separation, lie about it.

Still more interesting is not so much when and how children lie, as why they do it, especially since it does take less energy, most of the time, to tell the truth. But telling the truth may be complicated for a child. Think of the six-month-old deceptive baby. She cries because she wants attention. In this instance, she seems to be truth telling. Then she stops crying to see if anyone is paying attention. If no one is, she may try out another cry or two, but recognizing that her tears are wasted, since no one can hear them, the typical baby will take up some other activity. If, however, she hears someone in the next room, she will immediately resume her crying and indeed will exaggerate it in order to get the attention she needs.

In one sense there is nothing the baby is crying *about*; she hasn't hurt herself and isn't hungry, though she will pretend to be in need (as Robert Trivers has pointed out, baby chimpanzees and even baby pelicans will feign grievous need and indeed pain simply in order to get their parents' attention). But in another sense there is something she is crying *for*: she's crying for love, and she doesn't have any other surefire way to get it. Her means look deceptive because she isn't "really" upset; she won't cry unless she knows a parent is there to hear it. She's perfectly happy entertaining herself until she becomes aware that a parent can hear her. And she also has other means, though they are probably less effective, of getting her parent's attention: children can holler without crying. But if she starts bawling, which is what she will in fact do, she will get the attention she wants. If the parent doesn't respond, she'll howl with greater indignation and desperation. But what counts as deceptive here is a bit odd because "the lie" is her best means of communication—sometimes her only effective one. In some sense she means to deceive; she's not really as upset as she pretends. In another sense she is simply using the best communicative technique to get what she wants. But a lie—here a howl—may often turn out to be the best communicative technique to get what we want. That the deceptive intention is a bit slippery is helpful for us to remember because especially in contexts of love like these, deceptive intentions will be similarly slippery regardless of what age we are. With age, our howls simply become subtler, more refined, more cunning.

Of course, like adults, some children lie more and some children lie less. If you have a child who lies a lot, you may take consolation in a recent study (that I note in the prologue) that shows that the more a child lies, the higher her IQ is likely to prove and the more likely she is to succeed in later life. My wife's mother, a neurological research nurse at Stanford, told me that she had worried about her daughter's intelligence when she was young because "she just didn't lie as much as a smart kid ought to." We all lie for dozens of different reasons by the time we are adults, and even as young children we can discern multiple reasons for lying. Moreover, natural selection may well select for excellence in self-deception among both children and nonhuman offspring.

But some reasons for deceit are more fundamental and compelling than others. Just as believing a lie and then discovering it to be false may thrust us out on Rich's dark precipice of formlessness, so we tell lies to avoid finding ourselves abandoned on that same ledge. We tend to believe lies we would otherwise subject to closer scrutiny so as to avoid that feeling of nothingness. How many times has a friend come to you believing outrageous lies her partner is telling her or him, lies that are transparent to everyone except the person who, paradoxically, knows the liar best? We very often lie as children—and, perhaps for many years to come—because we are afraid of the separation that telling the truth may create between us and those we love most and feel closest to. Current research shows that very young children are prone to lie to avoid hurting the feelings of even relative strangers. By the time we are two or three we are telling people what they want to hear—or what we think they want to hear.

The best liars must also be mind readers: at age two we are already practicing the skill of imagining what another person is likely to be thinking and what that person is inclined to believe or disbelieve. Playing is of course a crucial part of this: when we make-believe, we are not only influencing what we ourselves think but are also doing our best to create an illusion for the others we are playing with.

A fierce advocate for truth telling, especially in the context of love, bell hooks accurately observes:

> Among any group of kids it is never clear why some quickly learn the fine art of dissimulation (that is, taking on whatever appearance is needed in order to manipulate a situation) while others find it hard to mask true feeling. Since pretense is such

an expected aspect of childhood play, it is a perfect context for mastering the art of dissimulation. Concealing the truth is often a fun part of childhood play, yet when it becomes a common practice it is a dangerous prelude to lying all the time.

One of the great dangers of lying is wrongly supposing that you know what someone else wants to believe or, still worse, that what they want to believe is good for them to believe because it happens to agree with your own (usually immediate) interest.

Remember the dreadful time your mother or father first told you: "I just can't trust you anymore"? You would have done anything for a giant mental vacuum cleaner to erase her or his memory of whatever you had done or said to lose that trust! It is not only the person who no longer trusts who feels separated, who feels threatened by nothingness—especially not when one of those people is an adult and the other a child—but also the person who has violated the trust. And so, when telling the truth means admitting to having done something that we fear is a violation of trust—and a child has no sense of proportion in these matters—we would sooner lie than be cast out. This, I'm arguing, is the most fundamental source of childhood lying: the suspicion by the child that telling the truth will create emotional distance between the parent and the child. "If I admit what I did, she will be angry with me, she will love me less; if I lie, she won't know, and she will love me just the same, or perhaps still more, since the lie will reassure her." Of course the double bind is that in lying, not only do we risk further separation, but we also alienate ourselves. Every lie we tell is itself a small separation, an assertion of loneliness, a reminder that you know the contents of your own mind and the other person does not. You cannot lie without hiding what is in your mind.

Every lie we tell is also, and for the same reasons, an expression of freedom. "It is the law of obedience which produces the necessity of lying in children," writes Rousseau, "since obedience is irksome." Deception is a way of asserting our autonomy. The parent expresses her separation from the child in the lies she tells the child; the child must also, as she separates from the parent, learn how to lie and to lie well. Lying is an essential step in the development of our independence from our parents. Satan, God's most difficult child, is the greatest liar because in his pride and independence, he will not obey his Father. Milton writes, in the voice of Satan:

> To bow and sue for grace
> With suppliant knee, and deify his power,
> Who from the terrour of this arm so late
> Doubted his empire; that were low indeed,
> That were an ignominy and shame beneath
> This downfall. . . .

This is the voice of the child who will no longer submit to the parent. Satan's downfall of course is into the lonely darkness of hell (what we might suppose Adrienne Rich is thinking of when she envisions her "dark, formless place"). When we lie as children, we introduce ourselves to these dark, perhaps desirable, and in any case inevitable companions: loneliness and freedom.

The first great love story about lying in the Western tradition is in the Book of Genesis, when Adam and Eve were still in the Garden, like children, before coming into the tough adult knowledge of good and evil. There, in paradise, Satan lies to Eve, and Eve in turn lies to Adam. They in turn are expelled from Eden and learn for the first time about freedom and the loneliness that accompanies it.

Again, the paradox of childhood lies is that we so often tell them out of fear of rejection, fear of separation, fear of being alone, and yet the lie is itself an expression of our independence. We lie in order not to be alone, and yet we cannot lie without accepting the fact that fundamentally, alone is where we are. Our minds are entirely private—and especially so when we lie.

HOW TO TEACH YOUR CHILD TO LIE

I am often asked by other parents: "How can I discourage my child from lying?" The first thing I like to do in these situations is quote (or, in truth, paraphrase) Robert Trivers:

> Are you investing in a child or exploiting it? Do you love the child or not? Do you have in mind a separate self-interest in the child that you are willing to support or is the child entirely conceived as instrumental to your larger projects? It makes a whale of a difference to the offspring which of these is true, and there is plenty of scope for deceit and self-deception on the part of the parent, as well as of the offspring . . . There are many opportunities for conscious and unconscious manipulation, including induced self-deception, in which the parent can induce a pattern of self-deception in the offspring that serves the parent's interests but not those of the offspring expressing the self-deception. The child may grow to believe that its parents are acting in its true interests when they are not.

Although there are lots of contemporary books that offer antilying prescriptions in the course of telling you how to raise your child, the best advice I have found on the subject comes from Jean-Jacques Rousseau in his book *Emile*. Rousseau was himself a confessed childhood liar and an incorrigible liar in his *Confessions*, despite his opening promise: "I am commencing an undertaking, hitherto without precedent, and which will never find an imitator. I desire to set before my fellows the likeness of a man in *all the truth* of nature, and that man myself" (emphasis mine).

Rousseau recommends that we not punish our children for lying but teach them why wiser persons in older age learn through hard experience to avoid deception whenever possible:

> I have said enough to make it understood that punishment as punishment must never be inflicted on children, but it should always happen to them as a consequence of their bad action. Thus you will not declaim against lying: you will not precisely punish them for having lied; but you will arrange it so that all the bad effects of lying—such as not being believed when one tells the truth, of being accused of the evil that one did not do although one denies it—come in league against them when they have lied.

He adds: "In the natural and free education why would your child lie to you? What has he to hide from you? You do not reprove him; you punish him for nothing; you exact nothing from him."

Without getting into the details of how Rousseau recommends we raise our children generally, we should notice that according to Rousseau, children lie because as parents we give them reasons to lie.

My favorite example of lie-inducing behavior in parents is the "Did you break the cookie jar?" type. When a father asks his child, "Did you break the cookie jar?" knowing full well that there are no other cookie jar–breaking candidates, not only is he creating the opportunity for the child to lie, but he himself is deceptively (since he knows the answer to the question but pretends not to) encouraging his child to lie to him, so that he can administer a lesson about—and often apply a punishment for—deception. The parent creates the temptation to lie, and if the child is savvy enough to see through her parent's motives, she may conclude that the parent does not deserve the truth. Another uncomfortably honest observation from bell hooks: "How many of us can vividly recall moments where we courageously practiced the honesty we had been taught to value by our parents, only to find that they did not really mean for us to tell the truth all the time. In far too many cases children are punished in circumstances where they respond to a question posed by an adult authority figure . . . And so they learn that lying is a way to avoid being hurt and hurting others."

As long as we are teaching children not to lie by punishing them in the practice of it, all we will succeed in doing is instructing them in being more cunning liars. The child is learning only that lying results in a punishment without ever understanding why the parent, whom any child will observe practicing deception from day to day, insists that lying is wrong. As a result, the child may in fact be encouraged to deceive still more, in order to avoid deception punishments (it has long been observed how one lie tends to weave itself into a tangle of many, and not just among children). Furthermore, for Rousseau, when adults extract promises from children, they are doing something still more blameworthy, because a child does not understand a future commitment in the way an adult does.

> If he could avoid the whip or get a bag of sugared almonds by promising to throw himself out the window tomorrow, he would do so on the spot . . . It follows from this that children's lies are all the work of masters, and that to want to teach them

to tell the truth is nothing other than to teach them to lie. In one's eagerness to control children, to govern them, to instruct them, one finds one never has sufficient means for reaching the goal. One wants to give oneself new holds on their minds by means of maxims without foundation and precepts without reason; one prefers that they know their lessons and lie, rather than remain ignorant and true.

What is the solution, then, according to Rousseau, to teaching your child not to lie? Simply not to provide occasion that the child should need to do so. Structure the child's life and environment in such a way that lying seems unnecessary to her. Cultivate a preference in her for telling the truth because it is easier to do so and succeeds in achieving the things that she wants. Above all, avoid coercing the child. Of his imagined pupil Emile, Rousseau writes: "It is quite clear that the more I make his well-being independent of either the will or the judgments of others, the more I reduce any interest in him to lie."

The interest in Rousseau's account, for my purposes, is that there is no force more powerfully coercive in the life of a child than the love (or withdrawal of love, or absence of love, or conditional love) of her parent. And of course, when it comes to love, we so often coerce without knowing we're doing it.

CARTWHEELING UP MOUNT OLYMPUS

In *Symposium,* Plato's famous dialogue on love, Aristophanes describes our original state as being combined with another human being: we are sewn together back to back, so that we have four arms and four legs (some of us are men sewn to men, some men sewn to women, and some women sewn to women; this will turn out to have erotic implications in later life). Because we have four legs and arms, rather than walk, we simply tumble, and we do so with such adroitness, and at such great speed, that displaying the hubris humans always do, we decide to roll our way to the top of Mount Olympus. The gods are suitably alarmed at all these humans tumbling like circus clowns up the mountain to crash the party.

> At this Zeus took counsel with the other gods as to what was to be done. They found themselves in rather an awkward position; they didn't want to blast them out of existence, with thunderbolts as they did the giants, because that would be saying goodbye to all their offerings and devotions, but at the same time they couldn't let them get altogether out of hand. At last, however, after racking his brains, Zeus offered a solution. I think I can see my way, he said, to put an end to this disturbance by weakening these people without destroying them. What I propose to do is to cut them all in half . . . They can walk about, upright, on their two legs, and if, said Zeus, I have any more trouble with them, I shall split them up again, and they'll have to hop about on one. So saying, he cut them all in half just as you or I might chop up sorb apples for pickling, or slice an egg with a hair.

Aristophanes uses this as a myth to explain the feeling of completeness we have when we are in the throes of romantic love, and indeed, I myself have used the story, more than once, and honestly, to describe how I was feeling with a romantic partner. In Aristophanes's version of the story we are always searching for our missing half, and when we find her or him, we feel completed; I think the myth is psychologically profound and accurate, but also believe that, for better or worse, we can achieve that feeling of completion with more than one person over the course of a life. (The first sentence of Samuel Beckett's *The Lost Ones* has a nice echo of Aristophanes's myth: "Abode where lost bodies roam each searching for its lost one.") But what occurred to me, when I was thinking about the love as identification theory of early childhood connection to one's mother, is that there is a time when Aristophanes's myth is nearly literally true—that is, when we are in the womb. Then we have four arms and four legs, and we are at one, inseparably joined, with the beloved.

Perhaps the greatest meditation on the child's need for the love of his mother, and the agony of the mother's complete control of that love, is in Proust (the passage, which I mention above, is long but unforgettable):

> My sole consolation when I went upstairs for the night was that Mamma would come in and kiss me after I was in bed. But this good night lasted for so short a time, she went down again so soon, that the moment in which I heard her climb the stairs, and then caught the sound of her garden dress of blue muslin, from which hung little tassels of plaited straw, rustling along the double-doored corridor, was for me a moment of the utmost pain; for it heralded the moment which was bound to follow it, when she would have left me and gone downstairs again. So much so that I reached the point of hoping that this good night which I loved so much would come as late as possible, so as to prolong the time of respite during which Mamma would not yet have appeared. Sometimes when, after kissing me, she opened the door to go, I longed to call her back, to say to her "Kiss me just once more," but I knew that then she would at once look displeased, for the concession which she made to my wretchedness and agitation in coming up to me to give me this kiss of peace always annoyed my father, who thought such

rituals absurd, and she would have liked to try to induce me to outgrow the need, the habit, of having her there at all, let alone get into the habit of asking her for an additional kiss when she was already crossing the threshold. And to see her look displeased destroyed all the calm and serenity she had brought me a moment before, when she had bent her loving face down over my bed, and held it out to me like a host for an act of peacegiving communion in which my lips might imbibe her real presence and with it the power to sleep.

Marcel is happy to lie to Françoise, their maid, to persuade her to take a note to his mother; he is also happy to lie to his mother—within the constraints of her credulity, he's a cunning liar, and he knows she anticipates his moves—in order to persuade her to return to his bedroom. In fact the only constraint on what Marcel will say in order to get more of his mother's time at bedtime is not the truth—far from it!—but the fear that he might push his mother too far, that he could increase his separation from her by pleading or misleading too much. He sometimes dares send an urgent note—"I must see you! There's something important I have to tell you!"—though all he wants, as his mother well knows, is to see her one more time. And how many of us, in later life, in the midst of heartbreak, have sent just the same sort of note, in an e-mail, or a text, or a voice mail? How many desperate lies have we told in order to seize the beloved's attention, if only for a few hours, or even a few minutes, for even the briefest reply, for the mere acknowledgment that we still exist, are known to the beloved, and are still in love?

Marcel's deceptive attempts to manipulate his mother's attention are no different from the kinds of games we all play as grown-ups, when we measure out our texts or phone calls to a love interest—waiting perhaps twenty-four hours before sending a text, at least forty-eight hours before making a call—and indeed, in an established love relationship, when we, in the course of a fight, say only as much as allows us to maintain our emotional advantage. Strike too hard a verbal blow, say something too cruel, and suddenly the tables have turned; you're in the wrong, and now you are the one who must apologize, again, regardless of what the "truth" of the matter may be, even though you "know" you are "in the right." At the end of the day does the truth really matter—suppose we can find it—when love is at stake?

Proust is a subtle enough psychologist to show how completely irrelevant considerations of truthfulness are for his young narrator, desperately in love as he is with his mother. All this taking place, remember, over a kiss, and at bedtime. Marcel, as he ages, will in his love relationships show this same disregard for the candle of truth whenever the game is love. Both he and his mother—and too his father, who unsurprisingly cannot tolerate these bedtime scenes—have collaborated to train him to be a particular kind of lover and perhaps even to fall in love with a particular kind of woman.

CRYING WOLF

Aesop writes:

> There was once a young Shepherd Boy who tended his sheep at the foot of a mountain near a dark forest. It was rather lonely for him all day, so he thought upon a plan by which he could get a little company and some excitement. He rushed down towards the village calling out "Wolf, Wolf," and the villagers came out to meet him, and some of them stopped with him for a considerable time. This pleased the boy so much that a few

days afterwards he tried the same trick, and again the villagers came to his help. But shortly after this a Wolf actually did come out from the forest, and began to worry the sheep, and the boy of course cried out "Wolf, Wolf," still louder than before. But this time the villagers, who had been fooled twice before, thought the boy was again deceiving them, and nobody stirred to come to his help. So the Wolf made a good meal off the boy's flock, and when the boy complained, the wise man of the village said: "A liar will not be believed, even when he speaks the truth."

When I was a kid, I knew I told lies too often, and I was worried and frightened by the story of "The Boy Who Cried Wolf." It also seemed unfair to me. At first I thought the poor kid was only trying to get attention. And then, next thing you know, he's trying to protect the flock. He's *lonely*. But in his attempt to deal with his loneliness, he winds up losing his friends entirely.

There may come a time in the life of any person when he has lied to some other person often enough that she or he no longer believes anything the liar says. Does the possibility for love end with that? Suppose a father has concluded that his son is an incorrigible liar: Will he stop loving him? Should he?

Not long ago I was telling my teenage daughter a true story about a baby I had found in a car. I was walking through a very poor neighborhood in Kansas City, and there, in a closed SUV, was a baby crying. I looked in the apartment building next door, yelled, knocked, finally opened a door, and smelled that delicious pepperminty aroma, familiar from my college days, of crack cocaine alight and smoking. At that point in the narrative my daughter interrupted me and said, "Dad, I really hate it when you make up these stories . . ."

My feelings were hurt. But her skepticism was justified. She's the daughter of a fiction writer. I've already admitted it many times in this book; putting it generously, I'm "prone to exaggeration." Just to make matters worse, when I protested, she added: "Dad, I believe that *you* believe it."

When you lie and people doubt you, it's annoying. But there is nothing more frustrating to the liar—especially to the child liar—than when you are telling the truth and no one believes you. Especially the people you *want* to believe you; still worse, the people you need to believe *in* you.

How closely tied are these two phenomena: to believe what someone says and to believe in that person? Believing and keeping promises, trust, integrity (what philosophers and psychoanalysts sometimes call the jargon of authenticity): all these are at the intersection of believing what someone says and believing in that person as a person.

As children we are not merely depending on our belief in what our parents say and believing in them as parents, as the ones who will love us; we are at the same time learning to believe or distrust what we ourselves say and cultivating belief or doubt in ourselves.

What I want to call attention to here is not just the tension between Aesop and Rousseau: for Rousseau, Aesop's shepherd boy is already in an odd, lie-producing situation (he's quite naturally lonely), and the adults in the fable are not performing very well (they don't perform any due diligence after the first lie the boy tells). In Rousseau's account, it is the adults of the village in this situation, and not so much the shepherd boy, who have created a situation that naturally encourages deception and its unfortunate consequences.

That said, it is not just Rousseau's point that in encouraging children to lie—for reasons of love and loneliness—we are influencing or even determining the strategies for communication they will deploy later in life. We are, on Rousseau's account, in fact influencing the kind of people they will become. I agree with Rousseau that if we give our children fewer reasons to lie, and less fear of lying, they may become psychologically healthier people and, perhaps paradoxically, will be more inclined toward honesty. But I also want to make a stronger claim, which is that given that we know children will lie—just as adults do—if we continue to trust, respect, and love our children while acknowledging that fact, we ourselves may be better, more loving parents. I would not encourage my child to lie. But to accept lies of little or no consequence and continue to trust the child; to openly discuss lies and other deceptions without condemning them; to talk about why a lie seemed like the best solution to a problem: surely these are kinder, more adult ways of showing a child how to think about and deal with deception and the truth. As parents we should bear in mind that as many love relationships may be destroyed by unrealistic expectations about truthfulness as by a tendency to deceive, just as a too brutal honesty can be as harmful as a blatantly manipulative deception.

HOW I BECAME A REAL BOY

Like "The Boy Who Cried Wolf," and for the same reasons, when I was a boy I was made distinctly uncomfortable by, and even tried not to think about, the Walt Disney movie *Pinocchio*.

In Carlo Collodi's *The Adventures of Pinocchio* (serialized in 1881–1883)—the original text for the Walt Disney adaptation—Pinocchio, unlike Rousseau's ideal of the child, is created naughty. In fact he's badly behaved even before he's created: while still a stick of wood, he starts a fight between Geppetto and his owner, and once he is a marionette he immediately wreaks all kinds of havoc: he insults Geppetto as soon as he has a mouth, laughs at him, runs away from him, etc. He behaves, in short, like a fairly typical two-year-old when the two-year-old is misbehaving. Collodi seems to have had Rousseau in mind. When the wise hundred-year-old cricket asks Pinocchio why he wants to run away from home, Pinocchio tells him: "I shall be sent to school and shall be made to study either by love or by force. To tell you in confidence, I have no wish to learn; it is much more amusing to run after butterflies, or to climb trees and to take young birds out of their nests." Contra Rousseau, Collodi thinks that a young boy who does not undergo a traditional education will get only naughtier and will "grow up a perfect donkey" (as the cricket warns—and prophesizes—and Pinocchio does indeed later become a donkey).

The first real lie in the story is not told by Pinocchio, who does, however, repeat various fanciful inaccuracies almost as soon as he can speak, but by Geppetto, who sells his coat in order to buy Pinocchio a schoolbook and lies to the boy, telling him that he sold it "Because I found it too hot." (This is a classic example of a paternalistic lie told with good intentions, of which both a Buddhist and perhaps even Plato would have approved.) Interestingly, Pinocchio understands what his maker has really done, "and unable to restrain the impulse of his good heart he sprang up, and throwing his arms around Geppetto's neck he began kissing him again and again." So Pinocchio does have a good heart and a subtle enough intelligence to understand that though Geppetto has lied to Pinocchio, he has done so out of kindness; it's simply that Pinocchio likes to misbehave, and he hasn't learned the ways of the world yet. When the fox and the cat come along, he is easily led into temptation.

Because Geppetto's lie is such a common one, before we continue Pinocchio's story, I'd like to remind my reader of Dietrich Bonhoeffer's notion of the living truth. Bonhoeffer argues that it is naive and misleading, perhaps even dangerous to suppose that the literal truth always or even typically conveys what we mean when we talk about telling the truth. Of course we often tell a straightforward lie, and for morally blameworthy reasons. But we also often make statements that are not literally true—that are in fact literal lies—while conveying a deeper truth that an honest statement of the facts could not communicate. So, for example, if Geppetto told Pinocchio, "I sold my coat in order to buy you a schoolbook," he would be speaking the literal truth, but his meaning might well be (or be understood by Pinocchio as) "Look what sacrifices I make for you!" By telling Pinocchio that he sold his coat because it was too hot—a lie—he communicates to Pinocchio something like "My coat doesn't really matter to me, and your schoolbook does, and I don't want you to feel bad about the fact that I sold my coat." This is a very nice example of what Bonhoeffer means by the living truth, the more important meanings in communication that may not, and sometimes cannot, be conveyed by strict reportage. So many of the stories we tell our children are of this kind—Santa Claus is the obvious example I use in the first chapter—and we should ask ourselves, as parents and also as lovers: How many stories might my child, or my boyfriend, or my partner, or my mom be telling me, not in order to mislead me but rather to tell me something that, if said outright, might be misunderstood or cause me harm?

Pinocchio does not tell his first real lie—the first lie that is identified by Collodi as a lie, and the occasion for the growth of Pinocchio's already enormous nose—until after he has been tricked by the fox and the cat, and he's learned that telling the truth (in this case, about the gold coins he has) may get him into trouble. He is telling a fairy his story of how the cat and the fox stole one of his gold coins and how he fell into the hands of assassins when she asks him: "'And the four pieces—where have you put them?' 'I have lost them!' said Pinocchio, but he was telling a lie, for he had them in his pocket."

A not unreasonable lie, given that earlier his honesty had led him to be cheated. Nevertheless, every time he lies, his nose grows—this time, two fingers longer—and then he tells two more lies in quick succession, while the fairy laughs at him and poor Pinocchio, "getting quite confused," finds himself with such a long nose that he can't even run from the house to hide his shame; his nose has grown to such an enormous size that it won't fit through the door.

The series of lies Pinocchio tells is instructive. He tells the first lie because he's worried about losing his three remaining gold pieces. His second lie is told to back up his first lie: the fairy asks him where he lost his gold pieces, and he has to provide an explanation (Walter Scott's familiar "Oh what a tangled web we weave / When first we practise to deceive!"). But the fairy is practicing the "broken cookie jar" style of interrogation (itself inherently deceptive, because it feigns honest ignorance and curiosity) in order to expose Pinocchio's lies. So, knowing that he's lying to her and that he is likely to continue to lie, she pursues: "If you have lost them in the wood near here . . . we will look for them, and we shall find them: because everything that is lost in that wood is always found." It is at this point that Pinocchio loses all composure and tells a still-clumsier lie: "I didn't lose the four gold pieces, I swallowed them inadvertently while I was drinking your medicine." In a familiar, rarely effective technique of argument, scrambling to extricate himself from the lies he has told, Pinocchio tries to put the blame back on the fairy. The fairy then "allowed the puppet to cry and to roar for a good half hour over his nose . . . This she did to give him a severe lesson, and to correct him of the disgraceful fault of telling lies—the most disgraceful fault that a boy can have."

Whether or not Collodi is tongue in cheek here is hard to say: the fairy is quick to forgive Pinocchio, and despite Pinocchio's historical reputation, the rest of the book is much less concerned with Pinocchio's lying than it is with other kinds of naughtiness he engages in. Collodi also, here agreeing with Rousseau, tells a lot of stories to illustrate how commonly adults mislead children into misbehaviors that the children otherwise might not have pursued. Moreover, the story is told by a writer of fiction, who is making veiled, often sarcastic observations about the politics of late-nineteenth-century Italy; perhaps Collodi is an advocate for truth in one way, but in another way, he is clearly someone who understands the subtleties of communication and the necessity for pretense, irony, and disguise.

One quick, delightful example of Collodi's trickery: Pinocchio asks the fairy how she knew that he was lying. The fairy replies: "Lies, my dear boy, are found out immediately, because they are of two sorts. There are lies that have short legs, and lies that have long noses. Your lie, as it happens, is one of those that have a long nose."

This is an interesting distinction, one worth remembering. Lies that have short legs are those that carry you a little distance but cannot outrun the truth. The truthful consequences always catch up with someone who tells a lie with short legs. Lies that have long noses are those that are obvious to everyone except the person who told the lie, lies that make the liar look ridiculous. In either case, according to our often-deceitful fairy, lies are bad because they result in bad consequences for the liar. And this conclusion of the fairy is noteworthy, because the vast majority of arguments against lying are made because lies are, so this line goes, unfair or harmful to the people who believe the liar. But it can also be—as another Italian, Machiavelli, advises—that lies should be avoided because they produce negative consequences for the liar. This is Aesop's argument as well, and much of what Aristotle says against lying also comes down to the idea that lies are harmful mostly to the teller of lies.

When at last Pinocchio is transformed into a real boy by the fairy, it is not because he's learned the value of honesty, but as the fairy says to him in his dreams, "To reward you for your good heart . . . Boys who minister tenderly to their parents, and assist them in their misery and infirmities, are deserving of great praise and affection, even if they cannot be cited as examples of obedience and good behavior. Try and do better in the future and you will be happy." So it is really for his good intentions that he is rewarded, and Pinocchio's few lies—and many misdeeds— were, though consistently misguided, never malicious. Pinocchio himself doesn't learn the lesson. Thinking about his life as a puppet, "he said to himself with great complacency: 'How ridiculous I was when I was a puppet! And how glad I am that I have become a well-behaved little boy!'" Here we know Collodi is laughing at his character: Pinocchio hasn't learned to be a well-behaved little boy—the fairy's told him so—and he's congratulating himself not with the resolution to be a better boy but with the "great complacency" of a job well done. The lesson, if there is one, is about trying one's best to be a good boy—the story was serialized in a children's magazine—and to please one's parents.

Before reading Collodi, when I was familiar only with Walt Disney's version of the story, I had the idea that the moral of Pinocchio's story was "The truth sets you free": as long as you are lying, you are dancing on the strings of others, but once you are brave enough to speak your mind—rather than worry about what others would have you say and do—you can be authentic; you can be a *real* boy. I still think there is some merit to this view, and I imagine it must be part of what Disney had in mind. But the reason I prefer Collodi's original, much longer version of the story is that he appears to moralize but in fact lets his hero behave very much as we expect a typical little boy will. Pinocchio is naughty, he lies, he breaks (well-intentioned, sincerely meant) promises, he gets into all sorts of difficulties—through hastiness, inexperience, and misjudgment. (Sound familiar?) But he is nevertheless a hero in the end, he is goodhearted, he loves Geppetto, and the fairy nobly gives him his just reward, which is, after all, just to be an ordinary boy. This is, as Nietzsche writes as the subtitle to his great final masterpiece *Ecce Homo*, "How one becomes what one is."

SEPARATION ANXIETY AND SECRETS

Many lies begin as secrets. Or as the pretense of a secret. Everything that is left unspoken may become the source of a lie, in order that it remain hidden or so that what is said should not be revealed as untrue.

Here I'm going to tell a personal story that is perhaps a bit gruesome, perhaps ridiculous, but in any case crucial to my own psychology, and I hope illustrative of the kinds of secrets children tell that ripen, over time, into deceptive behaviors and downright lies. This is also the story of the very first lie I remember telling as a child, and it is something like a classic Freudian case study in separation anxiety.

Not long after my little brother was born, my mother decided to toilet train me. I was too young, about eighteen months old. But with an alcoholic and abusive husband, a brand-new baby, and an already wild nine-year-old boy (my big brother Darren) she had her hands full, and she didn't need to be changing diapers for two of us.

The toilet training didn't take. The first lie I remember telling was on Christmas Day. I remember my little brother playing in a pen, standing there, supporting himself with his fingers in the netting and his blue eyes that seemed at that time to be half the size of his head. It was Christmas, so he was about fifteen months old, and I was two and a half. We were in our sunken living room, and there was a fire going. I remember the brass fire tools by the fireplace. More than that I remember the hard feel of the brick hearth against my bottom. I had not defecated in days or perhaps weeks, and my intestines were rebelling. The cramp at the bottom of my stomach was acutely painful and overwhelming. I sat on the corner of the bricks that surrounded the fireplace and pushed it as hard as I could against my rectum. "This is helping," I thought. "That will not come out of there."

"What are you doing, Clance?"

I had been concentrating. I looked up. It was my dad. I was relieved it was not my mom. Because I could lie to him—he wouldn't immediately know—and because I wasn't accountable to him for this.

"Why are you rubbing your bum against the bricks like that? Do you need to poop, buddy?"

With difficulty I stopped, clenching my bowels back so that it was like a swallowing in my throat, left the fireplace, and pretended to be playing again.

Many years later my dad and I were in Palm Beach, driving in his car—he was taking me to the doctor for acne—and he asked me if I was "still having problems on the shitter." My father was not a man who used foul language, but in this context it was a way of trying to make me less uncomfortable. "You know Freud had a theory about that, son," he said, before I could tell him that my problems with that had ended about a year before, when I moved into my college dorm. "There may be some other things you're not letting go of, son," he said. "You know the divorce was hard on all of us. You can thank your mother for that."

"I don't have those problems anymore, Dad," I said.

"Uh-huh," he said. Then he launched into one of his stories about my mother and "that dummy she married."

"I know it's hard for you to hear these things, son," he would add, "but it's important. You need to know the truth, son."

From age two forward, lying about defecating became a habit for me. I would hide the medicine my mother tried to make me ingest. Those little white or yellow or blue pills, the stool softeners, and the laxatives that she would use to excavate me: I feared them. Often she asked me to put them in my mouth and swallow them, just like a nurse in a psychiatric hospital, and then she checked the inside of my mouth, though I was cunning at secreting them in unexpected places in my mouth and then spitting them out later. My tongue was dextrous and misleading. We had a rule that she would see the excrement before I flushed, which I always broke. "I'm sorry," I would say. "I forgot."

We tend to think that this lie—the "I forgot" lie—is a very common feature only of childhood, but it turns out to be perhaps the most pervasive form of deception in ordinary human life. Especially among adults, the claim that we have forgotten quickly transforms into actually forgetting, and deception is perfected in self-deception; we tell the lie sincerely, with a clean conscience.

"I forgot," I would tell my mother, though she knew I was lying, and even I knew she knew I was lying. But sometimes the lie need only control the possible discourse; she was not in a position, at that point, to accuse me of lying (though, in her frustration and worry, she sometimes did). I was not crafty enough, at four and five, to flush sometimes when I actually had gone. Or rather, I knew that I ought to flush, at least a few times, when there was shit in the bowl, but I could never make myself do it then. There was too much pride in showing her that I had accomplished what she'd asked. What she did not understand was that after days or weeks of my keeping it safe in my belly, it was like a spike coming out. In pain, I postponed the day.

Another time, in third grade, I think, I remember the walk home taking hours—I arrived after dark; my mother was in a panic—because I had to stop every block, often more than once a block, in order to sit on the sidewalk or the curb and keep my bowels from expelling. The snow was high, and there was ice on the sidewalk, and when I got home, my pants were wet. "Where have you been?" my mother said, and I lied and told her that Tom and I had been sliding down Elbow Park hill—thus my wet pants—and apologized for worrying her.

Growing up, we always locked the door when we went to the bathroom in my house—when my mother remarried, there were all these new stepkids, and there were only two bathrooms, so you had to lock the door—and when I was going to the bathroom to try to defecate, always because my mother insisted that I try, she would knock on the locked door and ask, "Have you had a bowel movement yet?" (Those ugly words "bowel movement" still disturb me.) I would call back from the toilet, "I'm trying. Not yet." Sometimes I was truly sitting there, working up the nerve to push, but often I was sitting on the toilet with the lid down and my pants on, or if it was really bad, I couldn't go near the toilet—the thought of that made it worse—so I was lying on my back on the cool tile, reading a book, or sometimes curled up, fighting a cramp.

When I try to inventory the lies I told to my parents as a child, the list I make is dominated by this one semisecret behavior that at the time, I naturally regarded with both shame and disgust. (Eventually I got to college, and alcohol solved the problem; there's nothing like four or five beers a night to keep you regular.) It would be many years before I understood that at least part of the difficulty was that I was fighting separation, that this was just the physical manifestation of the extreme separation anxiety I had suffered ever since I was an infant. Defecating was a kind of separation that I could control, even for a time prevent. That my toilet habits were also intimately bound up with my mother, her expectations, promises that I made to her and broke (about going to the bathroom), lying to her, etc., is, from a Freudian perspective, so transparently an expression of separation anxiety that it's almost comical that it took me years of thinking about my childhood before I recognized the connection. On Freud's view, this is when—and even how—my subsequent problems with jealousy began, the jealousy that plagued all my love relationships at least until very recently.

Try the exercise, if you haven't already, of remembering your first lie or any early-childhood lie. Most people I've spoken with about this can remember the first lie they told—or rather, they have a vivid memory of an early lie, whether or not it is in fact the first lie they ever told—and whom they told it to, and why they told it. Because love motivates so much of our early interaction with the world, it perhaps sounds tautological to suggest that the vast majority of our early lies are motivated by love: to gain it, from fear of losing it, because of insecurity in it. But this early connection between love and lying and the manner in which it develops may inform our later loves in profound ways that we as adults have yet failed to examine. (Psychiatrists have to make a living somehow.)

The first lie I remember telling to another kid, in first grade, wasn't really a lie at all. My father had bought a new Lincoln Continental while we were in Florida that Christmas visiting him, and I still remember my fascination with the chrome power buttons and toggle switch it had for the seats and mirrors, and the sunroof—this was in 1973, and I'd never been in a car with power windows before—and the red leather interior. I told my friend Tom Davis that my father had bought a car that cost a million dollars. At the time I wasn't certain this figure was accurate, but it seemed about right to me, and I imagine I had the show *The Six Million Dollar Man* in my head—it was one of my favorite shows—as a kind of barometer of relative value. I remember feeling genuinely indignant and dismayed when Tom came back the next day and told me that his father had said, "There is no such thing as a car that costs a million dollars," and I began to doubt myself at that point: Maybe my father had said a hundred thousand dollars? Or maybe he hadn't said how much it had cost? I still don't know, and my father was as notorious an exaggerator as I myself later became, that there's no telling what he might have said, but I dug in my heels with Tom Davis. As Adam Phillips writes: "Exaggeration, in the first instance, is a way of being taken seriously; and then one is ignored for exaggerating."

The argument ended in Tom's calling me a liar and our wrestling and punching each other on the wet grass of the playground—it was spring in Calgary, and I can still remember the mud next to the chain-link fence of Elbow Park Elementary—and my putting my best friend Tom in a headlock, an effective trick I had been taught by my big brother Darren, who was a medaling wrestler. The first-grade girls were pulling on my hair and shouting, "Let him go!" and "You're killing him!" In short order a teacher took us both to the principal's office, the only time I was in the principal's office until the first time I was expelled, nine years later, in tenth grade. As we've seen, I had been accused more than once of lying to my mother or father, but the incident with Tom was the first time anyone had ever called me a liar.

My favorite thing about the lies we tell as children is they tend to have a clarity about them that most of our later lies will not. Even faster than we become expert at lying, we become expert at lying to ourselves.

As Nietzsche puts it, "Lying to others is, relatively speaking, an occasional and very late occurrence in the development of our psychology, almost an aberration. All that we know about lying we first learn from lying to ourselves." On this account all the lies of love may originate in lies of self-love, but for me, even lies of self-love have a more primitive origin, in the lies we would tell—and would be told by—the one we loved most, Mom, before the time we understood we were separate from her, or in the desperate, doomed attempt never to be separated from her, or, once separated, somehow to be reunited with her again. And who could blame us for trying to lie our way back to her? Here the truth won't do the trick. For the truth is, as Freud boldly but also ruefully insists, we will never have her back.

The pediatrician and psychoanalyst D. W. Winnicott argues that childhood lies are a response to our estrangement from our mothers and that they may, in extreme cases, even result in a kind of doubling of the personality into, within the child's own head, a good child that tells the truth and an evil child that lies.

Because self-deception similarly may involve a doubling (or fracturing into multiples) of the self, one is tempted toward the idea that our early lies are seminal for our later self-deceptions. Doubling of the self through deception may also take place later in life. In *Anna Karenina* Tolstoy explicitly uses the language of the doubling of the self to account for the possibility of the deceptions each lover is practicing in love. One does not experience this feeling of doubling in an ordinary lie or even system of lies; the phenomenology, the way it feels, is peculiar to the lies of the lover. To quote Proust again, when Marcel is considering his love for Albertine, he says: "Everything, indeed, is at least double."

I remember, as a child, that feeling of observing myself telling a lie to my mother as I stood in the bathroom, explaining that I had flushed the toilet before she could see the excrement (which was of course still safely secreted in my intestines). I don't think I ever considered myself "an evil child." I think I divided myself, as best I can recall, into a child who was telling one version of a story and another who knew the truth of what happened. The child who was telling a version of the story—who was simply lying—seemed like a buddy of mine who was instrumentally useful at keeping *me* out of trouble. In fact, if there was a good guy and a bad guy in my narrative, I think the good guy was the me who was willing to tell the lie and the bad guy was the me who hid behind him and let him do the necessary dirty work of deception.

I was recently at lunch with my mother talking about the psychoanalyst Melanie Klein and her idea that problems with defecation are an attack, by feces, that the child makes on the mother.

"Do you think that Lite-Brite incident had anything to do with my problems in the bathroom, Mom?"

"No. You were an anxious child. That's all it was. Everything was a problem with you."

I laughed. "It lasted until I was eighteen, Mom."

"Those psychoanalysts always want to blame everything on the mother. I had some of the same problems myself. Not to the same degree as you, but similar. I could never go outside the home, for example."

I mentioned earlier that my mother prides herself on her ability to lie and on her ability to be honest with herself. So do I. Although lately I am a bit ashamed of my fluency in lying, and I even think, though I'm afraid I may be deceiving myself, that I'm not as good at it as I used to be. When people tell me, "I just can't lie," they are mistaken; the simple, statistical truth is that we all lie easily and with astonishing frequency. What they mean is: it's hard to tell a bald-faced lie. Lately I find it difficult to look someone in the eye and lie to that person knowingly. That difficulty may be relevant to how deception ought to be incorporated into a happy, flourishing human life. Perhaps some kinds or styles of lies ought to be hard for us to tell, even if they do no harm or even spare the feelings of others.

I have never asked my mother if her mother was a liar. As I remember my grandma Jarvis, she was ruthlessly honest, honest to a fault. When, in my mid-twenties, I called her to tell her I was getting married (this was my first marriage), she said: "You're a damn fool!" and hung up the phone. Later, when she met my first wife, she said to me: "Clancy, I like this girl. So I want you to promise me that you're not going to cheat on her, the way your asshole father cheated on my poor daughter." That's the kind of truth teller my grandmother was. I promised.

3. First Loves

> People say young love or love of the moment isn't real,
> but I think the only love is the first. Later we hear its fleet-
> ing recapitulations throughout our lives, brief echoes of
> the original theme in a work that increasingly becomes
> all development. —Edmund White

> Men always want to be a woman's first love. That is their
> clumsy vanity. We women have a more subtle instinct
> about things. What we like is to be a man's last romance.
> —Oscar Wilde

THE PARENT AS FIRST LOVER

I remember, as no doubt many of us uncomfortably do, my first explicitly sexual encounter with a parent—in my case, my mother. I was eight or nine years old—the same age that I started masturbating—and I brushed past her in the kitchen while she was ironing, and her buttocks grazed my groin, and I got, to my pleasure and horror, an erection. If I had not been as sexually inhibited as I am, I could perhaps have put this experience to some use, in my youthful experiments with masturbation or my later erotic life. But here, writing this now, is the first time I've allowed myself to think it through.

Reminding us of what we've learned about love so far, Freud writes: "Childhood love is boundless, it demands exclusive possession, it is not content with less than all. But it has a second characteristic: it has, in point of fact, no aim and is incapable of obtaining complete satisfaction; and principally for that reason it is doomed to end in disappointment."

At least since Freud, a standard way of describing our first feelings of love, as an infant and as a small child, is as the feeling of identification with the beloved; we are one with our mothers. "A child suckling at his mother's breast," Freud continues, again sounding like Aristophanes, "has become the prototype of every relation of love. The finding of an object [of love, in later life] is in fact a refinding of it." And of course this is all the more true before we emerge from the womb. Being born is the first violent separation from one's mother, and you might say that it's all downhill from there. The psychoanalyst Jacques Lacan argues that as soon as we say, "I am," we are saying, "I have lost"—that is, to discover one's own separate identity is already to reject, or be rejected by, the love that comes with unification. How much more so, then, are we rejected from love—and have our own identity asserted—when we lie or realize we have been lied to and the isolation of our minds from one another is confirmed?

For Freud, as children, insofar as we are separated from our mothers, we all intensely desire to return to our mothers, and we are equally as intensely vulnerable to them because it is our mothers of course who control our access to and intimacy with them. "From the child's point of view the mother is—as the father will soon be—a model of promiscuity," Adam Phillips writes. "She has a thousand things to do. She knows other people." It is not a question of whether or not our mothers will leave us; we simply have to accept the fact that they will and do, in ways that are entirely out of our control. This takes place from the time we are infants, although it may be years before we fear or resent it. The question is rather: How do we control that separation, that (one hopes, temporary) abandonment? And how does that separation inform or determine the way we conduct ourselves as we discover other lovers and other kinds of love?

For the feminist philosopher and psychologist Carol Gilligan, we never escape the separation anxiety that characterizes, to a greater or lesser degree, our love of our parents. "The real question is about love: if I love you, will you leave me?" she writes. "It is a child's question: if you leave me, how will I survive? It is every lover's question." Gilligan agrees with the thinkers we've considered thus far. As for Aristophanes, so for Freud and Proust—and, following them, Jacques Lacan—love is always a matter of identification; this is why Freud often describes love as a form of increasingly extravagant narcissism. Any difference between the mother and the child, and any separation of the two, is hated and feared. It is also Freud of course who famously argues that our subsequent erotic relationships are profoundly influenced by, if not explicitly modeled on, the love relationship we had with a parent or parents.

It is, most of us would suppose, natural for the boy to take his mother as a possible object of first love; a girl, her father. But it's more complicated than that—presumably, for girls and boys alike. Here is an analysis of the development of the love of the young girl—most complete in the phenomenon of first love—by the psychoanalyst and philosopher Melanie Klein:

> . . . a more positive relation to the mother, built up on the genital position [provides the foundation for] that part of the relation which is connected exclusively with the father. At first it is focused on the act of the penis in coitus. This act, which also promises gratification of the desires that are now displaced on to the genital, seems to the little girl a most consummate performance.

Her admiration is, indeed, shaken by the Oedipus frustration, but unless it is converted into hate, it constitutes one of the fundamental features of the woman's relation to the man. Later, when full satisfaction of the love impulses is obtained, there is joined with this admiration the great gratitude ensuing from the long-pent-up deprivation. This gratitude finds expression in the greater feminine capacity for complete and lasting surrender to a love-object, especially to the "first love."

For Klein, first love occurs when "full satisfaction of the love impulses is obtained"—that is, when the process of first love culminates in the (successful) experience of sex.

We don't want to get bogged down in differences about terminology. One way of understanding first love is as the first time one takes a love object other than the object of love in identification (typically, we've said, a parent), plus the experience of sex with that person. More simply, we might say that first love means the first person with whom we both fell in love and had sex. Obviously, for many of us, the first person we have sex with is not the first person we fall in love with, just as, for many of us, we never had sex with our first love. For Klein, love culminating in sex permits a release of long-pent-up energy; this in turn results in "gratitude" and "complete and lasting surrender," which traits, she suggests, are more characteristic of feminine than masculine love.

The first lovers we consider in this chapter will not, as a rule, enjoy the sexual release that Klein describes; first lovers, in our analysis, typically suffer from unrequited love. But the attitudes of gratitude and surrender are characteristic of the first lover, whether male or female, quite independently of the question of sexual satisfaction. The first lover is grateful to be in love; he wants nothing more than to surrender himself to his beloved.

LISA'S HAIR

My own first love was my stepsister Lisa. I did have a sexual encounter with Lisa, though it did not result in the kind of sexual release Klein describes (fair warning: my first real encounter with erotic love is described in chapter 4).

When I think of Lisa now, what I remember best is her hair. I remember an afternoon with her in a locked room in a psychiatric ward of Foothills Hospital, after one of her suicide attempts. I was eight or nine, so she was fifteen or sixteen. She put her head in my lap and cried, and in confusion, dismay—anger at our parents—I stroked her hair, which has since become one way I often try to console a girl or a woman I love.

Leaving Foothills Hospital that day, I scoured my fingers on the wall of the hospital until the tips bled. When we were getting into the car, my mother looked at my fingers and said, frightened, "Clancy, what happened to your hand?" I told her I had fallen.

But thinking about it now, I suspect that when I dragged my fingers along that hospital wall until they bled, like a Christian ascetic before I knew what a Christian ascetic was, I was engaged in a kind of boasting to myself of my love for Lisa.

Boasting is a familiar, forgivable, and almost comical form of deception. In book 4, section 7 of *Nicomachean Ethics* Aristotle writes: "he who boasts for the sake of reputation or honor is (though he is a boaster) not very much to be blamed . . . those who boast for the sake of reputation claim such qualities as will garner praise or congratulation."

It was as if I were saying, "Look how strong my love is, look what I am willing to suffer because of my love for her." I remember thinking, in a confused, childish way, that if I suffered, I could somehow reduce her suffering. It wasn't mere boasting, you might say. But all boasting is a way of making oneself vulnerable; it's an attempt to earn a love that one feels one doesn't deserve. A person confident that he was worthy of love would never feel the need to boast.

It would be odd to say that I chose to fall in love with Lisa. But I remember wanting to fall in love at about that time. And I know I actively participated in my "falling in love" with her: I daydreamed about her; I longed for her when she was away; I tried to be amusing to her friends; I liked the things she liked, tried to do the things she did. She smoked, so I smoked. She shoplifted, so I shoplifted. I still remember her teaching me how to look for the security cameras in Shoppers Drug Mart and how to identify and position what you were going to steal—in my first effort, a Green Lantern squirt gun, which had to be moved from a merchandise hook to a shelf—before you made your real pass at hiding it down your pants.

Trying to really remeber Lisa, I think of how she always wore her hair down. It fell halfway to her shoulder blades. She rarely had bangs, except one summer when I was six and she was thirteen. We were floating in an inner tube together down the Elbow River, in the mild June Calgary sun, smoking du Maurier cigarettes. I remember looking then at her bangs, wet on her forehead from the river, the sun on her face, and her bare, skinny shoulders. I think at that time I understood I was in love with her. I remember lying on the floor of my bedroom, thinking about her, and listening to Donny and Marie Osmond's song "Puppy Love" on my plastic record player.

Perhaps my stepsister's hair made such an impression on me because it was as close as I would allow myself to her body. The hair is both the body and not yet the body. There is a tension in all love between the spiritual and the physical; perhaps the tension is created at birth, when we are separated from the bodies of our mothers. But there is a tension perhaps most especially in first love, when the lover has yet to reconcile the idealization of the beloved—how perfect she is!—with his physical desire for her and what can be done with that perfection. The ecstasy of first love differs from childhood love in its exaggeration of this tension, in its emerging consciousness of it, which oscillates the lover between fact and fantasy. That oscillation may create the well-known giddiness of first love, its raptures and despairs, its tendency to see the hand of destiny everywhere it turns, its seizing onto coincidence as proof, its ability to twist reality—whatever counts as reality for this intoxicated consciousness—into the many different forms, demonstrations, and terrors of its love. First love is an introduction into the imaginative world of romantic love, and like the first time swimming or the first time drunk, it is completely disorienting. We don't yet know the rules; we don't know what we're doing.

What does the first lover want? To be loved in return. But what would he do with the beloved if she returned his love? What would I make of my stepsister Lisa had she loved me in the way I loved her?

A couple of years after the float down the river, we were camping at Bragg Creek. Lisa and I were sharing a tent, and she suggested I get in her sleeping bag with her. It was cold. She used one of her hands to put my hand under her pajamas. With her other hand she was scratching the hair on my head.

"Feel my stomach. Slide your hand down," she said.

(I had felt pubic hair only once before, on one of my stepbrothers. He had lured me into his bedroom with the promise of rose seeds and trailed them from his belly button to his penis. I was perhaps five years old at the time and cannot remember if I understood that the activity was sexual. My stepbrother interrupted it before anything happened. He was a teenager at the time and not dangerous.)

"Put your fingers inside," Lisa said. "Do you like that?"

She took my other hand in hers and placed it on her breast. Her nipple got erect in my fingers.

"Do you know what that is?"

She put her hand down my pajama pants and wrapped it around me. I was embarrassed that I had no pubic hair. She kissed me and taught me how to put our tongues together.

The next morning I woke with a terrible sore throat. I lost my voice. I understood it was punishment for what we had done the night before. She was healthy and untroubled. She swam in the creek, and I watched from the bank. It was sunny, her hair was like an otter's fur, and she seemed like an animal to me. I avoided my mother for days after that.

Like many first beloveds, Lisa was a troublemaker. She could not get along with my parents and often ran away from home. I remember one time—my mother denies that it happened—when my stepdad dragged Lisa, his daughter, up the stairs to her bedroom by her hair. He had her hair in one fist and a toilet plunger in the other. The plunger was for her beating. I do not know if he unscrewed the red rubber part before using it.

If she were alive today, Lisa would be fifty-two years old, and she would have gray in her hair. The one picture I have of her was taken when my mother married her father, and her hair had been permed for the wedding. It really looks nothing like her hair. She went to foster care at fourteen. I think it was two years we lived in the house together.

My great betrayal of Lisa—our betrayal of each other—came when I was in seventh grade. To get to Rideau Park Junior High School, we crossed a swinging bridge made of wood, cable, and chain-link fencing. Often the junior high school students stood in the middle of the bridge and, coordinating the sway of our weight—you began simply by pressing down with one foot and then the other—caused the bridge to twist itself until the wooden planks of the walkway were almost perpendicular to the river. At the end of the bridge were a pair of concrete pilings with iron rails where the popular ninth graders, the rulers of the school, smoked cigarettes or hash or made out. The first few days of seventh grade were a test: you had to brave the end of the bridge, where the ninth graders would jeer at you, give you a push or a kick, try to make you cry.

One day, crossing the bridge, I saw Lisa on the other side. She was with her boyfriend, the handsome, long-haired Indigenous Canadian who, five years later, murdered her with a baseball bat. I was overjoyed to see her. I hadn't seen her in over a year. I disciplined myself not to run to her. There were other kids standing around: ninth graders. I could see the way they feared and admired Lisa and her boyfriend. She was wearing his leather jacket; it was too big for her and had fringes on the arms. He was wearing a cowboy hat with a blue feather in the hatband.

She looked at me coldly. "You told Mom I shouldn't smoke pot," she said. "I ought to beat you up."

She had the story both right and wrong. She had heard it from my other stepsister. We'd been sitting at the breakfast table—I, my little brother, and our stepsister—when my mom told us that Lisa smoked pot and asked us if we thought that was a good idea. Of course we all immediately agreed that Lisa shouldn't smoke pot. It was one of Rousseau's lies, the lie an authority coerces you into telling.

I was too shocked by the fact that Lisa'd threatened me to try to tell her the truth. Anyway, it was one of those things you couldn't explain without sounding guilty.

"Hey, give the kid a break, Lisa," her murderer said. "You're scaring him. He's shaking."

I looked at Lisa then and promised myself I would never

speak to her again. I wasn't trembling from fear. I was trembling with rage.

Often Lisa called, in the years after this, to try to get me to talk on the phone. My mom would pick up and say, "Your sister's on the phone." I'd listen to Lisa repeat my name a few times, and then I'd hang up. This went on for five years, and one afternoon my mom called me on the phone in my dormitory at Stetson University and told me: "Your sister's dead."

The only apology I can make to Lisa for that five-year grudge is, I think, in the retelling of this story. Benjamin Constant (who famously contests Kant's claim that lying is always wrong) writes: "Of all feelings, love is the most egoistic and, consequently, the least generous when it is wounded." I'd like to excuse myself by saying that I held the grudge as long as I did because I loved her as much as I did.

I see now that both Lisa and I were suffering from the natural exaggerations of love. She felt as betrayed as I did. We had each of us created impossible lovers in our imaginations. For years I simply could not believe she had spoken those words—"I ought to beat you up"—to *me*. The fact that we both felt betrayed showed that she was not simply an object of my love. I must have imagined that she loved me in return. And of course she did, though it is impossible for me to say how the character of our love differed. Obviously, it differed in several fundamental ways that we'll spend the rest of the chapter exploring. I suspect that it was a typical first love relationship, when the beloved (Lisa) has real affection for the lover (me), probably recognizes and even enjoys the ardor of the lover, but simply does not, cannot see her lover in romantic terms. In this way, first love is a transitional stage between the purely other-directed romantic love for the parent and requited erotic love.

In my falling in love with Lisa, what need did my first love fill? At this stage, I think, my relationship with my mother was changing. Perhaps I did not want or need to know my mother in the way I previously had, and only understood my mother's knowledge of me insofar as I failed or succeeded at hiding my thoughts or actions from her. The need to know another who was not my mother, and to be known by that other, was just beginning to arise in me.

This is why the lies, loneliness, and freedom of the child are so important. That loss of innocence, which is just the discovery of separation in love, prepares the way for the first attempt at recovering what has been lost. To lie and to be lied to by a parent are how we expel ourselves from the Garden; first love is the initial, naive, self-deceived attempt to return.

As far as I can recall, I never had a sexual fantasy about Lisa, but my love for her, and my perception of her betrayal of me, further informed the structure of my later romantic life. What I only suspected in my mother was confirmed, in my confused and developing notions about love, by my experience of first love. I became a fiercely jealous lover.

THE L WORD

A friend e-mailed me recently. She explained that she'd been with her boyfriend for about a year but that she hadn't told him she was in love with him yet. "I've never said, 'I love you,' to any man," she wrote. "When I scratch the back of his neck, I think he knows."

I understood the question in her e-mail. "Tell him," I wrote to her. "Tell him you love him."

The next day she wrote back. "Well, I did it," she said. "And he said back to me, 'I love you.' I couldn't tell if he was terrified or just confused. I think I fucked up." It wasn't terror or confusion, I told her, though I had no way of knowing that. But it got me to thinking about why that first time telling someone "I love you" is so momentous. It is a stage in erotic love of course, and the transition from knowing—or strongly believing—that you love each other to actually declaring it is a crucial transition in the development of erotic love, just as the decision and formal declaration of marriage and the marriage vows are another. It is a risk we take. What if he had said nothing in return? And what's happening in his head now? What's he saying to his friends? But it's also, I think, a recollection of that fear and hope we first experienced when we realized that we were in love—or tried to be in love— with someone other than our mothers. Saying "I love you" to someone for the first time is to throw oneself out into that abyss all over again. No matter how many times you've done it before, in some sense it will always be the first time if it is done sincerely. (Discussions of first love are strangely hard to find in the enormous literature on romantic love. One notable recent exception is Lisa Appignanesi's terrific *All About Love*.)

We often distinguish between "love" and "being in love" or "falling in love." Superficially, of course, the distinction is obvious: When I say, "I love my dog," or, "I love my work," I mean something very different from when I say, "I love my wife." The English word "love" is used much too broadly, but we tend to understand what is meant by it through the context in which it is being used.

The ancient Greeks had four different words for love: *agape, eros, philia,* and *storge.* These are a bit difficult to sort out into English equivalents, but I'll try to do so sufficiently for our purposes. Agape might be translated as "unconditional" or "spiritual" love; it is sometimes used to refer to the love one has for one's children and generally used, after the advent of Christianity, as the love one has for God. It is usually taken to have a "selfless" quality to it. Eros is passionate or romantic love, the kind of love with which we are chiefly concerned in this book. Philia is the kind of love shared by good friends. Storge usually refers to domestic love. It can be the

bonds of love within a family (like agape, it is often used to refer
to the love one has for one's children), it can be the love one has for
a spouse, and it sometimes has a vaguely pejorative meaning, like
the kind of tolerance a citizen might have for a mediocre ruler.

Even in romantic or erotic contexts, it makes sense to say, for
example, "I both love my wife and am in love with my wife." Because when I say, "I love my wife," I am saying something very
similar to what I am saying when I say, "I love my children": my
well-being is intimately connected with their well-being; they
are in a special, very small set of people for whom I would make
sacrifices that I would not make for others; they can make claims
on me that others cannot; their emotional states impact me in a
way that the emotional states of others do not. Accordingly, if I
were an ancient Greek, I would appeal to agape or storge or both
to explain that kind of love. But I would not say, "I am in love with
my children." My eros is for my wife. When we are "falling in
love," we are beginning to experience eros, and pace Freud and
Freudians, first love might be our first real taste of eros. When my
friend e-mailed her lover, what she was expressing was eros.

But her choice to express her love to him was not a trivial one.
Pascal puts it strongly: "By force of speaking of love we become
enamored." Declaring love is, as we all know, an enormously sig-
nificant act because the beloved is obliged to reply—even if that
reply is silence, which can be the loudest reply of them all. First
love, like obsessive love, is often nonverbal: we fall madly in love
with someone, we never tell her or him, and eventually it passes
away. To speak the words "I love you" is to dare what the first
lover may not be willing to risk, to hear back from the beloved
what the first lover fears must be the truth: "But I don't love you."
That said, to continue to love someone even though you know he
or she doesn't love you the same way in return is characteristic of
first love. But the countless self-deceptions of first love—that

perhaps she does indeed love me back, that she does not love me now but may one day, that she loves me but does not know it herself, that she loves me but dares not speak it—tend to be nonverbal. When we say something, we are more inclined to scrutinize it. It is easier to lie to ourselves when we don't verbalize our beliefs, although of course speaking our beliefs and repeating them, both to ourselves and to others, are one familiar way we consolidate self-deception. And Pascal's point is well-taken: declaring love can be a crucial part of bringing it into existence.

The cases of first love we shall be discussing in this chapter are mostly nonverbal: I never told Lisa I was in love with her, and toward the end of the chapter we'll discuss another of my first loves, my cousin Anna (I never told her); Woldemar's first love for Zinaida in Turgenev's *First Love* (Woldemar declares his love for Zinaida only to himself); the narrator's love for Mangan's sister in "Araby"; Simone de Beauvoir's first love for a girl she sees across a park (she never gets the chance to declare the love until she writes her memoir, forty-some years later). Nevertheless, these instances of love are deceptive, in a way that is different from the lies of love we tell as children; first love, I argue, is when self-deception becomes crucial to the structural development of romantic love.

We shall also be looking at the love of Werther for Lotte in Goethe's *The Sorrows of Young Werther* (we hear about his love for her all too often, as does she), but Werther's is in its way an imperfect case of first love because we learn, at the outset of the novella, that he is escaping from a love affair gone wrong. This is not Werther's first love, though in many interesting respects he acts just like any other first lover.

Of course the expression of love need not be verbal. We declare our love in all sorts of ways—as my friend wrote, every time she stroked her lover's neck she was telling him she loved him—but coming out and saying it are something more. It has often been observed that our initial encounters with the erotic are a particularly intense combination of the physical and the supersensible, the body and the imagination.

Think of the fantastic mental extravagances and self-tortures the first lover suffers, the erotic and emotional worlds she invents. As Shakespeare writes in *A Midsummer Night's Dream*: "Lovers and madmen have such seething brains, / Such shaping fantasies, that apprehend / More than cool reason ever comprehends." Reason will have its role as well, I shall argue, though it may not be particularly "cool." Or as Molière puts it more simply in *Tartuffe*, in the words of Dorine, "All lovers are crazy! It's sad, but true." Indeed, as in the courtly tradition of troubadours like Marcabru—"I approve that my Lady should long make me wait and that I should not have from her what she promised me"—the first lover may well fear or avoid the thought of physical, that is, sexual, expression or consummation of her love.

"I love him." "I love her." Or, "I love you," spoken romantically for the very first time. What are the ways in which that declaration changes over the course of a lifetime of (learning to) love?

Edmund White claims that the first love is the only true love and that all subsequent loves are echoes or elaborations of it. For White, subsequent loves eventually become "all development"—that is, entirely made up, 100 percent fiction based on a long-lost fact. And when Lisa Appignanesi discusses first love, she appeals to the example of Vladimir Nabokov's Humbert Humbert, who is pathologically unable to escape the idea of that first prepubescent love he enjoyed on the seaside.

That we fictionalize our way into erotic love is crucial to the view of love I am developing in this book. But that there is a "fact" of an initial love that we then progressively fictionalize away from, such as White suggests, is the dangerous and common notion I want to combat. I think the activity of the first lover—a self-deceptive activity—is our first, awkward attempt at loving in the way we will love erotically and in marriage (where marriage means simply any long-term, committed, monogamous, or mostly monogamous romantic relationship). But I think, like any other activity, the activity of first love, when first practiced, is fumbling, inept, mostly unconscious, a bit too self-conscious, usually silly. Loving requires at least as much practice as tennis. And although there may be prodigies—such as Don Juan, for example, whom we shall discuss in "Erotic Love"—I don't think any of them would claim that her or his first love was the only love.

Nevertheless, I think that like Aristophanes's myth that finding love is like finding our missing half, there is some truth to Edmund White's view that our first love is the greatest (Cat Stevens agrees: "Baby I'll try to love again but I know / The first cut is the deepest"). Many of us check back against that first love when thinking about later loves, but presumably, most of us also check back, in greater or lesser degrees and depending upon the particular love affair, against other previous loves we have suffered and enjoyed. That's how learning works. I will always remember the first "grown-up" book I read (*Papillon*), but I've read a lot of books since then.

If we believe too insistently that first love sets the pattern for our later loves, we commit ourselves to a sad view of romantic love because first love tends so often to end in heartbreak. Sadder still if we hold Edmund White's view that the first, heartbroken love must be the best.

In his autobiographical novella *First Love* Ivan Turgenev has one of the several foolish characters courting Zinaida claim: "I had no first love. I began with the second." He goes on somewhat more sensibly to admit: "To speak accurately, the first and last time I was in love was with my nurse when I was six years old." Turgenev gets it right: the first love, properly speaking, is almost always a parent figure. But for our purposes, first love represents the first time a lover looks beyond the parent; in effect, the first lover is seeking a replacement for the love of the parent.

TURGENEV'S "FIRST LOVE"

In *First Love*, the object of love, Zinaida, twenty-one years old, tells the sixteen-year-old "first lover" Woldemar: "you must always tell me the truth . . . and do what I tell you"(Turgenev's ellipsis). She plays the parent to Woldemar, continuing: "Look at me . . . Why don't you look at me?"

We understand why Woldemar can't look at her. For him to look at her would be to reveal the truth of his love, which he is not yet ready to do; to "look someone in the eye" is always one of the marks of truthfulness (one of the five "tells" of a lie is to look away, especially down and to the left). Moreover, as Jean-Paul Sartre famously details in *Being and Nothingness*, the recognition we experience of another human being, another mind, is fundamentally through "the look," through that mysterious, often frightening, and always intimate exchange that takes place when we look into each other's eyes. For Woldemar to look at Zinaida is to make himself entirely vulnerable to her.

A quick literary side note on the significance of these first glances of lovers: when Proust's Marcel first sees Albertine, he thinks, with the intimation that he is already falling in love with her: "I knew that I should never possess this young cyclist if I did not possess also what was in her eyes." And from Thomas Mann in *Death in Venice*, before Aschenbach and Tadzio meet:

> There can be no relation more strange, more critical, than that between two beings who know each other only through their

eyes, who meet daily, yes, even hourly, eye each other with a fixed regard, and yet by some whim or freak of convention feel constrained to act like strangers. Uneasiness rules between them, unslaked curiosity, a hysterical desire to give rein to their suppressed impulse to recognize and address each other; even, actually, a sort of strained but mutual regard. For one human being instinctively feels respect and love for another human being so long as he does not know him well enough to judge him; and that he does not, the craving he feels is evidence.

But back to Woldemar and Zinaida: "To tell the truth and do as one is told": that is, as we have seen, the deceptive imperative of the parent who (whether or not she means to do so) encourages a child to understand that love will require duplicity. Of the beloved women in great world literature, Zinaida is one of the most shamelessly deceitful, in part because she herself is very young, in part because she has so many suitors, in part because the suitor who loves her most sincerely is Woldemar—a younger boy, her inferior, not someone she is ready to love in return—and in part because she is in love with a married man, Woldemar's father.

For his part, Woldemar is incapable of deceiving his beloved. He imagines that "[s]he understands everything; she sees everything." But he is willing, as a jealous lover, to spy on her secretly and, in protecting his love for her, to lie to himself:

> I didn't want to know whether I was loved, and I didn't want to admit to myself I was not . . . avoid Zinaida I could not. Her presence seared me like a flame . . . but what did I care what kind of fire this was in which I burned and melted, when it was bliss to burn and melt? I gave myself freely to my sensations as they came, telling myself lies and hiding from my own memories, and closed my eyes to what I sensed was coming.

Woldemar makes two demands of himself: first, that he be completely transparent to Zinaida—this, for him, is "true love"— second, that he not require that she love him in return, because if he were to make that demand, he would have to engage in a kind of truth seeking that might threaten the love he has for her. The older, wiser Woldemar who is our narrator identifies the self-deceptive game that as a first lover he had to engage in. If he knows for certain that she does not love him, then his own love for her looks like pure childishness: Why would he desire what he is certain he cannot have? But as long as there is hope that she may love him in return, as long as he can close his eyes to the disappointment that he senses is on its way, he can continue to maintain his belief in his own love. "I was afraid of looking into myself, if a boy of sixteen can be said to do such a thing; I was afraid to face anything—whatever it might be—consciously."

Woldemar is in the state of self-deceptive suspension characteristic of the first lover. He has not been in love before, so he is not aware of his own state of emotional being in the way he will later be; he can lie to or avoid himself in a way that later he may be unable to do. Of course, as everyone knows all too well, self-deception in love does not end with first love. On the contrary, the kind of self-deception we learn to practice in self-love will be necessary for our subsequent experiments in erotic love and in our commitment to marriage. No real lover is a cynic, and the greatest among them—Abelard and Heloïse, Don Quixote, Don Juan, Beatrice and Benedick, Anna Karenina—are all experts in self-deception. But what Woldemar is aware of in his love for Zinaida is both his distance from her and his need to overcome that distance by making himself transparent to her. It is not a love in unification, like the love of a mother. (Woldemar is a teenage boy who, incidentally, never goes to bed without saying good night to his mother and asking for her blessing.) It is a love in separation that seeks reunification. To disclose himself to Zinaida—to say, "This is me! Take me as I am!"—is how he expresses his love for her. He hopes that he understands her as well as he needs her to understand him: "It seemed to me that I had known her for a long time, and that before her I had known nothing and had not lived . . . 'And here I am sitting opposite her,' I was thinking, 'I have met her, I know her. God, what happiness!'"

I know her, she knows me, God, what happiness! This is one of the great hopes of first love. It is also a hope that we recognize as intimately bound to the desires and frustrations of childhood. To be fully known, understood, and accepted by the parent is what every child hopes for, and indeed, this hope may well continue long after childhood (I am still frustrated at times by my mother's inability to understand me, and I'm sure I'm not alone). But Woldemar's is a hope that by definition will not be fulfilled: to enjoy first love is to indulge oneself in the desire for, but not the achievement of, knowledge of the beloved, much less the beloved's knowing the lover. The first lover neither knows nor is known; he only believes.

LOVE AS HOPE

Woldemar, like all first lovers, lives in an agony of hope. (In chapter 4, we shall see that hope is an essential stage in Stendhal's famous account of how we come to fall in love.) What kind of state of belief is hope? When, in the most famous statement about love and hope in all of Western literature, Paul separates out three kinds of belief in 1 Corinthians 13:13—"Faith, hope, love; but the greatest of these is love"—he is both asserting their interconnection and showing the dominance of love over and on faith and hope. To have faith might be to believe without sufficient reason for belief, a popular definition that we can trace from Kierkegaard through Anselm back to Augustine; to hope is to believe without quite believing yet, to want something that could be the case and is not yet; to love: that is the big question. Our enterprise here is to try to sort out what, if any, relationship love has with the truth.

"Faith, hope, love": for Paul, these are the belief states that make life worth living. They are also, to refer back to the discussion in the prologue, excellent examples of what we might intend when we say that "Truth is subjectivity" or "Meaning is subjectivity." None of these three belief states "points at the truth" in the way we ordinarily take our belief states to be related to the truth ("I believe the sun is shining because I can see that it is"). Kierkegaard thought of it in this way: if one *knows* the truth, one need not *believe* it. If I knew that God existed, why would I need faith?

The first lover spends so much of his time hoping. He is in a giddy state that is suspended from truthfulness. Nevertheless, truthfulness—knowledge—is precisely what he desires and expects. It is this paradoxical condition that creates so much space for deception and self-deception, but also imagination and creativity. To allow oneself to hope, to accept the condition of loving, might be simply to admit that the truth is more complicated than we like to pretend, maybe even more complicated than we need to know or even can attempt to know. Perhaps our relationship to the truth is, like our relationship to love, more creative than we naively suppose.

SELF-DECEPTION AND BAD FAITH

A magic trick of self-deception: it can make a lie true. Remember from the prologue the technique I used to teach my jewelry salespeople: (1) There is something you want to believe—and want

others to believe—that you know doesn't happen to be the case;
(2) identify the false belief; (3) convince yourself it is true; (4)
once you believe it, when you repeat it to others, it's no longer a
lie, because to lie is to report as true a belief you hold to be false.
Once you believe that it's true, you can report it honestly with a
good conscience.

Nietzsche observes:

> In all great deceivers, one thing is noteworthy, to which they owe
> their power. In the actual act of deception, with all their prepa-
> rations, the thrilling voice, expression, and manner, in the midst
> of their effective scenery, they are overcome by their belief in
> themselves; it is this, then, which speaks so wonderfully and
> persuasively to the spectator. The founders of religions are dis-
> tinguished from those great deceivers in that they never awake
> from their condition of self-deception; or at times, but very
> rarely, they have an enlightened moment when doubt overpow-
> ers them; they generally console themselves, however, by as-
> cribing these enlightened moments to the influence of the Evil
> One. There must be self-deception in order to produce a great
> effect. For men believe in the truth of everything that is visibly
> and strongly believed in.

Given Nietzsche's unfortunate and undeserved association
with Nazism, it's hard for us not to notice how he anticipates the
coming spectacle and mass deception of Bayreuth, Wagner, and
Hitler. Nietzsche clearly has political leaders in mind here, and
in a typically Nietzschean move, he points out the dangerous
power of self-deception, which power, in other contexts, he will
recommend as one of our most important possible strengths.

But Nietzsche also very nicely describes how the first lover,
whether or not be declares his love, comes to create in himself

the emotional fervor necessary to attain the feverish pitch of first love. It is not that Woldemar—or the young Clancy Martin—set out to deceive Zinaida—or Lisa—about our love. It's true that we loved. But what might also be true is that we wanted to love— that we were curious about love, desirous of falling in love, ready to know the answer to that young person's urgent question "What is love?"—and so, through "preparations, the thrilling voice, expression, and manner, in the midst of their effective scenery" we caused ourselves to believe in our love.

To cause oneself to fall in love in the very act of persuading someone else that you are in love with her or him—the discovery and practice of this activity—is, I think, why first love is so important to all subsequent attempts at and experiences of romantic love. This is the model we build.

When Jean-Paul Sartre discusses the particular form of self-deception that most interests him—he calls it *mauvaise foi,* "bad faith," which is self-deception with the added baggage of moral blameworthiness—one of the examples he uses (now the most famous and, among some feminist circles, notorious) is that of a woman on a first date. The long passage is worth quoting in its entirety:

Take the example of a woman who has consented to go out with a particular man for the first time. She knows very well the intentions which the man who is speaking to her cherishes regarding her. She knows also that it will be necessary sooner or later for her to make a decision. But she does not want to realize the urgency; she concerns herself only with what is respectful and discreet in the attitude of her companion. She does not apprehend this conduct as an attempt to achieve what we call "the first approach"; that is, she does not want to see possibilities of temporal development which his conduct presents. She restricts this behavior to what he is in the present; she does not wish to read in the phrases which he addresses to her anything other than their explicit meaning. If he says to her, "I find you so attractive!" she disarms this phrase of its sexual background; she attaches to the conversation and to the behavior of the speaker the immediate meanings, which she imagines as objective qualities. The man who is speaking to her appears to her sincere and respectful as the table is round or square, as the wall coloring is blue or gray. The qualities thus attached to the person she is listening to are in this way fixed in a permanence like that of things, which is no other than the projection of the strict present of the qualities into the temporal flux. This is because she does not quite know what she wants. She is profoundly aware of the desire which she inspires, but the desire cruel and naked would humiliate and horrify her. Yet she would find no charm in a respect which would be only respect. In order to satisfy her, there must be a feeling which is addressed wholly to her *personality*—i.e., to her full freedom—and which would be a recognition of her freedom. But at the same time this feeling must be wholly desire; that is, it must address itself to her body as object. This time then she refuses to apprehend the desire for what it is; she does not even give it a name; she recognizes it only to the extent that it transcends itself toward admiration, esteem, respect and that it is wholly absorbed in the more refined forms which it produces, to the extent of no longer figuring anymore as a sort of warmth and density. But then suppose he takes her hand. This act of her companion risks changing the situation by calling for an immediate decision. To leave the hand there is to consent in herself to flirt, to engage herself. To withdraw it is to break the troubled and unstable harmony which gives the hour its charm. The aim is to postpone the moment of decision as long as possible. We know what happens next; the young woman leaves her hand there, but she *does not notice* that she is leaving it. She does not notice because it happens by chance that she is at this moment all intellect. She draws her companion up to the most lofty regions of sentimental speculation; she speaks of Life, of her life, she shows herself in her essential aspect—a personality, a consciousness. And during this time the divorce of the body from the soul is accomplished; the hand rests inert between the warm hands of her companion—neither consenting nor resisting—a thing.

This is emphatically not a case of first love. It's just a first date. What is fascinating is the strategy that the woman uses in order to deceive herself: she, to use Sartrean terminology, "projects herself into transcendence"—that is, she moves out of the realm of the physical and into that of the mental, the imaginary, the creative. She is "all intellect": well, that's not quite right. She is all "consciousness"; she is all "soul"; she is all "mind." This is a technique she has practiced specifically in the context of romance; it is the maneuver made by the first lover. But what is deployed here as a strategy—in order to maintain and enjoy "the troubled and unstable harmony which gives the hour its charm"—is, in first love, the very activity that allows one to fall in love. To transcend the facts of her or his situation is the entire project of the first lover.

We should also notice several other conditions at work in the woman's self-deception. She pretends her lover is "sincere" in his praise, while knowing, but not admitting to herself, that the compliments are part of a sexual agenda. And why? Because "she does not quite know what she wants." She is in an epistemically and volitionally unstable condition; she is, in short, uncertain. The "truth" of her desires is specifically what she is avoiding knowing, if indeed, those desires are as yet sufficiently well formulated to be known. The fact is, especially when it comes to the initial stages of romance and love, we very often don't know the truth of what we want. We are engaged in the process not so much of discovering it as creating it, inventing it, imagining it.

It is not always the case, as with our woman on her first date with this seducer-in-action, that the self-deceptive may-be lover (the woman) moves into her mind in order to accomplish the requisite state of self-deception. Sartre also acknowledges that self-deception takes place in precisely the opposite way, through the use of the body and one's material or psychological circumstances. We can self-deceptively transport ourselves into either our "transcendence" (the mind) or our "facticity" (our bodies and material circumstances).

To say, "I can't help it, I'm in love!" or to appeal to the extreme physical impulse one may feel toward the beloved is, according to Sartre, to fail to recognize one's own radically free and independent *choice* in the act of loving. For Sartre, one decides to love. (He later softened this position in a famous debate with Jean Genet. Genet claimed that he was born attracted to men, that there was no choice in the matter; one of Sartre's examples of bad faith involves a homosexual man. Sartre reluctantly admitted in the course of the debate with Genet that the body must play at least some role in determining whom we love.) Our first lover too will often claim to be a mere victim of his physical passion—while engaged in imaginative transports. To think of blaming the body for love might initially sound absurd, but how many one-night stands, unexpected pregnancies, bad romances, and destructive affairs have resulted from precisely this source? "I couldn't help it; it was just so hot!" "I was a bit tipsy, and the next thing I knew . . ." We can think of countless examples of this kind of self-deception. What first love calls our attention to, and what Sartre here illuminates, are the way in which both the mind and the body can lie to us and can be employed by us in order to lie to ourselves.

YOUNG WERTHER AS FIRST LOVER

I think most of us have several first loves. But they all can't come first; the idea of course is that we have only one initial experience of romantic love, the one that answers the question "But what does it feel like, to be in love?" All subsequent experiences of romantic love are in some way different from this first love, at the very least because they are influenced by the first experience of love. To be fair, it's hard to imagine Woldemar's falling for another Zinaida, and in fact this would seem to trivialize his love for her. The question of whether subsequent loves are trivialized or enriched by previous loves is one of the most interesting questions in the literature on love and of course may vary from person to person. My suspicion is that love tends to be like almost everything else: we improve with practice.

When another famous young lover, Werther of Goethe's short novel *The Sorrows of Young Werther*, kills himself at the end of the book, we understand that his love for Lotte was meant to be his only love. Werther kills himself not just from misery and revenge but out of respect for the purity of his love.

Goethe describes the hero of his famous novel in a letter to a friend: "I present a young person gifted with deep, pure feeling and true penetration, who loses himself in rapturous dreams, buries himself in speculation, until at last, ruined by unhappy passions that supervene, in particular an unfulfilled love, puts a bullet in his head."

Werther was in his way following the Japanese tradition of *shinju*, when two young lovers commit suicide at the same time because both recognize that their love can never further increase but only be diminished. That said, it should also immediately be noted that *The Sorrows of Young Werther*, like Turgenev's *First Love*, is loosely autobiographical, and Goethe himself did not commit suicide over his love for the "real" Charlotte Buff.

As in the cases of both Woldemar and Werther—or in my own case, with Lisa—the experience of first love generally ends in heartbreak for the first lover. (Although it has typically been argued by psychologists that first love may be a kind of imprinting—such as how many warm-blooded creatures imprint on mothers or mother figures—the psychologist Nancy Kalish found, in a 2009 study, that most people report that their first loves tended to be "models for the kind of person they never wanted to date again.") It's hard to find first love stories that end happily, still harder to find first love stories that end with the breaking of the beloved's heart. More often than not, in first love the lover falls for a beloved whose heart remains ultimately unknown, or at best partially known, to the lover. Whether or not the beloved has loved before is somewhat tangential in the case of first love. First love is narcissistic in this way: it is understood entirely from the perspective of the lover (interestingly and unsurprisingly, most first love stories, as far as I've been able to find, are in fact told by first-person narrators). However, first love is not narcissistic insofar as the lover's heart is offered as a gift to the beloved. In fact first love is impossible as pure narcissism; there is the presumption of separation between the lover and the beloved, which the first lover hopes to bridge with her gift. In this way it differs importantly from childhood love, to which separation is initially unknown and in which separation emerges only over time. And to be fair to mothers, is one ever estranged from the love of one's mother in the way one is estranged from the love, say, of a college girlfriend or even a first wife? At least according to a long-standing cultural cliché, a mother's love is reliable and relied upon, is *present*, in a way perhaps no other love ever will be.

"The magic of first love is our ignorance that it can ever end," Benjamin Disraeli observes, and in this way first love does follow the model of the love of our mothers; but where it may be true that a mother's love never ends, and perhaps even that our love for our mothers never ends, in first love the (almost without exception false) belief that this first love will never end is vigorous and is not necessarily dependent upon *willful* self-deception. We may fail and fail in love and yet still remain optimists about love; that said, with each failure in love we ought to begin to wonder if enduring love is possible. Every time the fury of love diminishes and then dies, we should believe, if we are rational, that the next love, though just as furious, will also pass away.

But maybe that's just one more good reason to be irrational. Yes, first loves fail. But to suppose that repeated instances of failure in love confirm the view that romantic love will always come to an end is also to suppose that we cannot learn to love better. Perhaps one reason most, if not all, first loves fail is the innocent conviction that the love is incorruptible. The unhelpful psychological move here, it seems to me, is to conclude from the fact that one first great love failed that the very nature of love is somehow bound to failure. It's simply too easy, too convenient, and too childish to draw such a grand conclusion from a first experiment. By contrast, to recognize the fragility of love, rather than to insist on its impermanence (a self-defeating, self-fulfilling belief), might be the hope for enduring romance. Yes, creating enduring love is very difficult. But the fact that we tried once and failed should not convince us that it is impossible.

When Hamlet says to Ophelia (Ophelia is another of literature's great first lovers): "You should not have believed me . . ."

she, heartbroken, believes she can never love again and, like Werther, kills herself. This is the saddest, most desperate of all possible solutions to the agony of disappointed first love. First love had better not be our best love, and we have every reason to suppose it will not be, as our first attempt at almost everything in life is rarely our best. I think it's just because the failure of first love is so intensely painful that we tend to exaggerate its importance in our lives and loves that follow.

CHOOSING TO FALL IN LOVE

"It is asked whether it is necessary to love?" Pascal writes. "This should not be asked, it should be felt. We do not deliberate upon it, we are forced to it, and take pleasure in deceiving ourselves when we discuss it." I fell in love with Lisa. Woldemar was overcome by his love for Zinaida. Werther is famous for his uncontrollable passion for Lotte. But it is also true of each of these first lovers that he was curious about love, that he was at an age when falling in love is common, that he was even, so to speak, "looking for love."

It is probably superficial to suppose that falling in love is either passive or active. In the philosophy of emotions, for centuries it was generally supposed that love, like the other passions, was something inflicted upon a person, that love and other passions were involuntary. Many of us still understand falling in love in this way. The French call this *coup de foudre*, the "lightning bolt" that strikes the lover who then realizes he is in love. First love, like obsessional love, is often characterized in literature by just such an involuntary realization. "Did my heart love till now? forswear it, sight! / For I ne'er saw true beauty till this night," Romeo says after first seeing Juliet, declaring himself a first lover. (It should be admitted that even Romeo sounds a bit self-deceptive here.)

But I don't think the lightning bolt is characteristic in particular of first love or of any kind of love; dangerously, the lightning bolt may strike, we shall see, in all cases of romantic love. A wife may be struck by a coup de foudre when seeing her present husband. Either spouse may be struck by the lightning bolt from someone outside the marriage, and suddenly a disastrous affair begins. Coup de foudre, to my way of thinking, is an aspect of romantic love—it's part of the phenomenology of love—but it is not a special mark of it and certainly does not exhaust it.

In the twentieth century, especially with the work of Jean-Paul Sartre and, here in America, that of the philosopher Robert C. Solomon, emotions, and in particular love, were understood as activities, choices that we make. Now the prevailing view—articulated in the work of Jesse Prinz, for example—is that a complex emotional experience like falling in love has both voluntary and involuntary components.

One reason the question is philosophically difficult is that it reflects a more fundamental debate about what it is to believe at all. Let's say you truthfully tell a friend, "I'm in love." Is this the same kind of statement as when you truthfully tell a friend, "It's raining outside"? On the one hand, insofar as you hold both beliefs and both beliefs are true, they look the same. On the other hand, the first belief can be known with certainty only by you, while the second belief is known by anyone who observes the state of the weather where you are. Also, many of us suppose that your will is somehow involved with the first belief, while in the second case your will has nothing to do with whether or not it's raining and little or nothing to do with your belief that it is raining.

An involuntarist holds that our beliefs are inflicted upon us, independent of our wills. A voluntarist holds that our wills are involved with our states of belief. Once, when I was arguing for voluntarism with a philosopher friend of mine, he pointed at the sun and said, "Okay, prove it. Tell me that you don't believe the sun is shining." If I am sincere, I am incapable of believing that the sun is not shining when I can plainly see that it is. But when some philosophers advance this view, they begin by admitting that certain sorts of beliefs, such as moral beliefs and the belief in the existence of God, may be by their nature at least not involuntary (using double negatives is a philosopher's way of discussing a view that she is afraid either to defend or to deny). Of course, for most of us, precisely these sorts of beliefs—Does life have a meaning? Is there a God? Does my wife love me? Is it wrong to lie?—are the ones we care most about. Most days it is a matter of relative indifference to me whether or not the sun is shining. But every day it is of the utmost importance to me whether or not my children love me, and the love of my children, even most robust involuntarists will admit, may be at least partially under their own control.

The philosopher José Ortega y Gasset writes: "In falling in love, one's attention is voluntarily focused upon another person; whereas, in vital obligations, the fixation of attention is obligatory, against one's inclination." Now, love may be a vital obligation; furthermore, as we shall see when we look at Marcel's obsession with Albertine, love can certainly involve a fixation of attention against one's inclination. But at least in first love, I think Ortega y Gasset's point is well taken; our attention, if not entirely the inclination of love, is a voluntary matter.

In my own experience, love always involves the choice to love—even in the case of the love of one's own children. But I admit that love can force itself on you—most of us do love our children as soon as we see them or even before we see them—and most people I talk to about the subject are willing to admit the possibility of love at first sight.

Love might work a bit like the way the process seems to work in other life-defining commitments. Here we are back in the territory of "Subjectivity is meaning." In some sense, one could say I was destined to become a professor. My older brother started me reading books at an unusually young age, and my father had me reading philosophy before I was in my double digits; I was always most comfortable in a classroom (it was where I felt best about myself as a person); I loved college; and even when I took a seven-year side trip into the jewelry business, I would, as I've mentioned before, visit college campuses on stressful days. Surprise surprise, now I teach college for a living. But in another sense, when I left the jewelry business to return to graduate school, I was making a conscious, deliberate, momentous, and risky choice about the future and what mattered most to me. "College" imprinted itself on me, and I chose it.

In the classroom, when introducing the subject of love, I'll often ask my students, "How many people in here have never been in love?" Usually at least four or five people will raise their hands. I am no longer surprised when I get this response, and I don't doubt the sincerity of the people who are claiming they've never been in love; they clearly, however, have a particular kind of love in mind: romantic love, which seeks sexual satisfaction, or at least erotic involvement. I also suspect that those are the people who are waiting for love, who hold the view that love will strike, as the sun struck me on the face in my discussion with my philosopher friend. The coup de foudre set: "I'm still waiting for it to happen to me."

The ones who are curious about love, in my view, will initiate a process of falling in love that is at least partially voluntary, that involves that person's participation. If you want to fall in love, sooner or later you'll find someone to fall in love with. The process, as we've seen, may well involve self-deception, but that's okay; that's not a complaint against the process.

Here again the career analogy may be helpful. We all know people who still haven't found their callings. If you have a friend like this, you might ask her, "Well, what do you want to do? What do you like to do?" If she replies that she has no idea what she likes and she is waiting to discover it (the coup de foudre view), there wouldn't be much more you could say to her, other than perhaps encourage her to try a variety of different jobs. Haven't fallen in love yet? Well, keep on dating. But until you accept that most major commitments are not purely passive—that to feel passionate about something, your own will must be involved—it seems unlikely that a life-defining commitment (like love or a career) will develop.

To choose to fall in love is, we might think, in some way to fabricate or even to falsify love. But that's the very notion I'm combating. I want to challenge the idea that love forces itself upon us with all the strength of truth. There is a tradition, which runs from Diotima's lessons to Socrates in the *Symposium* through Christianity to bell hooks and the popular consciousness today, that love leads us to the truth, or depends upon the truth, or reflects the truth, or begins with the truth (and maybe all these and more). And I agree that trust and intimacy, essential components of enduring love—and of love at its best, even when it is short-lived—depend upon honesty, openness, and truthfulness. But I also think the way we get to love is much more complex and involves a more nuanced idea of both truthfulness and deception than we are normally willing to admit.

JAMES JOYCE ON FIRST LOVE

In James Joyce's (again, semiautobiographical) story of first love, "Araby," the first-person narrator has fallen in love with a playmate's older sister. We know her only as Mangan's sister. She is an object of fascination for many of the boys, but our narrator is obsessed:

> Or if Mangan's sister came out on the doorstep to call her brother in to his tea we watched her from our shadow peer up and down the street . . . I stood by the railings looking at her. Her dress swung as she moved her body and the soft rope of her hair tossed from side to side . . . Every morning I lay on the floor in the front parlour watching her door. The blind was pulled down to within an inch of the sash so that I could not be seen. When she came out on the doorstep my heart leaped. I ran to the hall, seized my books and followed her. I kept her brown figure always in my eye and, when we came near the point at which our ways diverged, I quickened my pace and passed her. This happened morning after morning. I had never spoken to her, except for a few casual words, and yet her name was like a summons to all my foolish blood.

He does not tell us how he came to fall in love with her but simply describes the state of passion he is in:

> Her image accompanied me even in places the most hostile to romance. On Saturday evenings when my aunt went marketing I had to go to carry some of the parcels. We walked through the flaring streets, jostled by drunken men and bargaining women, amid the curses of labourers, the shrill litanies of shop-boys who stood on guard by the barrels of pigs' cheeks, the nasal chanting of street-singers, who sang a come-all-you about O'Donovan Rossa, or a ballad about the troubles in our native land. These noises converged in a single sensation of life for me: I imagined that I bore my chalice safely through a throng

of foes. Her name sprang to my lips at moments in strange prayers and praises which I myself did not understand. My eyes were often full of tears (I could not tell why) and at times a flood from my heart seemed to pour itself out into my bosom. I thought little of the future. I did not know whether I would ever speak to her or not or, if I spoke to her, how I could tell her of my confused adoration. But my body was like a harp and her words and gestures were like fingers running upon the wires.

The physiology Joyce describes is familiar to all of us who have been or are in love: the susceptibility to tears, wishful and uncontrollable thoughts, the transfiguration of the ordinary world around us into something more fabulous and beautiful, as though the image of the beloved were woven into the fabric of our every-day life. Our own words are completely inadequate to our feel-ings, and indeed, before the love has been declared, even speaking to the beloved seems impossible. Any thought of the beloved, her movements, her words are physically felt. This is the state we think of when we look at a friend who is drunk with love and laugh: "Look at him! Guess who he's thinking about." With this incapacity to control or conceal our feelings comes the need for self-protection, which is found in admitting to oneself that what we are experiencing is first love. Joyce writes: "All my senses seemed to desire to veil themselves and, feeling that I was about to slip from them, I pressed the palms of my hands together un-til they trembled, murmuring: 'O love! O love!' many times."

At last Joyce's first lover is noticed by Mangan's sister, and she speaks to him—until then he can't find the courage to speak to her—asking him if he plans to go to Araby, the fair that is open that weekend. She can't go because she has to go to the convent that weekend; she too is longing for the romance of love, repre-sented here by the exotic and the forbidden (*The Arabian Nights*), but the church is keeping her chaste. She probably has some idea of her young lover's fascination with her, but typically for the beloved of the first lover, she is not interested in him. When she tells him that she's jealous that he can go, she gives us an intimation of something that we have not yet considered: that the first lover may know something that his or her beloved does not. To fall in love with someone does not mean that the person you fall in love with herself knows or has experienced love, and she, while unable to reciprocate your love, may well want what the lover has, the feeling of being in love.

"If I go," Joyce's narrator tells her, "I will bring you something."

After difficulties and delays—the frustrating obstacles we expect the young lover to encounter—Joyce's narrator makes it to the bazaar, only to find it mostly closed, disappointing, and offering nothing he can afford or feels would be equal to the love he wants to express. Joyce here gives us a physical description, through the disappointing place that Araby proves to be, of the disillusionment that will come from first love. Araby is of course a metaphor for the first lover's emotional position or, perhaps we should say, the first lover's emotional conclusion. Two young men are talking to a young woman who is working at the stall; they are engaged in just what the narrator feels love should not be, a kind of trivial, ugly flirtation that at best offers sex and is predicated upon the competition for sex. The young woman offers to help him, and there is nothing she has that he wants. And then the final, famous last sentence of the story: "Gazing up into the darkness I saw myself as a creature driven and derided by vanity; and my eyes burned with anguish and anger."

We have not yet discussed vanity, though the narcissism of the first lover is part of what Joyce has in mind here, and his presumption that his love is a gift, a gift that would be welcomed.

Suddenly it hits him: he has nothing to offer this girl. He is of course too hard on himself; he is willing to give her anything, and his heart is worth more than the few, insufficient pence he has in his pocket. But he recognizes that any gift he could give her would be at best a childish approximation of what she might actually want, and in that he is right. She does not, and will not, want his love, and contained within his love was the vain hope that she might love him in return. He is derided by no one but himself; his disillusionment is his derision, and so he suffers and is furious—again, only at himself or at the belief he held. Perhaps he is angry at love, the false promises his love made to him, the misleading hopes it gave him. His love has betrayed him; he has betrayed himself. Love seems to him now, perhaps, to be a sham. It is all and only self-deception, he thinks.

As Adam Phillips puts it, "the disillusioned always think they are being realistic, and the realists always think they are telling the truth." But if we persist on this way of thinking about (subsequent) erotic love, insisting on our innocence, our "realism," then we get what we deserve. As we observed above, on this way of looking at things, there will be no happy lovers.

Joyce's first lover does not really expect Mangan's sister to return his love, and yet he can't help hoping that she will. When he realizes that he has lied to himself, then he cries his tears of self-recrimination. Using Phillips's analysis, we see that both innocent illusion and exaggerated, angry disillusionment are destructive lies we tell ourselves. Joyce gets the phenomenology of first love exactly right: it is exaggerated in its aspirations and then equally exaggerated in its disappointment. It oscillates between wildly irrational optimism and utter despair.

These states are understandable in the young. But as we come to know ourselves better, we can't indulge in them with a good conscience. Romantic love has to become less earnest, more playful, less arrogant, more ironical, less insistent upon the naked truth, more tolerant of conscious illusion—perhaps even more superficial, more seductive. In short, more interesting.

THE YOUNG SIMONE DE BEAUVOIR

Here a quick (yes, autobiographical) sketch of first love from Simone de Beauvoir will help clarify the view we are developing. She tells the story in her *Memoirs of a Dutiful Daughter:*

> Already I was beginning to want to escape from the narrow circle in which I was confined. A way of walking, a gesture, a smile would suddenly touch me deeply; I should have liked to run after the stranger turning the corner whom I might never see again. One afternoon in the Luxembourg Gardens a big girl in an apple-green tailored suit was playing with some children; they were skipping rope; she had rosy cheeks and a gentle, radiant smile. That evening, I told my sister: "I know what love is!" I had a glimpse of something new. My father, my mother, my sister, and all those I loved were mine already. I sensed for the first time that one can be touched to the very heart of one's being by a radiance from the *outside*.

In Simone de Beauvoir's brief account of this "big girl" there are three elements crucial to the experience of first love:

1. The first lover sees the beloved as someone whose world is significantly different from her own. It is a world that she believes she does not know, but wants to know. Unlike the love of our mothers, our first love is a love defined by being separated from the beloved. This difference will be

crucial for our subsequent erotic efforts, as our recognition of separation and our attempts to overcome it are the substance of our attempts to love and to be loved in return by the beloved. In some cases, this may mean our resignation to the inevitability or even the desirability of our own separateness from other people, beloved or not. In first love we are still certain this separateness can be overcome.

2. The first lover wants to see the world through the eyes of the beloved. This aspect of first love is characterized in Joyce's short story as the desperate need to understand how the beloved thinks and to demonstrate to the beloved that the first lover can understand the world in the way that the beloved does. In "Araby" we saw that the young lover desires to buy a gift at the fair suitable for his beloved in order to show her that he loves her, and loves her well. "If I go, I will bring you something." This is of course one of the principal reasons for gift giving, from offerings to the gods forward, in giving a gift, one hopes to be loved in return but also, and more urgently for the first lover, to demonstrate that he loves in the right way, that he understands, that he knows her well enough to give her something she would want. His tears of frustration at the end of the story reflect Joyce's worry that it is simply not possible for the first lover to achieve his end of completing the transparency that the young lover seeks. Whatever it is to love, we shall see, has only a little to do with transparency and, consequently, cultivates only a certain species of truthfulness and truth seeking.

3. The first lover's love, again, is rarely requited. In Simone de Beauvoir's story she never sees the girl after the first encounter, though she has already learned what she

takes for the central lesson of love (especially as she
characterizes feminine love in *The Second Sex*): love is
essentially unfulfilled desire. It is wanting and not
getting what you want.

At this point in the book Simone is ten years old. There is no
erotic element—at least, as eroticism is usually understood.

That said, her phrase "touched to the very heart of one's being
by a radiance from the *outside*" might be an unconventional but
compelling definition of the erotic. Proust, for example, has the
older Marcel comment: "The belief that a person has a share in an
unknown life to which his or her love may win us admission is,
of all the prerequisites of love, the one which it values most highly."
Or, as Anne Carson puts it in a commentary on Marcel and
Albertine, "Marcel's theory of desire [is that] which equates possession of another person with erasure of the otherness of her
mind, while at the same time positing otherness as what makes
another person desirable." Here desire is a necessarily self-
deceptive and entirely self-destructive paradox. I think here
Marcel still has a youthful, even immature understanding of
love—more first love than full-blown erotic love. But I agree with
de Beauvoir, Proust (and Carson's interpretation of Marcel) that
the desire to understand "the unknown other" is an important,
perhaps even an essential stage in learning about erotic love.

For the young Simone de Beauvoir, her will is involved in her
discovery of love; she feels restless; she wants to escape. She is, we
might say, looking for love, though she doesn't know that love is
what she's looking for. She is so secure in the love of her family
that she experiences what few of us do: complete identification
with not just her mother but her father and sister as well. They
belong to her. For her up to this point in her life, to love is to be
completely inside; she is, as far as love is concerned, still within

her mother's womb. But she wants more than what she has; she wants to be born into a larger world. When, in the same memoir, Simone describes her meeting and subsequent falling in love with Jean-Paul Sartre, she describes it in terms that exactly echo Aristophanes's myth. She writes that she was "half a person" before meeting Sartre, that he "completed" her, that he was the "missing half" she was destined to meet. We should not take this as support for Aristophanes's view of love: de Beauvoir speaks of her love for Sartre, and of romantic love generally, as an ongoing source of anguish, betrayal, frustration, and disappointment. As long as we insist upon the Aristophanic view of love, I think de Beauvoir's disappointment is precisely what we all should expect, what we deceive ourselves into. This book is in part a polemic against taking Aristophanes's—the *comic's*—view of love too seriously.

For the process I am trying to describe, first love self-deceptively establishes in our psyche the illusion that the love relationship is a truth relationship: there was the known (love as identification), now there is the unknown (the beloved object of first love), and for the love to be satisfied, the unknown will become known again. As in Aristophanes's myth, the lovers are reunited. The fact that the first lover does not achieve this goal only increases its urgency and exaggerates its importance in the lover's imagination. To say to the first lover, "You will always be alone; you will always be lonely," is not a defeat but a challenge.

Much depends on what we mean by "being alone." There are degrees of loneliness, as there are degrees of intimacy. Once we admit degrees of intimacy, shades of truthfulness, gradations of illusion and deception, we are beginning to understand the erotic as adults. As adults we understand that not all love needs to be so anxious. Or at least we can seek ways of cultivating love that don't depend upon anxiety.

The tears of frustration and rage of the narrator of "Araby" are the tears for the first lover who understands that his love will not be realized. Simone de Beauvoir thinks that this kind of love is particular to women. For de Beauvoir, the frustrations of the first lover in "Araby" could serve as an archetype for feminine love generally (on this account, Joyce simply chose the wrong gender for his lover). She thinks it is in the nature of masculine love simply to take and never to return, but she is recognizing only one kind of love. The frustrations of love are not a function of gender; it's simply that both the young Joyce and de Beauvoir agree on the psychology of one particular way of being in love. This is a way of believing in love that, in our analysis, presents an opportunity for learning to love well, and less painfully.

FIRST LIARS

In first love the first lover does not expect the truth from his beloved; he wants to disclose himself to her, but he does not expect her to disclose herself to him. Woldemar sees what an incorrigible liar Zinaida is; Werther does not want Lotte to tell the truth; indeed, he fears that she may do so.

This is not to say that if the first lover were lied to, and the lie had been exposed, he would not feel betrayed. Expecting the truth and expecting not to be lied to are two very different things. It's hard to determine how Woldemar feels when he realizes that Zinaida has loved his father all along. He does not appear to be angry with her. He pities her; after all, he knows how she feels.

The first lover hopes, but probably does not expect to get, what he wants; he knows it's out of reach, and that may well be part of the appeal. This is also precisely why Joyce's lover in "Araby" is so angry. He realizes that he's been lying to himself. "Love itself is a lie!" he seems to conclude, in the brokenhearted state of first love defeated. But that of course is the self-consoling lie that first love tells itself in its attempt to recover from its self-deception.

I know many people—including my present wife, in the early days of our romance—who, because of the feeling of self-betrayal suffered by the first lover, insist for a long time that romantic love is a kind of collective fiction we've all invented. On this line the open secret is that there is no such thing, really, as love. It's sexual desire plus a lie.

They, the first lovers who have been hurt and become skeptics, are right in their way. Erotic love is a kind of tailoring of invisible clothes for the emperor. We will experience only so much as we are willing to believe in what is not "really" there. But love for a child, love for a parent, love for a book—the same is true for all our values if we look at them more closely—none of that is "really" there. We think we live in a world of facts, but all our decisions are based on our values. We can't grab hold of values any more or any less than we can grab hold of love. "Subjectivity is meaning": what matters to us is what we ourselves project out into a world that, absent of us, is a collection of indifferent facts.

Perhaps love informs us about truth better than truth informs us about love. Maybe we've been getting a lot of things backward. Or as Nietzsche thought, we get things right in the way that we actually practice them—we actually do embrace deception, fantasy, imagination, creativity, illusion, falsehood when we practice the activity of loving—but we get things wrong once we start thinking about them, about arranging in our heads how we value them because we are trained from a very early age to suppose that "the truth" is something objective and independent of us. We suppose that "the truth" is somehow more important than we are as individuals.

Or consider the phenomenon of "truthfulness" from the perspective of the first lover. The first lover longs to be transparent to his beloved and also hopes that ultimately, his beloved will be transparent to him. That is the earnestness, the possible "truthfulness" of his love. In its deepest hope, that transparency is a religious impulse: in God's love, we are seen entirely by him and loved entirely as we are. (It is interesting to note that like the young lovers we have so far observed, the religious lover does not expect God to be transparent in return.) But transparency—what Freud called clarity—is only one way of understanding truthfulness.

Another way of thinking about truthfulness in love is to consider what makes us seek the truth. Adam Phillips writes: "Freud . . . thought that clarity is trivial (that is, defensive in essence) and that being interested—having one's attention engaged—is one criterion of truthfulness." In this way of thinking about first love, we seek to be clear—transparent—to our beloved because we fear that nothing less than true love can accept us entirely as we are; similarly, unless the beloved becomes transparent to us, we will always live in fear that some unknown aspect of the beloved may in time betray us. For us to have perfect clarity of who we are is to be completely secure in our love. To think this way about it is to ignore what we have seen: that the exercise of first love is, above all, an exercise in self-deception.

Freud's plausible view is that we never have perfect clarity, in love or any psychological matter—and certainly not with ourselves (how many of us could with a good conscience insist that we truly know ourselves?). In the context of love, Freud thinks, the desire for clarity is merely a desire to avoid being hurt by the beloved. This is why the jealous lover will seek clarity—his version of truthfulness—with such single-minded and usually destructive ferocity. But when we consider "having one's attention engaged" as a possible criterion for truthfulness—curiosity,

interest, focus, provocation (all traits that motivate our familiar seekers of truth, scientists, philosophers, psychologists)—how
much more "truthful" does the relationship of the lover become
with his beloved? Because there is no person more interested in
anything than a woman or a man interested in the one she or he
loves.

On this account, "truthfulness" looks more like "caring for,"
in much the way that Martin Heidegger meant the word: both
to be "anxious about" and to be "solicitous of." To "care for" is to
attempt to recognize where and how the particular individual
relates to another, to project a future for oneself and that other
cared-for person, and to recognize the particular circumstances
of that person, which includes a fascination for the person. When
we add erotic curiosity to this formula, to know a person truthfully just is to be in love with that person.

Freud's criterion for truthfulness, "being interested," is de-
rivative of Kierkegaard's notion of subjective truth and a close
cousin to Bonhoeffer's notion of the living truth. Both Freud and
Bonhoeffer take the relevant domain of truth to be not in the
sentences one person speaks to another but in the manner in
which one person relates to the other. When I say sincerely, for
example, "I'll love you forever," both I and the beloved to whom
it is spoken know that the sentence is literally false and factually
impossible, but it is not therefore either meaningless or deceptive. What I am expressing on Bonhoeffer's account is the living
truth of what Freud would call my very high degree of interest-
edness. Indeed, for me, at the moment I speak the sentence, what
could feel more truthful? What could be more urgent for me to
communicate? Doesn't every other sentence feel trivial compared
with this one, when it is spoken from the deepest feeling of
love? Insofar as the first lover is indeed interested in the object
of his love—insofar as first love is not merely an exercise in

narcissism—we would say, then, that it is unhelpful to characterize him as in a state of error or falsehood.

MY COUSIN ANNA

Let me illustrate the complexity of truth talk in the context of first love with one more brief autobiographical love story.

In her late teens my cousin Anna was giving her parents trouble, and she came from Winnipeg to live with us, for a year or so, in Calgary. I was ten, and she was seventeen, and I had a great crush on her. When I won tickets to Beatlemania from a local radio station, Anna was my date. We walked over Rideau Hill to the concert, and I remember the sun was low in the sky, and we sat in the grass for fifteen minutes or so and talked. I don't remember what we said, but perhaps we talked about my older brother Darren, with whom I later learned we both were in love. That Christmas Anna was still with us, and I bought a gold chain for her at the jewelry counter in Eaton's. She was tremendously excited when she opened it. I remember on Christmas that her surprise and pleasure in the present made me nervous. She was disproportionately impressed. A few days later my mom came to me and asked how much I had paid for the chain.

"Why?" I asked. I wanted to lie but was afraid to.

"We just want to make sure you didn't pay too much for it."

It was electroplated and had been turning her neck green.

I was humiliated. I had not wanted to fool Anna into thinking that the gift I had given her was any better than it was, but it was also the best gift I had to give—it was more expensive than any other gift I gave that Christmas—and it turned out that not only was my gift a fake (I wasn't yet aware of the difference between a karat gold and a vermeil or electroplated chain), but it appeared that I had been trying to make my gift seem more precious than it was.

I tell this little story about another first love of mine because I think it illustrates the kind of suspension of what we might call the truth-seeking faculty—for lack of a better term, because I don't mean something so broad as "reason"—when it comes to the lover's state of mind. As I look back on it, when I bought the chain for Anna, I didn't think it was adequate. Then, when she was so excited to get it, I certainly didn't want to diminish her excitement over it; on the contrary. But I remember that Christmas's being spoiled by my anxiety over her excitement. So I knew something was up. And when my mother approached me, I knew what she was talking about. But at the same time I managed to tell myself that I didn't quite know.

We could describe this event as straightforward deception if I had been older, if you gave a lover a CZ, say, and then it was later discovered not to be a diamond, we would correctly think, "Well, that nasty lie deserved to be exposed." But in "Araby" the narrator's recognition that he cannot find an adequate gift is an exaggeration, one that is a consequence of his naive view of love and the truth; my anxiety too was an exaggeration, though justified, and that I was at some level hoping to deceive is also true (if I could have made that chain never turn Anna's neck green, I surely would have). But none of these exaggerations, half-lies, or self-accusations seem blameworthy in the way that giving a trusting lover a CZ while pretending it's a diamond does. The more we know about love, then, the more we expect ourselves to be truthful in the practice of it.

But that can't be right. We become so duplicitous in our erotic lives—and for good reasons, including good evolutionary reasons, as we shall see. What we must mean is that our expectations about the kind and care of deception and truthfulness in love change. The more we know about love, the greater subtlety we demand. In that most subtle and thorough of all books ever written about love, the *Kama Sutra*, the demands placed upon the lover are as rigorous as we would place upon any scientist or philosopher. But the *Kama Sutra* is always extremely practical about love, so practical in fact that it lists many different kinds of deception as among the necessary skills of the lover.

When we are naive about love, by contrast, we are clumsy, even indignant dogmatists about erotic experience. All the first loves we've examined and perhaps almost all first loves are unrequited loves in the way that first love in particular demands it: as not being loved in return in the way that one wants to be loved, which also means as not being loved in the way that one loves.

This is the self-righteousness of first love. It is the love of Woldemar, who loves Zinaida unreservedly, finds his love unrequited, and is vindicated when he discovers that his beloved has a similarly unrequited love for his own father. The self-righteousness, the moral fervor, the sense of justice and injustice of first love give the first lover the false belief that his love has the power of truthfulness. When he discovers he has been betrayed, he feels vindicated. "My love was real!" I felt when Lisa threatened to beat me up at the end of that bridge, so real that it kept me from speaking to her until her death. The lover feels, and may always feel, now *this* is love and, later, now *that* was love. The misguided search to recover that lost love will lead the lover into many confusions, lies—to him or herself but also to others—and especially confusions in later attempts at loves. It may take Woldemar many years before he trusts another woman enough to love her in the way he loved Zinaida, or he may conclude that true love is always accompanied by mistrust. For years after my first love for Lisa—for thirty years, it's fair to say—I felt certain that when I loved a woman strongly, it was inevitable that she would betray me. The fact that her boyfriend—another man—was standing beside her when she did it no doubt also imprinted itself on my self-righteous pubescent brain.

TWISTED SELF-DECEPTION

First love is usually also the lover's first real taste of jealousy. Of course we all experience jealousy with our mothers. Recall Adam Phillips's acute observation "Our mothers are a model of infidelity." They have lives of their own. They know people we don't know, people we will never know. They take an interest in others. They spend time on the phone talking to—as far as we're concerned—strangers. But because we understand we must share our mothers—because our mothers have authority over us—we reluctantly accept the separation. In first love, separation from the beloved is already unbearable, but when that separation is a consequence of someone's enjoying the beloved's company, her sexual proximity to that other, her lover, the first lover goes wild with pain and anxiety. This may be the most intense experience of jealousy the lover will ever feel, or it may set a pattern for the lover's future relationships, as it did for me in my relationship with Lisa.

In a tempest of jealousy there is no act the lover may not perform, no lie she will not tell, no fantasy of betrayal she will not believe, no promise or moral code she will not break. The jealousy of Othello, who murders Desdemona, and the jealousy of Medea, who murders first Jason's new wife and then her own children by him, are the jealousy of the first lover. Both Othello and Medea share the immediacy and certainty of the first lover, and therefore their betrayal—or perception of betrayal in Othello's case—is that much more terrible and profound.

When we have less confidence in the "truth" of love, our jealousy may be as acute, but it will have different sources: rivalry, for example, or humiliation, frustrated desire, or indignation. We understand that love is uncertain, and we are less surprised when it disappoints us. Another way of saying it: in first love, the emphasis is on the experience of love; in later loves, the emphasis is on the experience of the beloved. One's experience of the beloved is also always of course mediated by the prior love experiences of the lover—that is, by one's own experiences of loving.

In ordinary self-deception, we believe what we want to believe. That is one of the surest signs of self-deception: when you wind up feeling certain of what you know you desired to be true. In twisted self-deception, by contrast, you believe precisely what you most fear may be the truth. This is Othello's self-deception; it is the self-deception of the jealous lover, of the first lover.

But we should also ask ourselves: Is part of the piquancy of first love the delight in being betrayed? Certainly, betrayal is part of what makes it so memorable. There is a strange, unhealthy, nasty pleasure in jealousy. "It is the green-eyed monster which doth mock / The meat it feeds upon." Jealousy satisfies an unattractive hunger. There may even be a pleasure in knowing that you are being lied to. It puts the person to whom the lie is directed in a position of superiority over the liar; it gives that person power over the liar. The first lover, when lied to or betrayed, feels himself to be "good," "moral," "true." As the public exposure of any beloved liar suffices to show—whether the liar is Bill Clinton, Tiger Woods, or Lance Armstrong—moral indignation is an enormously popular and satisfying emotion.

ONANISM

I would like to talk about kissing now because for a long time it seemed to me the natural transition between first love and erotic love. But of course we can have sex without kissing—tellingly, most prostitutes will not let their clients kiss them on the lips—and in fact, first love rarely involves a kiss. Zinaida kisses Woldemar repeatedly on the head and face when she tells him to leap off a wall for her and he does it, but they do not exchange a kiss. I did kiss Lisa, but I never kissed Anna.

A real kiss, even more than sex, may best summarize what we mean by erotic love. There is nothing more intimate, erotically speaking, than a kiss. In Alberto Moravia's *Contempt*, one of the more discouraging books on the possibility of successful love, the narrator believes he has killed his wife's love for him when she catches him kissing another woman: "Now tell me the truth—wasn't it perhaps that kiss that first came between us? Tell me the truth—wasn't that kiss the first thing that made you lose your love for me?" And he in turn is most profoundly wounded when he sees her kissing another man. A kiss often matters much more to us than sex. And learning how to give a kiss is part of that intimacy; our first double-jointed attempts at kissing are a long way from the real thing. So, because kissing may be the quintessence of the erotic, we shall look more closely at it in the next chapter.

But before we leave the subject of first love, we should briefly consider our own first experience of sex, masturbation.

As we noted at the outset, our first experiences with the erotic are a kind of explosive combination of the body and the imagination. Allow me to tell another embarrassing personal story.

I was eight or nine. It was after watching Woody Allen's *Everything You Ever Wanted to Know About Sex* / *But Were Afraid to Ask*. I was particularly excited by the famous scene in the restaurant where we see everything that takes place in the man's body as he is aroused by the woman sitting at the table with him. I lay in bed, fearful that my younger brother, who was in the bunk below, would hear me, and repeated that scene over and over in my mind, pretending to myself that some faceless girl or young woman was sucking on my penis like a straw, sucking the fluid up from it. It may have taken an hour, and at times I was tempted to give up, as one often is in sex later in life. But I didn't stop trying, and I still faintly remember that spectacular, hard-earned climax, because I was disappointed, for years afterward, that with each masturbation since then there was a diminishment in pleasure. (An echo, here, of White's understanding of love.)

These days, of course, as I expect it is for most of us in adulthood, masturbation for me is more like a cup of coffee in the morning than it is like sex, except that it is still like the opposite of sex, that lonely, dirty feeling afterward and the grubby, hurried cleanup—like making your way through airport security, putting your shoes on as quickly as you can, and grabbing your laptop. Contrast this with sex's relaxation, with the easy, peaceful intimacy of resting in each other's arms or side by side, breathing together, interrupted only by that too human, comical, woebegone moment when your lover makes her trip to the bathroom. Once my father explained to me that the sadness that comes after sex was the consequence of—and, in his mind, a proof of the existence of—the power of kundalini and its release. I didn't understand the remark at the time because for me, that sadness followed masturbation but did not occur after sex.

Whatever our personal experience of the emotions involved in sex may be, my father's remark helps illustrate the fact that sex is ultimately as much a spiritual as a physical phenomenon. I think this is true even when sex is in part a business transaction, as when one has sex with a prostitute; in fact the spiritual element in sex with a prostitute can be most pronounced, because of the mutually felt need for an intimacy that is next to impossible and yet occasionally, unexpectedly, achieved. The spiritual element of sex is one reason I want to discuss masturbation in the context of first love. Masturbation is the specifically sexual beginning of the fantasy life that will be necessary for erotic love and that is deliberately, necessarily imaginative, creative, counterfactual. Our earliest sexual experiences are both egoistic and invented. It should come as no surprise, then, that our subsequent erotic life depends upon these elements. But what is missing from masturbation is the spiritual feeling that comes from sex with another person—the communicative aspect of sex, the intense experience of being together, which includes both egoistic and nonegoistic components. So far as masturbation is spiritual, it is spiritual in the way that first love is: it is a creative projection of what the lover or masturbator would like to have, would like to be the case. But when another is as actively engaged in the sex act as we are, the simple sexual act of masturbation—like the psychologically onanistic act of first love—is exposed in its narcissism. We will not succeed as erotic lovers if we are pleasing only ourselves. Suddenly we are not merely hoping for someone else to live up to our own fantasy lives; that beloved is also asking that we live up to his or hers. Two imaginations are more fantastic than one.

4. Erotic Love

A person has no need of sincerity, nor even of skill in lying, in order to be loved. Here I mean by love reciprocal torture.   —Marcel Proust

Few relationships have more potential for deceit and self-deception than those between the sexes.

—Robert Trivers

SEX ON A BET

I am not sure what my oedipal relationship with either my mother or my father may be or have been. From what I have written so far, I'm guessing it's complicated; even Freud famously admitted, toward the end of his life, that his theory of libido was so complicated that he wasn't sure he himself understood it. That said, my own first experience of desired sex with a beloved was very much like what the psychoanalyst Melanie Klein describes as consummated first love at the opening of our chapter on first love, and the story of my own first erotic experience certainly has elements of first love.

Her name was Lila Gibbard, and it started with a bet. Nikhil Singh and I were walking down the hill to Western Canada High School.

"I'm sixteen and I've never had a girlfriend. What a loser! My big brother had sex when he was fourteen. My dad lost his virginity when he was twelve," I said.

We were kicking leaves as we walked. It was late September. We had become friends because we both were in the International Baccalaureate Program at Western, and most of the kids in the program were bigger geeks than we were. It was the only IB program in Calgary, Alberta, and it had gathered every geek teenager in the city.

"I've never even had a date," Nikhil said.

The air was cold and smoky, the smell of fall near the mountains.

"I had a date in sixth grade. Denise. And Debbie at prom. But Denise doesn't count because I didn't like her, and Debbie doesn't count because she didn't like me. She told me that during prom. She said, 'I hope you're not expecting anything, because I like Malcolm.'"

"Normal people have a girlfriend by now. Half the guys in tenth grade are already getting laid."

I said to Nikhil, "Why don't we make that a goal?"

"What? To get laid? I've had that goal for sixteen years. Or close enough."

"No. Just to get a date. We could put twenty bucks on it. Or a vial of hash oil. Whoever gets a date first owes the other guy a vial of hash oil."

"But it can't be just anybody," Nikhil said. "It has to be somebody you really want to date. I mean, anybody can get a date with some girl."

We both quietly contemplated the untruth of this.

"Okay. Who do you want to date?"

"There's one."

There was a girl for me too. But I wasn't going to say her name first.

"That girl Lucy. Lucy Johnson."

Lucy was the girl I was going to say. But now that it was out of his mouth, he had dibs. We both couldn't try to date Lucy; the problem was tough enough without creating unnecessary competition.

"Lucy? I know her. She went to my junior high school."

"Yeah, I think I'm a little in love with her."

This was one of the reasons Nikhil and I were such good friends. We could admit things to each other that we couldn't admit to anyone else. That aspect of intimacy is common among very close friends: the ability to confess without fear—or with only a bit of fear—what we wouldn't tell anyone else and sometimes not even ourselves. In seduction, pretending to confess an intimate secret about oneself is a familiar technique; one hopes, of course, that the revelation of such secrets will be a key component of enduring romantic love.

"What about that blonde. She's hot."

"Blonde?"

I knew the girl he meant.

"She sits behind Rob. She seems like she might be smart too."

To a sixteen-year-old boy in IB, it was unlikely that a girl could be smart, and being smart was not a recommendation, which Nikhil knew well enough. But I knew she was smart, and she was hot.

"She's sort of chubby, don't you think?"

I wanted to get his approval before I expressed my own. It would be about ten years before I would begin to overcome that habit, which I have since observed in people of all ages.

"She's got a big ass, I guess," Nikhil said. "But she's definitely hot. I'd ask her out if I wasn't going to ask Lucy."

We shook on the bet.

"Thirty days," I said. "If we don't set a deadline, we'll never do it."

When I try to think back on the lies I may have told Lila in winning her attention, I think they were the most juvenile kind: I tried to seem smarter than I was, I bragged about the accomplishments of my older brother—he was Calgary's most successful cocaine dealer at the time, lived in a penthouse, smuggled marijuana, LSD, and cocaine from California, and had many other extraordinary adventures—I wrote long erotic letters detailing imagined sexual scenarios. She loved those letters. I was a habitual liar at this time, I believe, but I think I was a bit too intoxicated with her to lie to her effectively. I didn't have much to hide from her.

The actual romantic life I was beginning to lead—my first specifically romantic experience—was already, at its outset, a fantasy life. Novice lover that I was, self-deception was more important to the initial stages of the relationship than the deception of her. I remember my lies only really got going once another lover, a competitor, entered the scene.

In short, I won the bet.

Our first kiss was in her bedroom. I had one of Lila's tits out in my hand. I remember laughing with our tongues all wrapped up, from the joy—the pure surprise—of knowing I was going to fuck her. But even with the anticipation of sex, with my cock harder than it had ever been—I was a sixteen-year-old boy about to have sex for the first time—the pleasure was more mental than physical, and the experience was fitting itself into a narrative of expectation and hopes: Lila would be my girlfriend, we would fall in love, dates, dinners, walks—we would be a couple: "There they go, Clancy and Lila." Holding hands. Kissing.

A PARENTHESIS ON KISSING

Freud wrote in his *Three Essays on the Theory of Sexuality* that we begin kissing other people because we cannot kiss ourselves. Freud seems like the sort of person who would have wished he might kiss himself, but the idea he was trying to capture of course is one he took from Schopenhauer: that one's desire always exceeds the object from which it seeks its possible satisfaction. Here again, Freud and I differ. It may be true that desire is unquenchable, but in a kiss desire is at once incited and satisfied. The good kiss is perfect.

You can do many things with a kiss: you can lie; you can promise; you can ask; you can control, threaten, or attempt to dominate, to overpower; you can confess; you can surrender, or retreat, or accuse. A kiss can be like a cry (like crying, or a cry of pain or of hope). One reason Thai prostitutes are so much better than Western prostitutes is that in Thailand a prostitute kisses you, and you don't feel that she is trying not to kiss you while kissing you. Everyone seeks to become a better kisser, attempts various techniques: holding the throat while kissing, relaxing the neck backward while kissing, devouring while kissing. There are good kissers and bad kissers. There is such a thing as too artful a kiss— and then it feels like a fake kiss. But Thai prostitutes, among the best and most practiced kissers in the art, know that to kiss well, one must merely kiss. The best kiss is entirely uncontrived.

I once heard a story from a Tibetan Buddhist Rinpoche who was trying to explain the many rituals of one of his practices. They seemed, to a Zen practitioner who was present, ornamental and not in keeping with the philosophy of emptiness. The Rinpoche said to her that her reactions to Tibetan heritage might be like his reaction, on first arriving in New Zealand, to seeing a man and a woman with their mouths pressed together. He had never seen kissing before. He said, "For you it is an expression of love. To me it looked disgusting." It isn't love, quite. It is, as Freud would have said, wanting to put the whole world in one's mouth. Wanting to put the whole person in one's mouth. Wanting to eat the other person and to be eaten.

Socrates, who has already taught us a bit about love, also has something to say about kissing. In his *Memorabilia of Socrates,* the general and sometime philosopher Xenophon—a student of Socrates, one of three sources of our knowledge about him—writes about his teacher:

> As to love, his counsel was to abstain rigidly from familiarity with beautiful persons; for he observed that it was not easy to be in communication with such persons, and observe continence. Hearing, on one occasion, that Critobulus, the son of Criton, had kissed the son of Alcibiades, a handsome youth, he asked Xenophon, in the presence of Critobulus, saying, "Tell me, Xenophon, did you not think that Critobulus was one of the modest rather than the forward, one of the thoughtful rather than of the thoughtless and inconsiderate?" "Certainly," replied Xenophon. "You must now, then, think him extremely headstrong and daring; one who would even spring upon drawn swords, and leap into the fire." "And what," said Xenophon, "have you seen him doing, that you form this opinion of him?" "Why, has he not dared," rejoined Socrates, "to kiss the son of Alcibiades, a youth extremely handsome, and in the flower of his age?" "If such a deed," returned Xenophon, "is one of daring and peril, I think that even I could undergo such peril." "Unhappy man!" exclaimed Socrates, "and what do you think that you incur by kissing a handsome person? Do you not expect to become at once a slave instead of a freeman? To spend much money upon hurtful pleasures? To have too much oc-

cupation to attend to anything honorable and profitable? And to be compelled to pursue what not even a madman would pursue?" "By Hercules," said Xenophon, "what extraordinary power you represent to be in a kiss!" "Do you wonder at this?" rejoined Socrates; "are you not aware that the Tarantula, an insect not as large as half an obolus, by just touching a part of the body with its mouth, wears men down with pain, and deprives them of their senses?" "Yes, indeed," said Xenophon, "but the Tarantula infuses something when it bites." "And do you not think, foolish man," rejoined Socrates, "that beautiful persons infuse something when they kiss, something which you do not see? Do you not know that the animal, which they call a handsome and beautiful object, is so much more formidable than the Tarantula, as those insects instill something when they touch, but this creature, without even touching, but if a person only looks at it, though from a very great distance, instills something of such potency, as to drive people mad? Perhaps indeed Cupids are called archers for no other reason but because the beautiful wound from a distance. But I advise you, Xenophon, whenever you see any handsome person, to flee without looking behind you; and I recommend to you, Critobulus, to absent yourself from hence for a year, for perhaps you may in that time, though hardly indeed, be cured of your wound." Thus he thought that those should act with regard to objects of love who were not secure against the attractions of such objects; objects of such a nature, that if the body did not at all desire them, the mind would not contemplate them, and which, if the body did desire them, should cause us no trouble.

"What extraordinary power you represent to be in a kiss!" The unhappily married Socrates—even as reported by the rather dull-witted and pedantic Athenian general Xenophon, a student who was not in love with his teacher in the way that Plato was—recognizes that the innocent lover wagers not only his fortune and happiness but indeed the health of his soul on a kiss. For Socrates, a kiss is the start of serious trouble.

In "First Loves" we saw that the distinction between what is nonverbal and verbal was crucial because all the young would-be lover's love is distilled in the pipes of what he cannot say. When he can speak—normally, we think, this is where lying could begin, and things get more complicated (if only because to speak is almost always to exaggerate at least a little)—his love is moving into a new form: out of first love and into erotic love. But when I think about kissing, and sex, and how much communication can take place in the nonverbal aspects of human experience—especially the experience of love—I recognize how much deception takes place outside the verbal. It is hopelessly naive—perhaps it is a writer's self-serving naiveté—to suppose that to be lied to in love requires words.

One lover kisses because he wants to love; the other kisses back because he wants to be loved, not because he loves in return. Isn't that the beginning of every heartbreak? Of every betrayal, every "I've been lied to!" in love?

But a kiss can also be a lie one tells to oneself. Take Chekhov's story "The Kiss," for example. The trouble starts when the members of a reserve artillery brigade stop for a night at a village and are invited by a nearby general to visit his estate. He entertains them, with games, dinner, and the waltz. One officer, Ryabovitch, a little man in glasses, with sloped shoulders and shaggy whiskers on the sides of his cheeks, not covering his chin, and without a mustache, keeps apart. He is modest and shy, and the social requirements of the evening are painful for him. At first he is almost blinded by the activity, and then he watches it with scrutiny. To him, the host family's interest in conversation is feigned, and so are their smiles. Then, by mistake, Ryabovitch gets lost in the house and winds up in a dark room, where a woman turns to him and says, "At last." She puts her arms around him, presses her cheek to his, and gives him a kiss. Then suddenly she shrieks, because she realizes he is not the man she was looking for, and runs away.

Because of the kiss, Ryabovitch finds that the evening is completely transformed. Chekhov writes:

> His neck, round which soft, fragrant arms had so lately been clasped, seemed to him to be anointed with oil; on his left cheek near his moustache where the unknown had kissed him there was a faint chilly tingling sensation as from peppermint drops, and the more he rubbed the place the more distinct was the chilly sensation; all over, from head to foot, he was full of a strange new feeling which grew stronger and stronger . . . He wanted to dance, to talk, to run into the garden, to laugh aloud . . . He quite forgot that he was round-shouldered and uninteresting, that he had lynx-like whiskers and an "undistinguished appearance" (that was how his appearance had been described by some ladies whose conversation he had accidentally overheard). When Von Rabbek's wife happened to pass by him, he gave her such a broad and friendly smile that she stood still and looked at him inquiringly. "I like your house immensely!" he said, setting his spectacles straight.

Ryabovitch spends dinner trying to guess which woman he has kissed, ultimately deciding he'd like to have the shoulders of this one and the face of that, and back that night with his brigade, he tells the story. He feels like a poet at the opening of an epic, but the story is over in three lines, as is the magic of the kiss, which fades as the other officers laugh at him. The truth of the fact that the woman clearly meant to kiss someone else sadly dawns on him.

The stolen kiss was a lie he told himself; that became the lie that first defined the night for him in one way: as the kind of man whom a woman would want to kiss, even, would want to steal a kiss from! Then of course it defined him in another way, as the kind of fool who wouldn't understand that the kiss was an accident.

For our purposes, the kiss is a terrific example of the dangers of the subjectivity of meaning; everything, for Ryabovitch, depended upon interpretation. Not unlike a young lover, he has misinterpreted in two directions: first, by failing to ask himself if he ought to be so transported by such dubious circumstances; second, by letting what was, after all, an understandable, even charming misinterpretation define him to himself as an unlovable, humiliated man. What's most important for our purposes is that Chekhov illustrates that a kiss is rarely just a kiss. It's hard not to worry that poor Ryabovitch will never have another real kiss again.

BACK TO MY LOVE STORY: A RIVAL AND REVENGE

For a brief time Lila Gibbard and I were lovers. I was a lucky teenage boy: she was kinky. She liked anal sex more than vaginal, eagerly gave blow jobs—once on a road trip, under a blanket, in the front seat of her mother's car, with her mother sitting beside us (we were in the mountains, and she went back down under the blanket every time we entered a tunnel)—and liked to have me come on her panty hose, her bra, her bared tits, her face. We did our physics homework together. When at Christmas her little sister went on vacation with their parents, leaving her behind with her little brother, I stayed with them during the day and did her sister's paper route for her in the snow. I enjoyed doing things for her, and she liked it, and a kind of understanding arose between us that I was more in love with her than she was with me.

We were watching a movie at night in her living room, drinking hot chocolate and eating popcorn, when I told her I loved her. I know I said it first.

She replied, "I think I love you. I think I'm falling in love with you, I mean." Which showed that she already knew. Neither of us was lying, but both of us were venturing. She was more honest about it than I was.

Then the rival appeared. His name was Paul. He was not from our high school. He was a year older. Lila turned skinny. Boys at Western, at the mall, in the grocery store were approaching her. She reeked of sex.

One night she wasn't answering the phone, so I rode my bike to her house. It was seven and a half miles in the Calgary winter, after dark, through the blowing snow. When I got to her house, there was a strange car in the driveway.

Lila's bedroom was in the basement; all our rough, fabulous, dirty sex took place down there, where her parents couldn't hear or open a door and accidentally see. They would call from the top of the stairs before they came down. She even had a shower and a bath for afterward. We had rope.

The light was on in her basement. We had caught her younger brother peeping once, so she kept a curtain drawn over the window. I propped my bike against the side of the house and got down on my hands and knees in the snow. I could see a crack of light through the curtains. I lay flat on my belly. I could see the ceiling and part of a wall but nothing else. All the action was going on beneath my line of sight. I listened carefully, but she had her music on loud. I knew what that meant. I considered knocking on the window. Then I considered kicking it in. I stood there for half an hour, watching the window for changes in the light, hoping the music would stop. At one point there was silence; then she turned the record over. It was one of our records. There she was, in bed with him, though after all, they could be sitting on her sofa. Maybe she didn't do the same things with him she did with me—screwing him, jerking him off onto her crotch, swallowing his cock into her throat the way she could—maybe they were just talking, doing homework; they could just be friends.

Lila Gibbard had a more powerful impact on me than any of my previous loves. As Melanie Klein warns us, the addition of sex to love makes matters particularly confusing.

Almost thirty years later I still remember the intensity with which I loved Lila Gibbard. And the excesses I committed loving and trying to prove my love to her: a suicide attempt; a convertible I gave her for Valentine's Day; dropping out of school, lying to her parents and claiming that I had been kicked out of my house by my stepfather so that I could live with her; living for a time at a gas station, another time in the streets; sleeping in malls; stealing from my parents so that I could buy her Caesar salads and mint-chocolate milk shakes that I would deliver to her at lunchtime. The lies I told her about my suicide attempts. The lies I told her about other lovers that I had. The lies I told her about when I had seen her with Paul. The lies she told me about where she had been the night before, who she was talking to on the phone, what was really happening.

This went on for two years. Then I turned eighteen, and as was traditional in our house, it was time for me to leave. I didn't have a high school diploma, so my mom sent me to live with my dad in Florida. He got me into college, and my relationship with Lila was over.

Or it should have been. There were two more encounters.

The first time I was visiting my mom for Christmas, and I took Lila on a date. I borrowed my mom's Toyota Corolla. After pizza at our old favorite restaurant—she loved Hawaiian pizza—I fucked her in the parking lot, with the car's motor running. First I took her from behind, in the ass, the way I knew she wanted— "I don't let boys do that to me now," she told me—and then we fucked a second time in the back, with the seats of the hatchback folded down. I wanted her to have rug scars on her shoulder blades and elbows. I fucked her just to tell her that I didn't love her anymore. Of course I was still in love with her. But the rough, impersonal sex—the kind of sex, mind you, I knew she loved— was a technique I was using to convince myself that she didn't mean anything to me.

Afterward she asked me if I thought I'd ever move back to Calgary. "No," I told her, but I also knew then that if she had asked me to, I probably would have. This was how it was for me when I was in the state between escaping from years of being in love with her and still wondering if there was a way to have her back.

In that state, so common for the lover, it is almost impossible either to deceive or to tell the truth, either to the lover or to oneself, because you truly have no idea what is the case and what is not the case. And this fact about love—that from one moment to the next the lover experiences so many different degrees and even kinds of certainty, uncertainty, self-awareness, and self-doubt—is what makes speaking about "truth" and "transparency" and "honesty" in love so dubious. Nevertheless, as we shall observe again and again, intimacy and trust will depend upon at least the possibility of these ways of being and knowing.

The second time I heard from Lila I was about a year into graduate school. So four years had passed.

She called me on the phone. She told me she had been dating a handsome French architect for a few years who, she said quietly, "is abusive." She did not specify what kind of abuse, and I did not ask.

"He's nothing like you," she said. "In fact the opposite. Maybe that's the attraction. To punish myself."

I did not comment.

To put it differently, I knew I was not vulnerable, but I still remembered those two years I'd been so in love with her well enough to worry that I could become vulnerable again. At the end of our second conversation, she called me Sunshine—her old nickname for me—and I knew I had her. I asked her to send me pictures of herself.

"What kind? What do you mean?"

"You know what kind I mean."

She sent twenty or more, Polaroids, most of them naked, some with her masturbating naked. She wore just black panty hose and garters in others. In one she was hitting herself on her reddened ass with a riding crop. It was taken from behind, with her on her knees, looking back at the camera. They were wonderful pictures. You could see her ribs through her skin—that alone made me want to fuck her—she was slender and had come into her beauty. Her skin was pale and lustrous, her hair a true bold yellow, her eyes bright green. From a different woman I would have masturbated to those pictures for weeks.

I threw them away, and I never wrote to her again. I changed my phone number so she couldn't call. She wrote to me a couple of times, and then she went quiet.

That was my last seduction of her and my final, shameful act of revenge. It was, it seems to me now, clearly modeled on the years I refused to talk to my stepsister Lisa. It was a strange act of deception: to pretend to be falling for her again, just so that she would expose herself to me, so that I could more thoroughly and viciously reject her. I wanted her entirely exposed, so that her humiliation would be more complete.

To me, at the time, this action had the flavor of truthfulness to it, that seamy truthfulness that certain acts of "justice" have. I enjoyed the moral indignation that we noted in our analysis of the first lover, feeling vindicated when I should have felt ashamed (as I do now, relating the story). "Morality," Bertrand Russell wrote, thinking of sex and echoing Nietzsche, "is simply an expression of the repressed desire to be cruel to others."

SEX AND DECEPTION

We've looked at kissing, and I've told my own case history of my first real erotic experience, my first real lover. Now let's step back to look at a few facts and some theory about the erotic life and how deception plays into it.

First, some interesting facts: other factors being equal, a lover who is cheating on her partner is more likely to become impregnated when she is cheating than when she is with her partner. Males are more likely to find sexual partners if they are deceptive about their own (especially, genetic) quality. Women report commonly being deceived about "partner ambition, sincerity, kindness and strength of feeling." Men report commonly being deceived about a future female partner's willingness to have sex, and it is much more common for women to fake orgasm than for men to do so. Men regularly self-deceive about female sexual interest; men are inclined to believe that women are more interested than they in fact are. Men lie about how much sex they've had; women lie about how much they haven't. Both men and women commonly imagine the faces, bodies, and provocations of other lovers during sex. Deceit is commonly accepted as a part of the process of seduction in both sexes.

As Robert Trivers reminds us, none of this should come as a surprise: "Even *within* our genomes, deception flourishes, as selfish genetic elements use deceptive molecular techniques to overreproduce at the expense of other genes. Deception infects all the fundamental relationships in life: parasite and host, predator and prey, plant and animal, male and female, neighbor and neighbor, parent and offspring, and even the relationship of an organism to itself."

Given the fact that the more highly developed the brain of an organism is, the more prone to and the more expert at both deception and self-deception that organism will be, and given that deception and self-deception are most prevalent and useful in the context of (at least potential) reproduction, we should expect that the erotic lives of human beings are riddled with deception. To claim that when we love, we lie, is almost tautological. What's more interesting, perhaps, is that we are so insistent on the connection between love and truthfulness. Maybe we are searching for the truthful lover, at least in part, because we are all too familiar with the lover who lies. Perhaps I even recognize that the lying lover I fear and want to escape is myself. That said, when I think back on my love for Lila Gibbard, if I am tough on myself and truthful, I feel much less regret for the lies I told her than I feel irritation with the lies she told me. This is due to the fact, so it seems to me now, that I told her lies in order to try to make her love me more, whereas she was telling lies to cover up the fact that she was losing interest in me and discovering her love for someone else. But isn't that awfully convenient for me . . .

To lie in love is not necessarily to be irresponsible. On the contrary, the notorious liar and lover Don Juan "was nothing if not conscientious," Adam Phillips writes. Nor is it necessarily morally blameworthy; Phillips could have immediately added, "But not nearly so conscientious as Scheherazade." Scheherazade, we remember, deceitfully offered herself to the shah in order to save the lives of her sisters, and then spun lies for a thousand and one nights so that she could bear the shah three sons and so convince him not to kill their mother. (He had resolved to sleep with a new virgin every night because he had himself been deceived by his former wife in love.) Our most famous literary lovers have almost always been both deceivers and remarkably scrupulous in their deceptions.

DON JUAN AND THE CUTTLEFISH

When in Byron's great treatment of romantic love and seduction *Don Juan*, the sultana Gulbeyaz sees the young Don Juan for sale in the slaves' market, she is seized by an unconquerable passion for him, but she knows she can never get a man—other than a eunuch—into the palace. So she brings him, has him disguised as a woman (well, really it is her servant Baba, "ne'er been known to fail / in any kind of mischief to be wrought," who concocts the plan), and he is brought to her. Before any real serious sexual mischief is wrought, however, while the sultana and Don Juan delay, posture, and size each other up, suddenly the sultan enters.

Byron couldn't have known about it, but a similar game is played by giant Australian cuttlefish during spawning season. There are not enough female cuttlefish to satisfy the passion of all the males (males outnumber females by four to one), so the largest, strongest male cuttlefish will gather up harems, leaving the smaller, weaker males to scuttle in frustration around the circle of their (dis)satisfaction. But certain cuttlefish—these are cuttlefish, remember, masters of disguise, one of nature's consummate deceivers—will dress in borrowed robes, making themselves appear to be female cuttlefish, so that he can sneak into the harem and have his way with as many of the females as he can woo. This alone would be noteworthy—few other species pretend to be the opposite sex in order successfully to get sex they otherwise cannot obtain—but what is particularly interesting is that the female cuttlefish prefer to have sex with the smaller, cross-dressing males. Some researchers have speculated that the evolutionary advantage here is the preservation of a "smart gene": the clever cuttlefish that outwit the big louts are selected and their succession is guaranteed. Or maybe female cuttlefish just like their men in drag.

Nietzsche would have liked the story of the cuttlefish. He thought that in all species, indices of intelligence and sophistication correspond with indices of dissimulation: whether vegetable, insect, or mammal, the more advanced and clever you are, the better a liar you are and the more prone you are to deceive to get what you want. Orchids like the Ophrys (also known as the prostitute orchid) have sex by making their labella appear, smell, and even feel like the rear end of a female bee, so that a male bee supposes she has simply lit upon the flower to eat and has her head buried deeply into her meal. Cryptostylis, the Australian tongue orchid (what is it about these Australians?), so closely mimics a female wasp that the male wasp, in the practice of having the orchid's pollen transferred to him through his vigorous exertions, will in fact ejaculate into the flower.

The point of course is that if orchids and cuttlefish lie to get lucky—and now we're talking about the cooler kind of flower or the cuttlefish wearing the sexier cut of cloth—perhaps you shouldn't feel too bad about the whoppers you tell about yourself at the bar. You're working your evolutionary advantages in just the way that so many other species do. Other people no doubt are working their evolutionary advantages on you. This is not to say that you don't have a choice about whether or not to deceive: of course, you can be truthful, and there are lots of good reasons for truthfulness. We've all lied only to find later that precisely the one unnecessary lie we told during a seduction was the untruth that has led your would-be lover to distrust you. In the first chapter we saw that there are many reasons to worry about the ethics of lying. But what we are noting here is that the frequency of deception in seduction is, from nature's perspective, not only commonplace but also desirable. From an evolutionary perspective, it's the doe-eyed sincere ones that ought to be worried. That said, innocence and vulnerability can be a very effective ploy: the sultana achieves her victory over Don Juan, in the end, by deceptively bursting into tears.

THE THEORY OF FALLING IN LOVE

There are countless times during the course of the day when someone catches your eye. I remember an incident from a few years ago. I was in Everyman's Espresso, a pleasant coffee bar across from a friend and editor's apartment with excellent espresso in the triple ristretto style—real espresso, like the ones you get in Italy, and always wonder, "Why the hell can't I get a coffee like this in the States?"—and there was a fine-boned woman behind the cash register with a neck like an antelope's, and we looked at each other in that appraising and mutually approving way that, had I been a single man rather than a happily married one, would have resulted in a conversation. That is, we provoke and are provoked by each other frequently, perhaps many times a day, and if our sexual antennae are up—in New York, when I visit,

as opposed to Kansas City, where I live, the array and inter-
twining of sexual antennae seem like a tangle of erotic interest, a
dangerous sensual spiderweb—we could begin the process of
feeling each other out (which would lead, one hopes, to feeling
each other up) in an almost daily way. Later that day I was with
another friend who also lives in New York, and she was complaining of the hopeless loneliness of the city. What I am pointing to now is the fact that we are constantly surrounded by
potential sexual encounters. An old Tibetan proverb relates that
in the realm of the gods, they make love by exchanging glances.
In a way, so do we.

Of course mere erotic interest—what we sense when we are in
crowded cities like New York or London—is a very different thing
from intimacy. And how different from these initial brief looks,
estimations, rejections, or approvals is the process of falling in
love! That tumbling down the stairs, that frightening loss of control mixed with willfully throwing oneself down the stairwell,
that choosing to fall in love—"But I want to be in love!"—suddenly
transformed into the helplessness of, "But now I am in love, and my
only fear is: Is she? Is he?" I've argued that one of the most interesting facts about falling in love is that especially in its first throes—
as with a similar state, depression—we cannot quite tell what part
of the process we are making up ourselves and what part is being
thrust upon us. "Is it me inventing these virtues in him, or does
he have these irresistible qualities; is it me seeking love and to be
loved, or is it really happening whether I want it to or not?"

It doesn't matter. We tell little lies about ourselves, we exaggerate, we fictionalize; meanwhile little lies are being told to us, and
we doubt, or believe, or half believe; we deceive while we self-
deceive. It's okay not to know whether or not you are falling in love
yet; it's natural to lie a little. That's part of self-protection and part
of allure. Furthermore, as we've seen, to want to believe is almost

always to self-deceive, and that, again, is part of the process of cultivating love, a good and necessary part of the process.

Consider again Aristophanes's story in the *Symposium*. The reuniting we seek, Aristophanes says, is of another, whom we were split from in the distant mythological past. Aristophanes is explaining that need we feel to reunite, the impulse we have to find another person, the insecurity we share that we are incomplete. (An echo of Aristophanes from Proust: "Love, in the pain of anxiety as in the bliss of desire, is a demand for a whole.") Perhaps Aristophanes does not mean to say that there is only one lover out there for you: he is speaking, among others, to Alcibiades, one of the most beautiful and sought-after men in all Athens, who has known countless lovers. Rather, what he may be arguing for is the feeling we seek when we are falling in love, and the emotional bond we experience once we are in love is the feeling of wholeness that truly is absent from us—at least much of the time—when we are not in love. But the process of falling in love is a poetic and dramatic one—Aristophanes is a poet and a playwright, after all—with all the inventions, poses, ploys, and conceits that any good poem or play requires.

"Delusional conceptions are necessary and salutary provisions of the instinct," Nietzsche writes, speaking especially of the erotic instinct. When you are angry with someone for telling you a lie, you are angry, in part, because he has manipulated you, he has taken a part of your freedom, but of course this taking of your freedom, and the relinquishing of your freedom, are not only essential to the process of falling in love but part of the good of falling in love. We don't want to be as free as we like to pretend we do. We'd give up half our freedom if only we could take half of someone else's away, and what contortions of limbs and pinwheelings of arms and legs (and beliefs and brains) won't we suffer and enjoy in order to accomplish it?

When we are in love, on this account, we may discover a kind of truth, even a kind of transparency that goes with wholeness. But in falling in love, when it's not just the antennae but suddenly all the rest of the body that is on the move, the process of finding and discovering the beloved is active and imaginative. In a passage that summarizes much of what I am arguing in this book, this is how Nietzsche describes falling in love:

> Here [in falling in love] it makes no difference whether one is human or animal; even less whether one has spirit, goodness, integrity. If one is subtle, one is fooled subtly; if one is coarse, one is fooled coarsely; but love, and even the love of God, the saintly love of "redeemed souls," remains the same in its roots: a fever that has good reason to transfigure itself, an intoxication that does well to lie about itself— And in any case, one lies well when one loves, about oneself and to oneself: one seems to oneself transfigured, stronger, richer, more perfect, one *is* more perfect—Here we discover *art* as an organic function: we discover it in the most angelic instinct, "love"; we discover it as the greatest stimulus of life—art thus sublimely expedient even when it lies—.

Plato too, champion for the truth though he remained, recognized that love, art, and deception are subtly interwoven; this is why he put the famous myth of the two halves in the mouth of Aristophanes, the greatest artist in the room. Plato understood that the goal of love was finding that other half, and that success in that goal will require lies, believing what one should not "truly" believe (as one believes in a play); that love required artfulness; that love itself was a kind of art.

How do we fall in love? We *create*.

CREATIVE CRYSTALLIZATION

In the summer of 1818 Stendhal was visiting the salt mines near Salzburg. He was traveling with his friend and a woman. His friend fell in love with the woman, and Stendhal watched as his friend's madness became more apparent daily in his actions and speech. His friend admired the lady's hand, which had been scarred by smallpox, and Stendhal wanted to name this process, which makes every quality of the beloved seem enchanting. At the moment he was seeking a name, the lady his friend loved admired a twig crystallized by salt. In the sunlight the salt crystals glittered like diamonds, and so Stendhal had his name, crystallization. It has since become the single most famous, controversial, and popular metaphor, among thinkers who worry about love, for characterizing the process of falling in love.

Stendhal defined the process of erotic love in four parts. Before one falls in love, one is indifferent to the object. Then one sets out on the journey, by no real choice. But once the lover has begun the process, he goes through the following phases:

Admiration—one marvels at the qualities of the loved one;
Acknowledgment—one acknowledges the pleasantness of having
    gained the loved one's interest;
Hope—one envisions gaining the love of the loved one;
Delight—one delights in *overrating* the beauty and merit of the
    person whose love one hopes to win.

Love, on Stendhal's account, first strikes you involuntarily but is subsequently pursued as a kind of autonomously chosen gamble. For Stendhal, all erotic love begins like the start of my love for Lila Gibbard, as a bet we make that all too often turns into a gambling addiction.

Whether or not the will is involved in the opening stages of love, the lover engages in deceptive and self-deceptive maneuvers in order to further cultivate the newly discovered love. This happens in both the process of seduction and the process of being seduced, and to be fair, both "seducer" and "seduced" are roles that we play, poses we assume in the development of love.

The seed is necessary for any supersaturated solution to crystallize; without the branches, the diamonds would never encrust around the strange candelabra of Stendhal's salt mines. But the process of supersaturation takes place in the heart of the lover, and the manner of crystallization follows the mind of the lover. Stendhal goes on to describe a second stage of crystallization that involves still more the creative imagination of the lover, in part because Stendhal (himself a famously clumsy seducer) recognizes that the beloved is in part seduced by the virtues the lover sees in her or him. To seduce and to love are to willfully imbue the beloved with virtues one projects out of the salty mines of one's own imagination, one's own soul, but once those virtues are there, they do indeed catch the light; you can see them. They are neither fake nor real, any more than any other value is fake or real. When you look at a beautiful piece of art and see it as beautiful, your mind is at work. The beauty is in the interaction.

To create is in some sense to falsify. Stendhal thinks that the crystals the lover attaches to his beloved "aren't really there" (at least no one other than the lover is likely to see them). But in another sense, he wants to insist that to engage in this activity *just is* what it is to fall in love. That is, the creative activity of crystallization is what constitutes the love of the lover. So Stendhal would not say that the love was fake—nothing could be more real to the lover than the love he has for his beloved—but it is certainly something different from "finding" or "discovering" love. It is an activity of the imagination.

Let's consider the process from the other side: suppose there's someone you'd love to seduce you. Now seduction almost always involves ploys, feints, disguises, manipulations, even downright lies, and often leaves the seduced feeling manipulated, used, or worse. (This occurs even in the insect kingdom. The female praying mantis, for example, seduces her mate without letting him know that she will eat his head during the process, which turns him into a mentally uninhibited sex machine.) Is it worth the lie to be seduced? Do we cooperate in the lies we are being told when we allow ourselves to be tricked into bed? ("Tell me lies, tell me sweet little lies . . .")

If we know that we are likely to be lied to when being seduced, and yet we want to be seduced, it's hard to say what's wrong about the lie. Nothing's a greater turnoff than the fumbling desperate would-be lover who spills his guts in the attempt to be loved in return. And a naked request for sex gets you nowhere, at least while the night is young. This leads us to the idea that it is not lying that is simply wrong, but the kind of lie that one tells—and perhaps also the kind of lie that one encourages or lets oneself believe. The question "Do you love me?"—asked too soon—invites a lie of the worst kind, and the only honest response might be the one Meursault famously gives Marie in Albert Camus's *The Stranger*: "No. I don't know. It doesn't matter, really." Maybe we are allowed to lie—and ask to be lied to—in little ways, but not the big ones. Without seduction there will rarely be falling in love, falling in love is one of our highest goods, and we have seen how the process of falling in love involves countless little lies we tell ourselves and must tell to the ones with whom we are falling in love.

Even Kant, who, as we remember, insisted that it was always wrong to lie, understood that the process of cultivating intimacy and overcoming mistrust would require us to "cover up our weaknesses, so as not to be ill thought of." And just as our lover (or our seduced) believes the version of ourselves we present, we may come to believe through our lovers' eyes the lies we tell about ourselves. As we seduce or are seduced, we seduce ourselves; in being seduced, we turn a trick or two; in seducing, we may provide the possibility of love.

SHAKESPEARE ON SEDUCTION

Here's a thesis: when it comes to love, the lies we believe are the lies we'd like to be told. Similarly, the lies we tell are the lies we'd like to believe.

In Shakespeare's great analysis of deception and seduction *Much Ado About Nothing*, we see that the two central characters, Beatrice and Benedick, accomplish the goal of falling in love with each other through the process, largely, of seducing themselves. That is to say, each of them tells the other the lies that would work best on the liar him or herself. Bizarrely, but convincingly, they manage to seduce each other through believing their own lies. The success of this convoluted process is made all the more intriguing because of the fact that each considers the other untrustworthy.

Let's try to see how it works. In *Much Ado About Nothing* both our hero and heroine have been in love before—indeed, they were in love with each other—and both have become cynics about love. Neither of them believes that love is anything more than a lie, a foolish illusion (in this they are much like our typical, disillusioned first lover of the last chapter). And yet Shakespeare has them not only fall in love with each other but actually seduce each other. And they lie the whole time, in order to come to the conclusion that love is a kind of truthfulness that embraces the deceptions of the romantic.

One revealing feature of the mutual seduction of Benedick and Beatrice in *Much Ado About Nothing* is Shakespeare's emphasis—the same holds true for the seductions in virtually all his plays—on the complicity that exists between the seducer and the seduced. The two love each other but have been trading insults for years. Their friends conspire and tell each that the other is in love. It might be fishy, but rather than ask questions, both Beatrice and Benedick fall headfirst into the sappiest and most foolish kind of love.

As I've said, neither Benedick nor Beatrice believes in romantic love, at least for himself or herself; moreover, each professes a distinct dislike for the other. Here's an early, typical exchange:

> BENEDICK: . . . it is certain I am loved of all ladies, only you excepted: and I would I could find in my heart that I had not a hard heart, for truly I love none.
>
> BEATRICE: . . . I thank God and my cold blood, I am of your humour for that: I had rather hear my dog bark at a crow than a man swear he loves me.

Both Benedick and Beatrice are plying deceptions and, in doing so, initiating the process of seduction. Benedick's boast that all ladies love him (a timeworn, if silly and ineffective, male technique for attracting a woman's attention, and one that Benedick should have outgrown) is obviously false and not really a lie; he says it so as to contrast all other women with Beatrice and to suggest that he could have any woman he pleases except for her.

The real deception that Benedick is practicing—the deception, repeated by Beatrice, that sets up both the seduction and the comedy of the play—is the claim that his heart is so hard that it cannot love.

Beatrice and Benedick open the play already in sexual tension, which both pretend does not exist between the two of them and which, furthermore, on their account, is not the sort of thing either of them desires. Benedick deceives Beatrice by insisting that he is not interested in love (he repeats the same claim to anyone who will listen to him throughout the first act of the play). By saying that he loves none, however, Benedick is also announcing to Beatrice that there is no woman he is presently attached to or even interested in. Should he take an interest in a woman, it follows, what a rare and fine thing that would be—and this is intended to pique her curiosity and vanity. Beatrice responds with the same deception but is more direct and to the point (she is more honest about her deception): I don't even want to hear promises of love from a man, she says, much less the real thing. Of course we know she has already been asking specifically about Benedick, and hers is also a familiar technique for interesting a lover: he is (in fact) a warrior, and she is raising a challenge. The conversations both Benedick and Beatrice have with friends shortly after this scene confirm their attraction for each other. All this is so transparent—such a clear and delightful example of schoolyard flirtation—that the audience knows, only a few minutes into the play, that these two will fall in love before it ends.

But the point of their deception is not only to begin the process of seduction but also to protect themselves, because neither is sure of the other's interest. They don't trust each other. Benedick puts it plainly: "Because I will not do [women] the wrong to mistrust any, I will do myself the right to trust none." Furthermore, they shouldn't trust each other: if either Benedick or Beatrice were to be too overt about his or her interest in the other, the other's pride and sense of him or herself as superior to love—to which they both at least pretend and may partially believe—would end the seduction before it could begin. Beatrice and Benedick mutually seduce each other because they regard each other as equals, and should that equality shift too much in one direction or the other—if one, in other words, came to feel that he or she were losing control or being controlled, if he or she were being diminished in terms of autonomy, the seduction would be frustrated. Beatrice is as clear about the importance for her of her autonomy as Benedick is about his need for trust: "Would it not grieve a woman to be overmastered with a piece of valiant dust? to make an account of her life to a clod of wayward marl?" When Benedick and Beatrice were involved before, something went wrong: Beatrice claims she lent Benedick her heart awhile, but that he won it "with false dice." So for Beatrice, there is a particular and we may suppose justified distrust of Benedick, born of a failed deception.

Here the earlier notion of romantic love as "an autonomously chosen gamble"—Stendhal's description of the cultivation of love—comes to the fore: Beatrice and Benedick have previously gambled at love, and Beatrice at least, in her account, lost the game. (Though as cagey as each is with the other, the feeling one has is that both suffered in the failed game.) The problem now is that because of shared mistrust, both are reluctant to take a chance, to gamble a second time. Beatrice and Benedick seem to view the very idea of gambling on love as a violation of their autonomy, and it takes several deceptions before either of them is willing to admit that "the die is cast," and they are willing actively to try to allow romantic love to take hold.

Nevertheless, the seduction continues. It is through another

deceit—one of Shakespeare's classic devices, the masked ball—
that the seductive tension between Benedick and Beatrice mounts.
They are dancing with each other, each clearly knowing who the
other is, but with the comfortable position of enjoying plausible deniability about their epistemic situation. Benedick asks
the masked Beatrice what she thinks of Benedick, looking for the
least encouragement—"Did he never make you laugh?"—only to
find Beatrice using the mask against him to say even crueler
things about him than she might say to his face, and the words
are that much sharper because, he is forced to suppose, she is
willing to say them to someone whose identity (he is forced to
pretend) she doesn't know.

The leitmotif of the play comes from the song that opens the
famous orchard scene and is a kind of playful leitmotif of this
chapter:

> Sigh no more, ladies, sigh no more,
> Men were deceivers ever,
> One foot in sea and one on shore,
> To one thing constant never,
> Then sigh not so, but let them go,
> And be you blithe and bonny,
> Converting all your sounds of woe
> Into Hey nonny, nonny.

Naturally the ladies can no more let the men go than the
men can the ladies—"can't live with 'em, can't live without
'em"—so the advice is ironical, meant truly, in a sense, on its face
but, in another sense, meant in just the opposite way: that though
we recognize and complain about each other's weaknesses and
bemoan them, they are part and parcel of a good we cannot do
without.

While Benedick and Beatrice are slow and reluctant to understand this ironic truth about love, their friends are not. So, growing impatient with the spectacle of Beatrice and Benedick trying to seduce each other but tripping over their pride, freedom, and mistrust in the process, three of Benedick's friends deceive him—while he thinks he is deceiving them by hiding behind the bushes—and have a "secret conversation" in order to convince him that Beatrice is passionately, desperately in love with him and all but dying from her fear to disclose it to him. In the very next scene, at the opening of Act III, Beatrice's friends, also part of the plan, have the same secret conversation designed for her eavesdropping ears, persuading her that Benedick is in just the same impassioned, prostrate position he supposes she is in for him.

By this point in the play we have Benedick benevolently deceiving Beatrice, Beatrice benevolently deceiving Benedick, and both Benedick's and Beatrice's friends benevolently deceiving each of them. It's comical and charming; seduction is taking place; no one's autonomy is being violated in a blameworthy way; and while trust is in some sense being betrayed (that is, by Beatrice and Benedick's friends, who are willfully exploiting their eavesdropping, though we should ask, as Shakespeare wants us to ask, if you can betray the trust of someone who is already betraying your trust by eavesdropping on you), the betrayal of trust does not look morally pernicious; on the contrary, it's a happy, well-intentioned, even praiseworthy act. There is deception here at every level of the cultivation of love, and yet none of the deception looks either unusual or unattractive; rather it seems familiar, reasonable, and even desirable.

The drama is not yet over: Beatrice will demand a proof of Benedick's love after he professes it, and the proof is intended to test their love. The great moment of suspense is captured by

Beatrice when she summarizes their position, and how much depends on whether or not she can trust Benedick. Benedick tells her: "I do love nothing in the world so well as you: is not that strange?" And Beatrice replies: "As strange as the thing I know not. It were as possible for me to say I loved nothing so well as you; but believe me not; and yet I lie not; I confess nothing, nor I deny nothing." Sounding a bit like the skeptical philosophers Pyrrho and Sextus Empiricus, Beatrice is about to ask Benedick to prove his love by killing his friend Claudio in recompense for the betrayal of her cousin. Shakespeare is subtle as ever: this proof of love is demanded as the enactment of justice for a betrayal of trust.

Happily, after several more demoniacally clever Shakespearean twists and turns, Benedick succeeds in proving his love, and at the close of the play the two are married. But right until the last few minutes of the play they continue to deceive each other, denying their love, because they find themselves in the classic lover's paradox: "Who will say the L word first?" This paradox is a paradox of trust, and when at last they are confronted with their own professions of love in writing (produced, naturally, by others), the Gordian knot of their distrust is cut, and to everyone's relief, they are at last free to bind themselves to each other. One of Benedick's friends is about to tease him about marrying, after all he has said against it, and he summarizes his position with one of the most plangent observations about the nature of love in all the vast literature on the subject: "In brief, since I do purpose to marry, I will think nothing to any purpose that the world can say against it; and therefore never flout at me for what I have said against it; for man is a giddy thing, and this is my conclusion." He has gained the good he desired, and however giddy, deceptive, and full of false belief the process was that got him there, now it doesn't matter.

Stanley Cavell, commenting on marriage comedies generally, writes: "It is a feature of this mode of comedy that the pair are shown at some point to become incomprehensible to the world beyond them. As if their arrival at true marriage is itself the mystery." And Benedick's statement, here at the very end of the play—"his conclusion," as it is Shakespeare's—emphasizes what we referred to at the outset as the complicity of the seduced: the willing self-deception that we have thus far sought to illustrate but not made explicit. Beatrice and Benedick are entirely complicit in their own seduction. They hide behind masks; they lie to themselves about their own feelings and reaffirm their self-deceptions by repeating them to others; they test each other's interest through insults and jabs; they eavesdrop in the hope of learning that their hopes of shared love might be fulfilled. Before long the audience realizes that Beatrice and Benedick would be willing to twist the truth in any direction she or he pleased in order to gain the good each of them seeks, the seduction of the other. Both are so complicit in each other's seduction and each in his or her own seduction—think of Benedick's giddy joy as he interprets and reinterprets Beatrice's innocent and casual invitation to come into the house after hearing his friends speak of her love for him—that it no longer makes sense to divide seducer from seduced. Not only does each seduce the other, but both recognize that a kind of mutual self-seduction, an allowing oneself to be seduced, is also necessary. Thus theirs is genuinely an autonomous gamble because they are involved in the risks of the game from the perspective of both the seducer and the seduced.

Benedick undoubtedly is a giddy thing, and maybe we don't want to go too far in endorsing giddiness. But the back-and-forth nature of the romance between Benedick and Beatrice, the alternation of true and false, of frankness and deception, and the very tentative small steps forward into trust: these, I think, are the elements of how the more usual kind of seduction occurs. In the case of Beatrice and Benedick, seduction is essentially tied to deception and is practiced to obtain a good in which they both share. There are elements of conceit, paternalism, and manipulation throughout the case, but neither Benedick nor Beatrice is wronged, and it would be silly to argue that the freedom or autonomy of either is compromised. In fact for both of them it is their proud insistence upon their autonomy—proud almost to the point of irrationality—that has made so many deceptions necessary in order for them to accomplish the mutual seduction they both desire. And though the case is exaggerated for comic effect, I think anyone who has been involved in this kind of seduction with the result of romantic love—whether or not that love endured—will agree that Benedick and Beatrice seem familiar.

The Beatrice and Benedick case of seduction illustrates why deception need not undermine autonomy. We might here recall, from chapter 1, that this is a common and persuasive account of why deception is wrong. If I put false beliefs in your head, I am illegitimately constraining the ways in which you can act, I am controlling your freedom—because your choices, after all, are made on the basis of your beliefs, and your beliefs, if they include beliefs you have acquired through your trust in me, are beliefs you hold to be true.

So, for example, in the movie *The Invention of Lying*, the one lie the hero refuses to tell—in a world where everyone else always speaks the truth and every statement is believed—is the lie that will cause a woman he loves to fall in love with him. That is, we may lie to seduce, we may lie to control, but at a certain point, when we love, we must be loved in return, and that love is the only kind of love we truly seek and need when it is given freely. That's one of the most frightening things about love: when I love you, it's entirely in your control whether or not you love me back. And perhaps, to truly love (we have to step carefully; here we're verging on cliché) is to give someone that freedom in return. Not to shortcut through his or her personality or to shortchange on your own.

A particularly surprising and interesting by-product of the Beatrice-Benedick tale is that deception, of both oneself and of others—at least in some love scenarios—may respect freedom and foster trust rather than betray or destroy those goods. In scenarios in which mutually interested parties begin a seduction with mistrust (and doesn't it usually begin this way?), some deception may be necessary in order for the process of trusting to get off the ground. If trust is importantly linked to autonomy in seduction, then it may be that some deceptions and self-deceptions actually enhance autonomy. So the story of Beatrice and Benedick suggests that autonomy, at least in the case of love, may not merely survive false belief but flourish in it. Beatrice and Benedick are like children again, lying in order to be free—and believing each other's lies, in order to free themselves from their own misgivings so that they can marry.

PROUST, SEDUCTION, AND HEARTBREAK

Perhaps the greatest story of a seduction and the pain of romantic love is Proust's probably autobiographical story about Marcel and his beloved Albertine (as André Gide, Anne Carson, and other critics have noted, Albertine is likely to be, in Carson's

words, "a disguised version of Proust's chauffeur, Alfred Agosti-
nelli"). Marcel falls in love with Albertine, but he can never possess her as completely as he likes; volume 5 of the novel is titled
"The Captive" because Marcel does everything in his power to
own and control Albertine while they pursue their love affair in
Paris. She will not be possessed, however, and escapes him for
other lovers—both men and women—as often as she can manage (it's difficult for us to know how often and with whom she is
actually cheating on him, as we learn everything about her
through the distorting lens of his own fiercely imaginative, self-
torturing jealousy). So long as he does not possess her entirely,
Marcel is obsessed with Albertine.

Over the course of volume 5 Marcel finally does come to control Albertine—or so he supposes. But once he has in fact won
her, he comes to despise her. Before long he declares to himself
that his love for Albertine provides at best a little pleasure while
preventing many other much better entertainments and perhaps
even real happiness. Then, once he is absolutely certain that she
means nothing to him, that he in fact despises her, she leaves.
His servant tells him: "Mademoiselle Albertine has gone." Marcel is certain that she meant nothing to him, that he had thorough self-knowledge at least on this score: "I believed that I had,
like a precise analyst, left nothing out. I believed that I knew
the very bottom of my heart." Then she leaves, and his pain is
so wrenching that "wondering retrospectively whether or not
she looked at a woman on a particular day in the corridor of a
little seaside railway-train causes one the same pain as would a
surgeon probing for a bullet in one's heart."

There is a debate in the philosophy of emotion about the level
of cognition in our emotional experiences. It began in American
academic philosophy with the work of Robert C. Solomon, and
in the context particularly of love it has been forcefully investi-

gated by Martha Nussbaum in her book *Love's Knowledge*. Part of the debate (here I am indebted particularly to Nussbaum) is about whether one comes to know love in heartbreak or whether the suffering of heartbreak is in fact constitutive of the love. Was Marcel simply wrong in thinking that he didn't love Albertine and didn't recognize that fact until she left him? Or did Marcel in fact come to love Albertine through the fact of her leaving him? I think I came to love Lila, for example, in a very different way, through the process of losing her to a rival.

Option one: when the lover leaves, we realize that we love. Option two: when the lover leaves, a new love, or new kind of love, is created. There is also a third option (and there are probably more than three): the pain we suffer in heartbreak is yet another layer of self-deception. It may be that there is no real bottom to the depths of our self-deceptions in love, that there is no final truth to be known about how we felt. On this account, while the pain we feel when we are having our heart broken is real, it is no more and no less real than the boredom Marcel feels when he was with Albertine or the love he felt for her when they were first seducing each other. All these feelings are creations, self-deceptions in a way; the fact that the painful ones may seem less comprehensible than the pleasurable ones doesn't make them any more "true." While pain, real suffering, seems to bear the mark of undeniable truth ("the lies I told myself just because I was happy!"), the pain may nevertheless be one more half-truth, or false belief, or strategic self-deception.

Let me give an example that may clarify the idea. Back in my college drug days—now very far behind me, thank God—I remember the end of a crack cocaine binge in Miami. I was sitting on the railing of the balcony of my hotel room, ten stories up, confronting, as I felt then, the irrefutable and unbearable truth about me and my place in the world. I was trying to let myself roll off the railing. The mental anguish I was in seemed to reveal the triviality and deceptiveness of my ordinary life. But in fact I was just coming down.

The reason cognition matters here is that pain seems primitive (and thus somehow "truthful") in a way that thinking does not. Recall our discussion of how first love threatened to be "the only true love" just because it was such a painful experience of love for the first lover. If emotions are involved with thinking, if they are, as Bob Solomon first put it (following Sartre), judgments or evaluations (Sartre describes an emotion as a "magical transformation" of the world, and that might be better than either judgment or evaluation), then they are more slippery than we suppose. And they are that much harder to grasp when they are swimming in the muddiest pond of them all, self-knowledge. It's hard even to say what we mean by the expression "self-knowledge." "For my part," the Scottish philosopher David Hume writes, "when I enter most intimately into what I call myself, I always stumble on some particular perception or other, of heat or cold, light or shade, love or hatred, pain or pleasure. I never can catch myself at any time without a perception, and never can observe any thing but the perception." The pain of heartbreak might be "truthful" in some trivial sense—we discover the perception of pain—but how we incorporate that into the larger structure of who we understand ourselves to be is precisely what is at stake in evaluating our emotional situation. If Marcel didn't "know" that he loved her when he felt he did, how can he "know" that he was bored with her? If he didn't "know" that he was bored with her, how can he "know" that he is heartbroken? Each self-deception implies at least the possibility of the next.

But if we can't know about ourselves when we are and are not in love, what can we know? Could it ever make sense for you to approach me and say: "You think you love her, but you don't"?

Could your arguments ever persuade me? If anything, we know—from experience with friends (whether they are the lovers or we are)—arguments of that kind tend to have the opposite effect. And if we can't know whether or not we are in love, does it make sense for us to say that we are self-deceived in love? For to lie is to lie about something you know to be true, so to lie to yourself that you are not in love when in fact you know that you are, but you cannot know that you are, so you cannot lie to yourself . . . and the pond becomes an abyss.

Maybe heartbreak—let's let love be for a moment—is not so much a state or a judgment as it is an activity, and so our usual way of thinking about the emotional condition ("truly loved," "falsely loved," "the truth of my love was revealed") does not fit heartbreak very well. There are certainly lots of judgments that go into heartbreak: "She didn't love me as much as I thought she did!" "I'm unlovable!" "I am a different person than I was before; part of me is gone!" "He is too good to love someone like me!" "If only he could see how much I really love him, if only he could hear me, he couldn't help loving me back!" etc. It isn't much of an exaggeration to say that about half of all our art, literature, music, and film is devoted to this subject. Judgments are part of the activity of heartbreak, I think, but are not sufficient to its description (the judgment without the heartbreak, Kant would say, is empty); just as heartbreak without judgments—what I have called primitive pain and Proust calls simply suffering—would be blind.

So what is heartbreak? And how does it relate to the problem of truthfulness and deception in love?

Denial, anger, bargaining, depression, and acceptance are no longer the popular model for thinking about grief for scientists who work on the subject, but it is so close to the familiar cycle we go through when suffering heartbreak that it is hard to imagine that Dr. Elisabeth Kübler-Ross did not have the loss of love squarely in mind, when she proposed her five stages, as the loss of a loved one. The difference of course is that in love lost, the lost beloved goes on living: you imagine how she looks at him, twisting her hair around her finger at her ear, how his eyes change when he sees her; or how she supposes she knows him so well, while you know that, in Tori Amos's words, you "knew him, better, better, better." And while you might feel like tearing out your own eyes with grief at the inability ever again to speak to a dead person, you will never have to suffer that conversation that is the very low point of heartbreak, when the person with whom you were once more intimate than any other in the world pretends that she doesn't understand what you are talking about, acts as though she simply can't hear what you are saying anymore. "It's me," you want to scream—or do scream—but it doesn't work. It has the opposite of the desired effect; everything you do or imagine trying only makes matters worse, only further sinks the lead weight of your hopes.

Sartre says of the lover, "He wants to be loved by a freedom but demands that this freedom as freedom should no longer be free." Funny how, in heartbreak, the first clause that sets up the paradox goes out the window. I don't give a damn anymore whether she comes back freely or in chains; I'd use any kind of potion or threat to estrange her from her new lover. Sartre insists that "if the beloved is transformed into an automaton, the lover finds himself alone," but the hell with that, the heartbroken lover thinks—at least the robot wouldn't have her cold legs wrapped around someone else's furious, eager, doubtless nimble hips. This first blind moment of irrational despair and infantile demand in heartbreak is straightforward denial.

Honor Moore writes very well about heartbreak in a poem of hers about denial, an homage to Proust, titled "Disparu." The poem is beautiful and short:

I spent the day with invisible you, your arms
invisible around me, holding me blue in your
open invisible eyes. We walked invisible,
invisible and happy, daydreaming sight as if
light were a piano it played on. Invisible
my hand at your well-cut trouser, invisible
speeding night, the invisible taxi, bare
the invisible legs, kissing the vanishing
mouths, breasts invisible, your, my invisible
entwining, the sheets white as geese, blue as sky.
And darling, how your invisible prick rose,
rosy, invisible, invisible as all night
galloping, swinging, we tilted and sang.

   I want to focus our attention on two elements of the poem, articulated in two lines: "invisible and happy, daydreaming sight as if" and "galloping, swinging, we tilted and sang." The first we might call the transparency feature of heartbreak; the second, the quixotic feature. Both transparency and quixotism are crucial aspects of the creative project of love generally, and we should not be surprised to encounter the same steps on the ladder both on our happy climb up and on our desperate slide down. But I take this as an example of a poem in early heartbreak because there is no acceptance here; no depression, no bargaining or begging, not yet even anger. This poem is overflowing with impossible hope. Like hope, it is all invisible, all imagination, and the lovers, because invisible, have nothing to hide from each other; they are completely transparent—light passes through them as though they were not even there—even seeing has become daydreaming; substance is as light as music (sight is like light playing on a piano); and we are out of the realm of cold truth and colder falsehood, in the happy fictional land of "as if," where anything might be.

There is denial, but denial that depends upon the Aristophanic myth of love: that we will know each other completely; that we will see through each other; that we will blend in such a way that we could hold each other in our eyes, become truly one.

A grown-up love, I think, will always believe that we can become more transparent to each other, while accepting that the transparency of complete visibility (which is an invisibility; to see completely through someone is to see him or her like glass) is impossible, probably undesirable, and maybe even threatening. Which leads us to the quixotic feature of this denial: "galloping, swinging, we tilted and sang," like Don Quixote on poor old Rosinante, swinging wildly in the saddle and tilting after his famous sail-armed giants in the name of the beautiful pig-tender Dulcinea. This love will believe the romantic dream it must believe in order to continue its love; it will deny all empirical evidence; it will love for romance's sake alone; it will sing where it cannot be satisfied. We cannot love without the imagination, without projecting ourselves and our lover into a realm of value that stands far beyond the pedantry of ordinary everyday fact— this is the great lesson of Don Quixote and why Miguel de Unamuno claims that for the Spanish, he is a greater religious figure even than Christ—but the price of that sacrifice of the ordinary world in love is that when love is lost, what was an imaginative transformation of reality now becomes a blindness to fact, a seeing that can occur only when everything is invisible. For Sartre, this is the far extreme end of one of his two poles of bad faith. Honor Moore's narrator has moved entirely into transcendence, into the world of possibility and is denying every fact (her "facticity," in Sartre's jargon) that might ground her in the opportunity to make a free choice to move into a new love relationship.

I began this meditation on heartbreak years ago, during my first divorce, by wondering what the relationship was between self-knowledge and heartbreak: What do we learn about ourselves and love when we have our hearts broken? I really thought my wife and I had understood each other, ourselves, and our love—and the way those three elements worked together—in a way that as it turned out, we did not. My first observation is that heartbreak sends us into a mode of escape from pain—which doubtless comes and goes—that mirrors how we fell in love in the first place. The first movement of heartbreak, then, is not self-knowledge (at least not as we ordinarily think of it) but self-deception. Which is what denial is—a necessary self-deception that allows you to survive and, eventually, to thrive again.

LOVE'S AUTOPSY

Raymond Carver's short story "What We Talk About When We Talk About Love" is, like Plato's *Symposium*—and perhaps as a kind of play on it—an analysis of "the truth" about love. As in *Symposium*, Carver's characters are engaged in a drinking party, and the most difficult and the most fascinating subject comes up, a subject suitable only for drunks: love. Carver's first speaker has the right to speak because he is a cardiologist (a heart doctor, who, according to his wife, "always has love on his mind"). These are all experts in love: married couples, one of the couples in their second marriage. Mel, the heart doctor, says that "real love was nothing less than spiritual love" (this view is also offered in *Symposium*). Terri, his wife, replies that the man she lived with before Mel "loved her so much he tried to kill her . . . He dragged me around the living room by my ankles. He kept saying, 'I love you, I love you, you bitch.'" Mel disputes his wife's claim that this could be love, saying that Terri is "of the kick-me-so-I'll-know-you-love-me school." As the group continues to discuss whether or not Terri's last lover could indeed have actually loved her, the story's narrator, Nick, tells Mel: "I think what you're saying is that love is an absolute."

What might that mean, to say that "love is an absolute"? In *Symposium*, it resembles the viewpoint of Diotima—the woman who teaches Socrates about love—that love is a ladder that leads us from bodily love up to the love of people generally, then the love of the state, the love of justice and ideas, and, ultimately, the love of the truth. In the Judeo-Christian tradition—and especially as this tradition is received in neo-Platonist Christians like Plotinus or the twelfth-century monastic thinkers on love like Bernard of Clairvaux—it is the idea that God is love and that, again, ultimate knowledge of oneself and the beloved is attained in perfect love. (Recalling this courtly view of love, Terri says of her husband: "Mel would like to ride a horse and carry a lance.") As for what Terri had with her previous lover, in Mel's view:

> "My God, don't be silly. That's not love, and you know it," Mel said. "I don't know what you'd call it, but I sure know you wouldn't call it love."
>
> "Say what you want, but I know it was," Terri said. "It may sound crazy to you, but it's true just the same. People are different, Mel. Sure, sometimes he may have acted crazy. Okay. But he loved me. In his own way maybe, but he loved me. There was love there, Mel. Don't say there wasn't."

After she left him, Terri's lover tried to kill himself twice: first with rat poison and then with a .22. Both times he bungled it. The second time he died, but it was a slow death. Mel continues to deny that he could have loved Terri, but Terri's insistence that he loved her enough to die for her gives Mel pause.

So, like one of the speakers in *Symposium,* and as they all get drunker, Mel tries again.

> I'll tell you what real love is, [he begins, and continues]: What do any of us really know about love? . . . It seems to me we're all just beginners at love. We say we do and I don't doubt it . . . You know the kind of love I'm talking about now. Physical love, that impulse that drives you to someone special, as well as love of the other person's being, his or her essence, as it were. Carnal love and, well, call it sentimental love, the day-to-day caring about the other person. But sometimes I have a hard time accounting for the fact that I must have loved my first wife too. [He goes on, but he is getting into deep water now.] ". . . the terrible thing, the terrible thing is, but the good thing too, the saving grace, you might say, is that if something happened to one of us . . . I think the other one, the other person, would grieve for a while, you know, but then the surviving party would go out and love again, have someone else soon enough.

If Mel meant to advocate absolute love, he's now taking it back; he is attacking the persistent myth that there is "one true love" or that we ever love one person in a way that outdoes all our other loves. The biggest lie we tell about love, Mel is here arguing, is that there is such a thing as absolute love between two people. At the end of his speech, now, about the relativity of love, he echoes Socrates's refrain: "I mean, I don't know anything, and I'm the first one to admit it."

The story gets most interesting when Mel starts talking about an old couple who were in a terrible car wreck. A couple, that is, according to Terri—she says sarcastically—"Older but wiser." The couple recover, but they are covered in bandages, and the old man is depressed "because he couldn't see her through his eye-holes.

Can you imagine? I'm telling you, the man's heart was breaking because he couldn't turn his goddamn head and *see* his goddamn wife."

Mel's story reminds me of a story my mother told me about my stepfather when he was dying. My mother was getting out of the shower, she said, when she heard a clatter in the other room. Then my stepdad came struggling around the corner in his walker. She said: "What on earth are you doing? Get back in bed!" And he said—she cried when she told me the story—"I'm not too sick to want to see my wife getting naked out of the shower." I did not particularly like my stepfather (he wasn't good with children), but I continue to feel grateful to him when I think about this story, for the sincerity of his love for my mother and the effort he made, in the last days of his life, to demonstrate it to her.

That said, my mother does not share Mel's view of absolute love. She recognized, when she told me the story, that my stepfather was doing something more than expressing his need to see her. He was saying: "Look, I'm not dead yet!" And also: "You're so beautiful you can get a dying man on his feet." Once, when I asked my mother how she succeeded in her second marriage, she said: "It's not complicated, Clancy. You simply refuse to give up." That's what my stepfather was doing. He was showing his love in his refusal to give up to death.

But let's return to Mel and the other members of Carver's symposium on love. The group proceeds to get drunker. Mel decides to call his kids but thinks better of it. Nick, our narrator, comments that he could "eat or not eat. Or keep drinking. I could head right out into the sunset."

"What does that mean, honey?" his wife, Laura, asks him.

"It just means what I said," he replies. "It means I could just keep going. That's all it means."

They all are at the worst stage of in vino veritas by now, the "pain is truer than pleasure" stage; loneliness starts to settle over the four of them, and they begin to look at love in a different, frightening way. They suspect that whatever it was that made the old man desperate to see his wife, none of the four of them feels as if they have it. Mel announces that the gin's gone, Terri asks, "Now what?" and the story ends: "I could hear my heart beating. I could hear everyone's heart. I could hear the human noise we sat there making, not one of us moving, not even when the room went dark."

What no one in the group is in a position to realize is that Mel, who, despite being a heart surgeon, is very confused about love, is the one who has put all four of these lovers into their drunken despair. The old man he describes in his body cast could very well have been any one of the four of them, years before; probably at some time he too sat at a table over drinks with friends, even propositioned his friend's wife (the way Mel does Nick's). Of course, when we are at death's door, we are going to long for nothing more than the people we love, and that's one perfectly legitimate reason we cherish the loved ones we have (who among us doesn't fear dying alone?). The old man in the story, like my dying stepfather, is in extraordinary circumstances, which lend themselves to a particular interpretation precisely because in those circumstances the stakes are so high. In the midst of everyday life we don't understand a simple action like turning to look at one's wife, or hurrying to see her get out of the shower, as proof of the certainty of love, the need for love, the purity of love. Mel and the rest of them feel more bereft than they ought to feel, because they are cherishing an illusion that is a lie. They have romanced themselves into despair.

Love like the kind Mel has just described is experienced in moments, in snapshots, in rare, happy, intimate glances. Anyone in a love affair or a happy marriage might argue (as I myself would, this week) that a really intense certainty of love can continue for days, even weeks. But ask that person the same question the following week, and he or she will probably give you a different answer. In any case, to think of the most intense and certain moments of love as a model for the way love ought to be is a bit like thinking that orgasm is the model for sex. It's not merely unrealistic; it's unhelpful, it's silly.

Furthermore, this view of love places an unreasonable burden on love as a belief state or set of beliefs. A dear friend of mine tells me that while making love, she often asks herself, again and again: "Am I in love with this man? Am I in love with this man? Am I in love with this man?"

Can we feel certain that she doesn't, simply because she asks? But few beliefs, if any, should be so certain that we are not permitted to interrogate them. What would it mean to say: "If you question your love, then you must not love?" I'm always asking myself: "Am I a good professor?" I also often ask myself: "Should I be a professor?" But that doesn't undermine the larger structure of my life as a professor, and many of us might argue that in fact I stop being a good professor when I stop asking those questions. In faith-based traditions, the profession of doubt is often described as proof of the fact that one believes—or that one is at least making a sincere effort to believe. Kierkegaard was right: if we *knew* that God existed, faith in his existence would be superfluous. But if we don't know it, then we must also be allowed to doubt it.

So is it unhealthy for my friend to ask the question "Am I in love with him?" What are the possible consequences of this question? Why is she asking the question? Is it so uncommon a question to ask? Mightn't it be more dangerous if we insisted that there are certain questions that the lover is simply not allowed to ask? That to be good lovers we all must be dogmatists about love?

THE EROTIC SOCIOPATH

A buddy of mine called me recently and told me that his wife had concluded he was a sociopath. (He had just been caught in an affair.)

"I think I really might be one," he said. "I might even be a psychopath. Or have antisocial personality disorder. I mean, I know she's mad and she's throwing these labels around. But I looked it up, and she might be onto something." He referred me to a list and to a quiz.

According to the *DSM-4* (*Diagnostic and Statistical Manual of Mental Disorders*), in order for a patient to be diagnosed with antisocial personality disorder (which is not quite as bad as being a psychopath, but close), the patient must have a persistent history of disregard for and violation of others' rights, the disorder should have existed since age fifteen, and it should be evidenced by three (or more) of the following seven traits:

- Failure to conform to social norms
- Deceitfulness, repeated lying, use of aliases, or manipulation of others
- Impulsivity or failure to plan ahead
- Irritability and aggressiveness
- Reckless disregard for the safety of his or her self or others
- Consistent irresponsibility
- Lack of remorse, indifference to or rationalizing having hurt or mistreated others

"I mean, sometimes I think I have all these," he told me. "I've never used an alias, I guess. But the rest of them, hell, sure. Manipulation of others? Every day, I think, since before age fifteen."

(I should perhaps note that my friend is a respected scientist at a prominent university—that is, not Jeffrey Dahmer.)

I told my buddy about a story I had heard on NPR about one of the leading researchers on psychopaths who had traveled around the country with an fMRI in a bus, looking at the brains of imprisoned serial murderers. His wife pointed out to him one day that though he had tested almost everyone he knew, he had never examined—he had "somehow forgotten" to test—his own brain. When he did, surprise surprise, his brain looked just like a psychopath's. Which is not to say that he was a danger to his family or the rest of us, but that (1) there is obviously an environmental component in what makes a psychopath and (2) his intense interest in the subject was probably related to some deep suspicions and corresponding self-deceptions he was entertaining about himself.

"I've always suspected I might be a sociopath," my friend continued, and I thought: "What about me?" I've spent years now working on lying, and my own mentor, Robert C. Solomon— himself the author of one or two of the best papers on lying— once told me: "You know, it takes an odd character to work on deception." All this got me to wondering about myself: Was the reason I'm so interested in lying that I am a pathological liar? That I am, still worse, a sociopath?

So, on a bright spring morning in Kansas City, I found myself in my office, taking a test to see whether or not I am a sociopath. Let me be perfectly honest, it wasn't just my conversation with my friend. Over the course of the last few years one of my dear friends (with whom I once nearly had an affair, and then didn't), a recent ex-girlfriend, and my second (now ex-) wife all have told me, for I think more or less independent motivations but on the basis perhaps of similar evidence, that I might be one of these unhappy individuals, a "sociopath," who, among other things, experience "general anxiety," "shallow emotions," and "egocentricity." In a funny way I was half hoping I might be a sociopath, as a kind of neurochemical explanation and consolation for why I've had such trouble with lying in my love life—and, for that matter, with loving (at least, within the context of a marriage; I've failed twice at being a faithful husband and am now working hard—and succeeding so far, but knock on wood for me—at number three). My friend had, I think, the same half desire to want to be able to label himself. It's a common enough psychological phenomenon (I encounter it a lot in my work on addiction): once you can label yourself as "an alcoholic" or for that matter as "a psychopath," some of the responsibility—especially *moral* responsibility—for your actions seems to be lifted from your shoulders. You've got a condition. We don't blame a diabetic for his problems with his blood sugar, do we? Though we might also insist that he work on his eating habits.

Okay, let's talk about love. I think—I hope—I'm pretty good at loving my children. It comes naturally to me. They seem to feel well loved. But children will deceive about that sort of thing. Moreover, if I am a sociopath, it is very possible that my children will be sociopaths—the best current research suggests a genetic link for the disorder—and then they would be genetically apt at feigning the appearance of feeling loved. I don't want my children to be sociopaths. It sounds like a miserable existence. But if they are, best to learn about it now, so their mothers and I can take appropriate measures. It's also true that if I am a sociopath, I have likely been one since at least middle childhood—especially given that as far as the whole lying thing goes, I think I've improved, however modestly, over the years and especially recently. (Granted, it's very easy to self-deceive on this issue.) Research on sociopaths suggests they are generally diagnosable as children. But isn't it a frightening thought that at any turn we may be surrounded by little sociopathic children all on their way to be-coming sociopathic adults? It sounds like *Lord of the Flies*.

I'm stalling. Let's proceed to the diagnosis. I can sympathize with general anxiety, that's for certain. As for egocentricity, it's a bit difficult for me to judge: seems as if almost everyone I know is much more concerned with his or her own little world than he or she is with the world of others around him or her. I spend a lot of time worrying about other people's opinions, but to be honest, I'm often worried about their opinion of *me* or whether or not I've hurt their feelings in some way, which again has a kind of hard-to-specify *me-ness* to it. I suspect most people are the same way, but that may just be my egocentricity flaring up: Is think-ing that most people are probably more or less like me further evidence of my me-centered way of thinking? As a rule the ma-jority of my students as freshmen are egoists; they tend to claim that all behavior is me-directed. Then I show them that such a claim is either vacuous or false: if all behavior is me-directed, it's as good as saying no behavior is me-directed (a concept isn't any good unless it differentiates between things; Hegel calls this way of overgeneralizing a concept "the night in which all cows are black"). If, however, as I think, at least some of our actions are done simply or at least primarily for the sake of others, even if it causes short-term difficulty, then the kind of naive egoism my first-year students tend to advocate, which is sometimes called psychological egoism, is false.

But "shallow emotions"? Life would be simpler. Not long ago I had my heart broken by both my soon-to-be-ex-wife and my ex-girlfriend. Now I expect that from either of their perspectives the fact that I could have my heart broken by both of them at the same time might count as evidence of shallow emotions. But I can assure you it doesn't feel that way on the inside. From the inside it feels as if a stiff steel spring had been screwed into the top of the breastbone and someone were persistently yanking on it. Hard. From the inside it's terrifying and miserable and like picking up the cell phone with desperate hope every time the text beeps and trying not to call all day long, day after day. From the inside . . . hell, you know what it feels like. But unless you're feeling it right now, you also know that you don't truly remember what it felt like last time. Interestingly, the physiological sensations, along with the phenomenology of panic and pervasive dread, are similar to the symptoms one experiences on the first day or two of withdrawal from the sustained abuse of alcohol. If it's fair to say that many of us like to get love drunk, then heartbreak is like an especially grisly hangover.

When I reflect upon the people I have known in my life, of how many of them would I say they were emotionally shallow? Three or four, and those are women I have loved, all of whom, I know, if I consider the matter from their side, have all the emotional fathoms that I've found everywhere I've honestly spoken with people: in classrooms, in jail cells, in psychiatric wards, in bed, driving in the car, at night in a darkened room with a friend. I don't think there are many "emotionally shallow" people out there. Frightened people, perhaps, who are less inclined to expose themselves than others.

Having satisfied myself somewhat about the list, which, like all such lists, seems to characterize anyone as a sociopath, depending upon how it is interpreted, I tried the quiz my friend supplied.

"Do you like to torture animals?" No. At least, not nonhuman animals. Since early childhood I've been absolutely crazy about animals.

"Do you often engage in aggressive behavior?" Almost never, though I once repeatedly lied to a girlfriend and told her I got in fights all the time, hoping it would make me sexier to her. She had a friend who found this trait sexy in men, so that might have influenced me. Also, after seeing the movie *The Boxer*, and because my dad was a boxer, I thought being able to handle myself seemed cool. So yes, I lied about that one, but I haven't been in a fight since high school.

"Do you think other human beings are worthy of a fundamental respect?" Well, even Kant says yes—he disliked people more than I do—and though I don't think Kant has particularly compelling arguments for the view, my basic intuition is that every human being (and perhaps every living thing) are due respect by virtue of that fact alone. I can't defend the view and think it is probably irrational, which is not to say that it is false. Reason may be insufficient to support or may even contradict many of our true beliefs, as love teaches us again and again. (Try convincing a lover he is not in love because his love is irrational.) I'm with the Confucian philosopher Mencius, Jean-Jacques Rousseau, and the contemporary anthropologist Frans de Waal on this one: we are all of us—excepting the unhappy sociopaths of course—wired for a kind of basic human empathy. I also believe in moral progress, which is relevant to this question, but that's not on the quiz.

"Would you describe yourself as hard-hearted?" I teared up during the preview for that movie about the fat kid who wants to become a ballerina. If anything, I'm a little too soft-hearted.

"Do you ever enjoy the suffering of others, especially of children?" No, again. I cannot read news stories, watch movies, see photographs, or appreciate poetry about the suffering of small children.

"Do you lie?" Okay, now we're getting somewhere. Yes, I admit it: I lie. As I've mentioned before, one of the reasons I wrote this book—one of the reasons I wrote a Ph.D. dissertation on deception—is that I know that it has taken me years to become a more truthful person and that I will always struggle to be as truthful as some of the people around me.

The possible answers to the "Do you lie?" question on the quiz are interesting:

a. Never.
b. Lying is fun! Whenever the opportunity presents itself.
c. Whenever I need to do so to further my ends.
d. Infrequently, but when politeness requires it.

I want (e): All of the above. (I should add that I asked several friends whose self-honesty I respect the same question, and they also wanted [e], with some worrying about [b]).

As far as (b), (c), and (d) go, though it's true that I'm working hard at becoming a more honest person, well, when another friend remarked about me, "I believe half of everything that guy says" ("that guy" being me), it stung, but I also thought: "Well, half is not so bad. That's a glass half full of truth."

I remember, when I was eighteen, a freshman at Stetson University confronting me about the fact that I wasn't as honest as I believed I ought to be. I did what any rational young man does in this situation: I called my mother on the phone and informed her that I was going to stop lying.

"That's a good goal," she said.

"It's not a goal, Mom," I said. "I'm just going to stop. There's no trick to it. I'll just tell the truth or keep my mouth shut. Simple."

"Well, don't let me talk you out of it," she said. "I'm just saying it might be more difficult than you think."

"She doesn't get it," I thought. I was surprised that she

doubted me, since I was quite certain at this time—back at age eighteen—that my mom told lies very infrequently, if at all.

I suspect one of the reasons that we continue to think of lying as being a rare event, despite the funny frequency with which all of us practice it—mostly without noticing we're doing it—is that we consider it unpleasant to think of ourselves as liars, much less call ourselves liars or hear someone else call us liars. I have friends I could call adulterers who would laugh that off and yet might well never speak to me again if I called him or her a liar.

Some lazy, curious, self-reflective day, when you're feeling as if "the unexamined life is not worth living," roll out of bed in the morning and try to scrupulously observe everything you say for that day, making a little mark somewhere every time you tell a lie, however innocuous the lie is. Count even lies of politeness and mild flattery, lies to avoid hurting the feelings of others. You have to pay extraordinarily close attention to catch yourself at it. That's one of the most fascinating things about it. This is at least in part because as we have noted, it works both to your evolutionary advantage to be good at lying and to your evolutionary advantage not to notice when you're doing it.

Of course, even if lying isn't always bad and may sometimes be good, we can get carried away—especially in love. At the very least lying too frequently carries the same penalty as not lying when polite interaction requires it: social exclusion—even, perhaps, exclusion from the very possibility of the romantic (the player who gets too much of a reputation as being only a player cannot really be a player anymore, so this line of thinking goes). Moreover, while thinking you are protecting others by lying, you may be doing all sorts of emotional damage to them (we've all been lied to, and we know what kinds of wreckage can result). The liar, who must try to be a mind reader in order to lie successfully, presumes to know what is in the head of another and is often wrong. Even if he gets it right, he is still attempting to control the contents of another person's head. To want to control what's in that person's head for her own good: Isn't that the greatest possible presumption? But isn't that precisely the game we are playing? Think back to the observations of the second chapter and the lies that the parent tells the child, and the child tells the parent, in their first experiments in love: we learn these techniques so early, and they are so deeply ingrained in our most basic emotional understanding of what it is to love and to seek love. What lover isn't also always attempting to be a mind reader? When we are in love, we care what the other person is thinking; we want to know her thoughts. We even dare ask that most dangerous question, the question that perhaps asks for the lie more than any other: "What are you thinking?" And we tailor our speech to what we think we know about that other person's thoughts.

Just a few mornings ago, I was lying in bed with my wife after making love. My eyes were closed; her body was resting on mine. I imagined, lying there, that she was looking down on my face—of course, with suitably adoring eyes. Or perhaps her eyes were closed, as mine were.

I opened my eyes and saw that she was staring in the direction of the window, her eyes focused at that middle distance that signifies serious thought. I watched her for four or five long seconds before she realized I was staring up at her. Then she looked down at me and realized I was watching her. Her expression changed, she smiled, and she looked, perhaps, slightly guilty, though that may have been my jealous imagination.

What kind of destructive, rash, egomaniacal, self-deceptive desire might have prompted me to ask at that moment: "What were you thinking about?" Would I dare such a question and expect the truth? Or would a reasonable lover let his beloved tell him what she was thinking, if she wanted to do so, and leave her to the privacy of her own thoughts, if they were best left unspoken? In its way it is a truly endearing question because it's a duplicitous way of saying, "I trust you to lie to me." If I didn't trust my wife to lie to me and yet asked this question, then I'd have to commit myself to accept the fact that she happened to be thinking about, say, the astonishing sex she'd had with a particular man back in her twenties. And God knows what goes through our minds from one minute to the next. Certainly not thoughts that are all appropriate to share with the person or people we care most deeply about.

"Ask me no questions, and I'll tell you no lies." We so often imagine that this piece of simple wisdom is supposed to be a moral reproach to its speaker.

Insist too much on transparency and the truth, and you will never be able to love. Would you demand to know the mind of your friend in the way that you demand to know the mind of your lover?

Most of the deceptions we practice in erotic love do not have the goal of harming the beloved, just as most of the truths we tell have at least the hope of helping our relationship with the beloved. The point for most of us, I think, is that love simply matters more than most if not all other goods, even such mysterious, celebrated goods as truth.

5. Marriage

Therefore a man leaves his father and his mother and clings to his wife, and they become one flesh.

—Genesis 2:24

Love is mutual loneliness, and the deeper the loneliness, the deeper the love. —Chögyam Trungpa Rinpoche

You can't be honest in a marriage-type relationship where you live together, not absolutely honest, not if you want it to last. That is one of the down things about marriage. —Anya, in J. M. Coetzee, *Diary of a Bad Year*

MARRIAGE AND SUICIDE

I was separated from my second wife; I was in the midst of an unhappy love affair that was going from bad to worse; I had relapsed in my alcoholism. Finally, after a scene in the street outside my apartment, I went inside, took what pills I had, drank a bottle of scotch, ran a hot bath, climbed in, and tried to slice open my wrists.

When the cops beat on the door, I was in a warm bath, pecking at my basilic vein with the Global knife my second wife had allowed me after expelling me from our house.

Did I intend to kill myself? The nasty, coldhearted question that you are always asked if you fail. Most people ask the question in the deceptive way they coyly say: "So how did you do it?" A suicide attempt can be very much like falling in love. You're not really sure, as you proceed, what is real and what you're making up as you go. You're genuinely uncertain how the whole thing's going to turn out. You want it, but you don't. It seems both inevitable and impossible.

The police took me to the psychiatric ward at Research Medical Center in Kansas City. I'd been there before. I tried to escape, in the night, in my slippers and hospital robe, and failed: I was trapped by a nurse, a security guard, and some locking exit doors.

I sat, most days, with a muscular, startlingly good-looking Irishman (Daniel Day-Lewis–style, truly handsome), who, the whole time I was there, spoke only once and never stopped crying. He was covered in tattoos, in his early thirties, with massive arms and shoulders, long black eyelashes, and heavy curls. Mostly he cried noiselessly. I never learned his name. He reminded me of a kid who had lost his mother at night at a county fair. But he could also have been a saint who had taken a vow of silence and now could do nothing but weep for the world.

One Sunday afternoon a group of us rebelled and refused to "go to group" because the Kansas City Chiefs were playing the New England Patriots. We put the game on; the staff turned off the TV and told us to get in our session. I went to the nurse's station and explained with all the authority of a tenured professor the demonstrated therapeutic effects of a little good clean fun. They turned the TV back on. About half of us watched the game while in the same room, separated by a few standing gray vinyl and carpet screens, the other half went through the sorry motions of one of our utterly ineffectual therapy sessions, where we mostly just complained about members of the staff while the staff member leading the group ate it up. My Irishman cried through the game too, though he laughed more than once while weeping and we even high-fived each other after an unlikely touchdown. Our team won that game and beat the undefeated Patriots, an unheard-of result for the Chiefs.

The morning I left Research was the one time I heard this sad man speak. That's when I found out for certain he was Irish, though you could more or less tell just by looking at him.

"So you're goin'?"

"Yeah. Thank God."

"It was a good football game, wouldn't you say?" He smiled at me. He was looking me straight in the eye, and the tears ran down his cheeks unceasingly.

"It was the best football game I ever watched," I said truthfully. In fact, I don't like to watch football. The last time I'd watched a football game was the last time I'd been in Research. Or perhaps the time before that.

We didn't shake hands. And then the orderly took me downstairs, where the dean of my college was waiting to pick me up and take me out for buffalo wings at The Peanut on Main Street. It was a place we liked, where we could be honest with each other about most things, one of those casual men's places where you talk about your wives, children, and the politics at work.

The kind of therapeutic, friendly place that is the opposite of a psychiatric hospital, come to think of it. People lie in psychiatric hospitals. The staff lies unremittingly to the patients, about meds, meals, messages, you name it; the patients lie to the psychiatrists, faking happiness and serenity; and the psychiatrists lie to the patients (I don't know how many times I've been told, "I think you're ready to go. I expect we'll release you tomorrow," only to find that the cliché holds: tomorrow never comes); we patients lie to one another, in group and out of it, about why we're here, what we've done, whom we've betrayed, who's betrayed us; we lie on the phone to the people who will take our calls on the outside; people from the outside call in and tell lies about what's going on out there, about what people are saying about us, about why we need to stay inside. It's a lot like jail that way. To this day, many psychiatric wards are much like jail cells, except there is more room to roam in a ward, and they are cleaner and have much better windows. Also, there's usually a snack time. If you can choose, definitely go with the psych ward. But in my own limited experience, there's not much difference between a psychiatric ward nurse and a jail guard, not much difference between a hurried psychiatrist and an angry warden.

I mention this Irishman because a bond of strong affection had formed between me and this solitary penitent or martyr, despite the fact that we never spoke to each other. We had not communicated much in even nonverbal ways. Perhaps the reason it made such an impression on me is that it was a kind of return to the preverbal love I must have experienced as a baby. I was—I am—so accustomed to thinking of love as something that is made (and broken) through words.

For most of us, to love is to talk to each other. Most especially, to begin to love is to begin to communicate: to know each other. And, one supposes, to know each other truly. Intimacy is a function of mutual understanding, and I don't want to understand some false you, as I hope you will try to understand me as I actually am. To create a fake me for you to love—a trick we all can perform, especially with words—doesn't get me the love I hope for; on the contrary, it seems to leave me more alone.

As many of us do, when it comes to thinking about marriage, I start with my parents. My father married twice. My mother divorced him because he was a drunk and a notorious philanderer. When I was twenty-one years old, finally bold enough to confront him, I asked my father, "Why did you cheat on Mom the way you did, Dad? I could never do that. I could never break my promise like that." And he said: "Sometimes one person's sex drive doesn't match the other's, son. It's not as straightforward as it seems. Try not to be too hard on your old man." But I knew very well that I could never cheat on a woman I loved, much less on a woman I had promised to be faithful to for the rest of my life.

I was, at twenty-one, not merely sincere that I could never cheat on my own wife (remember the promise I made to my grandmother, at the end of chapter 2?) but morally outraged at the possibility that any man might. At this time I was speaking from the perspective of the childish lover, the first lover, and the naive lover—my love experiences had been with my mother (as Adam Phillips says, a "model of promiscuity"), my stepsister, Lisa, and Lila Gibbard, all of whom had cheated on me, not the other way around—so although I was ignorant, I wasn't deceiving myself. I simply didn't realize, yet, how complicated love would become.

"The lie of a pipe dream is what gives life to the whole misbegotten mad lot of us, drunk or sober," Eugene O'Neill writes in *The Iceman Cometh*. Is marriage a pipe dream? If so, is the pipe worth smoking?

I have married three times. Both my previous marriages ended in a flurry of lies, lies told both by me and by my wives, both to each other and to ourselves. And at the end of any marriage all the lies that sustained the marriage—the good lies, I would argue—are exposed and accused, so that what may have been once useful, necessary deceptions are now used as weapons against the marriage itself, as "proofs" that the love never existed in the first place, that the marriage was doomed from the outset or at best had become poisoned somewhere along the way.

But a man who has married three times has already failed at it twice, and why should he suppose that this third effort will meet with better success than the previous two? What can he have to say other than "In marriage, cheating doesn't work"?

In the endeavor of marrying repeatedly, statistics show that practice does not make perfect: the more often we marry, the less likely it is our marriages will endure. (Why this is the case, though it has been the subject of much careless editorializing and anecdotal speculation, has never been carefully studied.) Either way, it is odd to rely upon an expert who willingly confesses that he has both failed and failed as consequence of lies. When a marriage ends, both partners have a tendency—at least for a time—to insist that the entire enterprise was a lie from start to finish, a destructive illusion that harmed both their lives. "What we had together, we always only pretended we had together."

All that is of course just more exaggeration and deception: the "truth" is that while there are better marriages and worse marriages and as we have already seen, love requires both truth and falsehood, and one is no more necessary than the other, it is simply easiest to scapegoat the lies when tempers are high and when—as at the end of a marriage or at the end of any long-term relationship—both lies and the truth are being used as weapons against the beloved person, against oneself, and against the relationship the two of you had together. Love, as we have seen, is not a thing of "truth" or "falsehood" exclusively: trust and intimacy may require understanding when to tell a kind lie as much as knowing when to bare a difficult truth. Similarly, the end of love—or its transformation into a different kind of love, such as friendship, when a marriage or a long-term monogamous relationship ends—is similarly a bewildering mix of the true and the false, of sincerity and guile, of knowledge and ignorance, of fact and belief.

But I started this, my last chapter, with a story. Much of this book has been made up of or about stories—one of the reasons I like stories is that they mirror the kind of activity we are engaged in when we love. In fact, and although I don't like appealing to fMRI studies when it comes to the discussion of philosophical questions, it turns out that something unique happens when we tell stories to each other: the exact same parts of our brains light up. When we tell stories to each other, we are in fact communicating better than at other times; we become, in a way, telepathic; we are in a uniquely intimate exchange. And that, perhaps more than any other observation in this book, is the key to understanding what kind of thing romantic love is. So I think the best way to make some progress in understanding my view of the relationship among love, lies, and marriage is to briefly tell the stories of my three marriages so far. Because both my previous two marriages ended when I had an affair, one of my themes will be adultery.

FIRST MARRIAGE

My first wife and I met in a Bennigan's in Texas during summer break when I was a junior at Stetson University. We both were waiting tables. It was 1988, the summer we both turned twenty-one. She was at Baylor. After the summer ended, we went back to our colleges, but I didn't even make it to the end of the week. I sold my parrot, Sigmund, to a local breeder to pay off my parking tickets and remove the boot from my car. Then I drove from DeLand, Florida, nonstop to Waco, Texas. I had my father's gas card, and I used it for fuel, Clorets gum, and coffee.

I arrived at her apartment at about five in the morning—I'd left at 7:00 a.m. the previous day—and I began to knock on the window. Her roommate came out with a hunting rifle in his hands.

"I'm Clancy," I told him. "I'm her boyfriend."

"Did she know you were coming?"

"Kind of."

"I don't know about this," he said. "I think you better get back in your car."

Then my ocean-eyed, suntanned future wife appeared at the door and saved me. She brought me to her bedroom. I transferred to Baylor, and then we went to UT Austin together for graduate school. We married. We traveled; we were together for that rainstorm in Portugal (from the prologue). We spent a year together in Copenhagen on a fellowship. That is where our first daughter was conceived. It is also where I conceived our future life together: I joined my older brother in his jewelry business. I would get rich quick so that I could become a writer, and I didn't get rich and didn't become a writer (that came much later), but I did ruin my marriage. About a month before our daughter turned two, I became involved with another woman, my assistant at the jewelry store, and within a few weeks I moved out of the house. I didn't tell my wife about the other woman—I lied and blamed the separation on our problems, though my wife suspected the truth—for about a year. The summer before our daughter was four, we divorced.

I should add that over the years my first wife has become one of my closest friends.

A PREMONITION

That was marriage number one. Two years passed, and I met my second wife.

It was September 2000, and three of us were sitting on the steps of Waggener Hall in the warm Texas sun, arguing about the German philosopher and mathematician Gottlob Frege. I was pretending to smoke because the beautiful, long-haired, long-legged twenty-one-year-old I had my eye on was a smoker. I didn't know yet that she was twenty-one, which was lucky for us both, because I don't think I would have had the nerve to ask out a woman twelve years younger than I was. I was back at UT Austin, attending the graduate school I'd dropped out of seven years before to go into the jewelry business. One of my friends from the old days was still there—he'd known my first wife, in fact—he was finishing his dissertation, and he actually knew something about Frege. I was sure the twenty-one-year-old had her eye on him. She later confessed to me that she had guessed I was gay.

On our third or fourth date a strange thing happened to me. I was standing in the men's room at a coffee shop called the Spider House. I was checking my look in the mirror when I had a vision. There's no other word for it. I had had visions before. I came back to the table and sat down.

I had a beer, and she had an iced coffee. We were in a booth, and she was sitting across from me. "There's something I have to tell you," I said.

"What?" she said. She was quiet at this time. Later, when she knew how much I loved her, she became the talker.

"I just saw something. I suddenly saw that we are going to be married and have two children together."

"What do you mean, you saw something?" she said. She was sane and skeptical.

I told her what I had seen, and it all came true. About eighteen months later we were married. Not long after that, after I had started teaching at the University of Missouri–Kansas City and she had started law school at KU, our first daughter was born; about two years later, as she was finishing law school, our second daughter was born. And on July 24, 2012, our divorce was finalized. Two daughters, just like the vision. Curiously, the whole ten years we were married, I also knew that it wasn't going to last. I think she knew. Our marriage had the feeling of a very important game we were playing together that had to come to an end. And it did when I cheated on her after I'd been sober for a year and we'd been together for ten.

The adultery was exposed quickly—after about a month of constant lying on my part—and there was no sincere attempt by either of us to put things back together. She threw me out of the house, and a new, harder life began for us and for our two daughters, who were at that time aged six and four, and for my eldest daughter, from my first marriage, then sixteen.

ADULTERY FOR ADULTS

"The greatest part of virtue lies in avoiding the opportunities for vice," St. Augustine taught, but this is the same saint who gave us "Make me chaste, Lord. But not yet, Lord, not yet!" C. S. Lewis writes about erotic love in *The Four Loves*: "this act, done under the influence of a soaring and iridescent Eros which reduces the role of the senses to a minor consideration, may yet be plain adultery, may involve breaking a wife's heart, deceiving a husband, betraying a friend, polluting hospitality and deserting your children."

When my second wife and I first started dating, I told her: "One day you might cheat on me, and I want you to promise me that if that happens, you will lie to me about it." She thought it was bizarre and unhealthy at the time, but I still stand by it. The problem of course of sticking your head in the sand like this is that a hyena can come along and bite you in the ass. As it turned out, she was not the cheater; I was. But suppose for a moment that she had been. Would my policy have been a sensible one?

What if, contrary to my express wishes, she confessed early on, while there was still time to save things? What if by encouraging her not to confess—making her promise—I was creating the future circumstances that could allow her to fall in love with someone else? I was quick to add: "But if it turns serious, then of course I would want to know." But by then it might be too late. By then, many of us know from hard experience—whether we are the cheaters or the cheated upon—it usually is too late.

And what about the coerced confession? Usually there is at least some coercion in any confession of infidelity: a question about a strange phone call, an e-mail "I opened by accident," a text you forgot to delete before your real lover—the one you are cheating on—borrowed your phone. "My friend said she saw you at a restaurant with ———. Weren't you working late that night?" Fight or flight: we usually put both to work, deploying indignation and lies on the spot. But then the decision process starts.

Here again, the thought of Adrienne Rich is useful. While offering a nuanced account of truthfulness, she also correctly argues that lies and secrets always undermine what we are really seeking when we love. For Rich, it may not always be possible to be truthful, but when we are seeking to create intimacy, we are at least trying to move in the direction of truthfulness and openness.

By contrast, when we lie, as we saw when we considered the lies of children, we are affirming our independence in a way that may threaten the intimacy of love. Because I myself have been a secret drinker and I understand that mode of deception, I like the way Mary Karr puts it in her memoir: "If you lie to your husband—even about something as banal as how much you drink—each lie is a brick in a wall going up between you, and when he tells you he loves you, it's deflected away."

Now, as any alcoholic will tell you, there's nothing "banal" about how much you drink if you're the sort of person who is already lying about his or her drinking. On the contrary, you are lying about one of the most important things that are taking place in your life at that time. And for Adrienne Rich, who admits that many truths are too trivial to concern us as far as our intimacy is concerned, a truth about "how much you are drinking" would count as a vital truth in the development or discouragement of intimacy between two lovers.

So much turns on what we mean by the most important truths. There is a new category of infidelity that seems to be growing in social currency (and, probably, popularity of practice): the so-called emotional affair. The emotional affair occurs when we establish a high degree of intimacy—and probably flirtation—with a potential lover, a level of intimacy that we know would be unacceptable to our partner (and which we may or may not have with our partner, depending upon the present state of the relationship). An emotional affair need not be a prelude to an actual affair, but it certainly looks like a violation of trust; it is the creation of a world of secrets that are emotionally relevant to the marital relationship.

Suppose that you are in an emotional affair. Now contrast that emotional affair with your sexual fantasy life. When we think about our own sexual fantasies, we recognize how harmless they are yet also how damaging they could be if revealed to our spouses. If, however, we think about our partners' sexual fantasies—the people we suspect they might involve, most upsettingly—we can bring ourselves into a rage of jealousy or a despair of insecurity (even if this rage or despair remains, and should remain, entirely hidden from our partners). "What is harmless and innocent when it takes place in my mind is dangerous and morally blameworthy when it takes place in yours." (The psychological plausibility, the evident ordinariness of even this modest piece of hypocrisy shows us how important it is for us to become more open-minded and honest about the possibilities and perhaps inevitability of deception and self-deception in marriage.)

The emotional affair is similarly kept secret from one's partner, but there is a crucial difference: it involves direct, emotionally fraught interaction with another *real person*. That other human being seems to fall within the realm of most important truths. But these matters get so complex so quickly. If we are straight women, are we having emotional affairs with our girlfriends? But does that mean we can't have friends who are men? And won't our friendships always involve secrets that we keep from our spouses (if only minor secrets like: "God, I wanted to slap him today because . . .")?

We might suggest that our ordinary friendships don't tend to intrude into our sexual consciousness; our emotional affairs, by contrast, always have the dangerous, seductive aroma of the erotic clouding them. The transition from friendship to emotional intimacy to the "must-be-revealed important truth" of the emotional affair, then, might not be so very different from the "important truth" of a real affair. The only difference may be that what is about to happen hasn't physically happened yet. How long might we cling to precisely that self-deceptive fact that "nothing's happened!" just because nothing physical has happened? The purpose of clinging to that belief is obvious: to persuade ourselves that our partners need not—indeed, should not, for their own sakes—know about this relationship, which is, after all, "really just a friendship . . ." (Wait, how many texts did I send her today? God, I don't even want to look.)

We should notice that fantasizing about having sex with someone else may be (and I think usually is) different from fantasizing about having an affair, which in turn may be different from fantasizing about cheating. The fantasy, either during sex with one's spouse or not, of having sex with another person can be mentally compatible (this is how complex our mental life is) with a horror of having cheated on one's spouse. Then there may be the fantasy of an affair, which may or may not be a sexual fantasy; a kind of imaginative foray into an alternative life that does not include one's spouse but retains the fact that one is married. Then again there is the fantasy of cheating, having sex that is specifically not with your spouse, the fantasy of betrayal.

I think it is because the mind is so creative, so adept in its fantastical prestidigitation, so expert at visualizing the not-yet, the better-not-be, the never-will-be, the impossible that we make the sensible moral division between imagining sex with someone else and actually having it. When we were talking about cheating and the most important truths above, I think we mean at the very least to include actual acts of having sex with someone else—or for that matter any instance of physical intimacy—among the most important truths. According to Matthew, Jesus taught: "Ye have heard that it was said by them of old time, Thou shalt not commit adultery: But I say unto you, That whosoever looketh on a woman to lust after her hath committed adultery with her already in his heart"(Matthew 5:27–28). Here again, we run up against our old enemy "the truth and nothing but the truth, so help me God" or "pure transparency" or "love as a ladder to the knowledge of the truth": if a married person sincerely believed that his fantasy life amounted to the same thing as adultery—or suspected that his spouse had a robust fantasy life and so was engaging in adultery—marriage and romantic love would be impossible.

DRUNKS AND CHEATERS

The affair that ended my second marriage was inextricably mixed with booze. Allow me briefly to discuss one analysis of the relationship among alcohol, truthfulness, and marriage, Chekhov's *Uncle Vanya*, in order to expose what I think really destroys love in marriage: lying to ourselves about the fact that we lie, pretending that all this is entirely and only about believing and telling the truth.

In *Uncle Vanya* alcohol plays an important role in the story, and I am including a few words on the role of alcohol in adultery because drinking is so commonly a part both of deception and of adultery.

While there is an enormous popular literature—and much terrific dramatic and fictional writing—on the relationship between adultery and alcoholism and other forms of addiction, I have not been able to find any serious scientific work that has been done on the subject. When I think of my second wife's claim that I might be a sociopath, I find a strange comfort in this observation from David Sheff's book *Clean*: "Addicts' impaired cognition can lead to behavioral changes. Also, with the prefrontal cortex dismantled and the rear brain in control, addicts are literally not in their right minds. The go system is raging, the prefrontal cortex offline, and, as a result, addicts appear to be pathological narcissists, unable to empathize or sympathize." In short, maybe I was a sociopath while I was a drunk, and so long as I'm stable in my recovery, there is hope for me yet.

My own personal experience in this kind of deception and self-deception comes from a three-year affair I had with booze, lying to my wife that I was sober, while drinking for weeks at a time, mixed of course with weeks of abstinence. I could never quite tell what she suspected, what she knew, what she remained totally oblivious of, and to this day she insists she was almost entirely unaware that I was secret drinking. She believed in me. I thought it ended when I tried to kill myself, but then, after two years of sobriety, I started an affair with a woman, and soon I was drinking again. Those two, the illicit affair and alcohol, collaborated together, and almost before I knew what was happening, the marriage was over.

Chekhov comes close to telling what happened in my own story. Chekhov's *Uncle Vanya* is a play about two failed love affairs—both with the same woman—attempted by two drunks who are also failures in their love lives. The drunken lovers are Astrov, a country doctor, and Uncle Vanya, a landowner and intellectual who hasn't satisfied any of his hopes for himself. The object of their ardor is Yelena, a coquette, who is married to the professor, Aleksandr Serebyakov. So it's a love triangle, from which the husband is excluded, as husbands usually are. If you haven't read the play recently, the plot is simple: the professor and his beautiful wife, half his age, have moved to the country for his retirement, where his daughter, Sonya, owns a farm that she runs with her uncle (Vanya). All the proceeds of the farm go to support Sonya's father, the professor. But when he and his sexy wife join their relatives in the country, the simple, stable harmony of the farm is destroyed, in part by the professor's posturing, endless demands, old age, and hypochondria, but more by the glamour and lazy boredom of Yelena, who distracts Astrov, Uncle Vanya, and even Sonya out of their normal, healthy habits. She is indolent and reeks with the sensuality of indolence, the privilege of beauty, which in this play is contrasted with the morality of hard work.

Chekhov is not a fan of country life, nor is he a fan of city life. We tend to forget that this great genius died at the age of forty-four, after a hard life of working as a physician in both the country and the city—he described medicine as his wife, literature as his mistress—because he had the studied, gentle skepticism of a much older man. Like any good doctor, he was an empiricist (two great empiricist philosophers before him, the skeptic Sextus Empiricus and the materialist John Locke, were also physicians), and he hesitates to attach ethical valence to any of the situations he creates, preferring to describe what he sees without judging it. "Only a great, rare, deep genius can catch what surrounds us daily, what always accompanies us, what is ordinary," Gogol writes, no doubt influencing how Chekhov saw the role (and the style) of the artist, and that is what he gives us in Uncle Vanya. "A writer must be humane to his fingertips," Chekhov tells us, and to be humane is among other things to withhold judgment when one can and, when one cannot, to be quick to forgive.

Nevertheless, there is a bit of moralizing in the play: drunkenness is bad, if all but inevitable; boredom is bad, the result of a weak mind or a weak character; life is worth living for love, though you are unlikely to find it; beauty is dangerous and destructive, work is healthy and productive; nature is better than civilization. All these are familiar Chekhovian themes and, after all, not terribly controversial. The underlying theme of the play anticipates the major themes of existentialism: In the absence of a God and traditional values, where shall we now find the meaning of life? Chekhov is too wise to give answers. Instead, he presents the situation: boredom turns to hope, hope to passion, and passion to drink. "We're all creeps," Astrov complains, and the main reason we're all creeps is that we're all bored, and boredom is unbearable. The one person who piques everyone's interest—Yelena, a flirt who refuses to cheat on her husband—complains of boredom more than anyone else in the play.

Chekhov wrote to his brother, advising on these matters:

What [good men] want in a woman is not a sexual playmate . . . They do not ask for the cleverness which shows itself in continual lying. They want especially, if they are artists, freshness, elegance, humanity, the capacity for motherhood . . . They do not swill vodka at all hours of the day and night, do not sniff at cupboards, for they are not pigs and know they are not. They

drink only when they are free, on occasion . . . What is needed
is constant work, day and night, constant reading, study, will . . .
Come to us, smash the vodka bottle, lie down and read.

Not that Chekhov was a prude. "Chekhov wrote of sex with
honesty and lack of fuss as he wrote of all human experience,"
Eudora Welty correctly observes, and in *Uncle Vanya* he gets the
temptations of adultery just right. What are they? Here's Chekhov's list, by character:

For Uncle Vanya:
(1) To sleep with Yelena is to prove his equality with the
professor, always part of a man's desire to sleep with
another man's woman, especially if he is a friend, most
especially if he is a friend one envies, resents, or admires.
(2) Yelena represents meaning in Uncle Vanya's life: he
knows and constantly reminds us that he's made nothing
of himself intellectually—he works an estate, does the
accounts, turns a profit, is a kind of middle manager—
but to take Yelena to bed would make real the passions he
has suppressed in service of the estate, would realize his
inner life (something he knows he will never do).
(3) Yelena is beautiful. For Vanya, she is an unapproachable
beauty. At one point she all but offers him a kiss, leaning
against him when she should pull away, and he turns
away, afraid to take what he wants.
(4) Yelena is an ideal: when he is drunk, Vanya lies to himself
and to her, insisting that she is the whole meaning of his
life. He means it, while drunk, but when sobriety returns
to him (and it doesn't really return until after he has tried
to murder the professor and finally the professor and
Yelena leave), he knows that all there is for him is work.

For Astrov:

(1) Yelena loves him.

(2) Unlike Vanya, Astrov wants to have sex with this
woman, and he knows she wants him: he grabs her; he
forces her to kiss him.

(3) When drunk, Astrov is Dionysian: he sings; he bawls; he
shouts; he is ribald; he wants to satisfy his desires, and a
woman who will cheat on her husband is exactly the kind
of lawlessness the drunk revels in. He wants her to *cheat*,
to betray, to be young, to care about nothing but passion,
no matter who is harmed.

For Yelena:

(1) Adultery is a celebration of her beauty, which she knows
she is losing; she tells her husband she will join him in
old age in just a few years.

(2) Adultery is vanity; she loves flattery and to know she is
desirable.

(3) Adultery is freedom from boredom; it is the spice of vice;
it is Augustine's stealing the pomegranates only to throw
them away for the sheer joy of sin.

(4) Adultery is the solution to her boredom. Why should she
work when she can flirt?

(5) When she is drunk, with Sonya, it is the desire to have
something more in her life than she has had—to expand
her life, to return to her piano, to play music again, to
believe in art, to which the professor says simply, at the
end of Act 2, before the curtain falls, "No."

These people are human: what is at stake is not so much
truthfulness and deception as vanity and frailty. We understand
this behavior without endorsing it. There is even a failed suicide

attempt at the end of the play—along with a failed murder—all of it driven by the same thing: booze, vanity, ordinary human stupidity.

Here we might repeat Augustine's advice: "The greatest part of virtue lies in avoiding the opportunities for vice." This, for me today, in my own marriage, is one of the most important maxims to remember. If I don't drink, if I don't put myself in awful situations—such as I did when I brought a beautiful woman to my hotel room several years ago, during my second marriage, "but just as a friend"—then I am far less likely to create self-deceptive scenarios, to lie to myself, to repeat the serious mistakes I've made in the past. I may be simply lying to myself in order to try to excuse my own past misbehavior, but I suspect that almost anyone, if he is honest with himself—and most especially if he is bored or if he is a drunk or, worst of all, both—can become an adulterer. He is vulnerable not in knowing this fact but in lying to himself about it.

For Chekhov, this is what we can learn from *Uncle Vanya*: how vulnerable to vice we all are.

THIRD TIME'S THE CHARM

At this year's Thanksgiving, in the turn-of-the-century house Amie and I just bought in old Kansas City, Amie, my third wife; Rebecca, my second; Alicia, my first; Amie's mom, Pat; and my three daughters sat around the harvest table. My first wife, Alicia, who has a large, ambitious heart, had proposed this act of holiday lunacy. My second wife, Rebecca, had suggested we just have fun without her but then came anyway. Amie had felt powerless to say no, and now it was taking place. Once the guests arrived, Amie hid in the kitchen. She spent most of her time there, making eggnog cappuccinos, roasting sweet potatoes, and baking pumpkin pies. I was afraid of the dinner table but took the head, my daughters flanking me. Amie's mother was at the other end, and she's what Amie refers to as a good storyteller. The four women and three girls all seemed to have a good time. My first wife and my third wife discussed cleaning supplies and ghosts. Three of the four women—everyone but Amie—were single mothers, I realized. They'd all been married; they all were presently single.

Coming out of the kitchen with one of the roasted chickens on a platter, I listened nervously to the conversation:

"I know the wood needs oil," Amie said, gesturing to the mahogany paneling in the dining room. "But you can't really do it before company comes."

My eldest daughter was musing aloud about what she would do if she had accidentally killed someone. She thought it would be best to hide the body.

"No," my first wife (her mother) said. "You would call me."

"I'd call my attorney!" my daughter said, and she pointed to my second wife (a divorce lawyer), who laughed. As my three wives discussed the scenario—the dead body, the mistake, and how to go forward—my mother-in-law grimaced at my two young daughters, as if to say: Why are we all talking about killing someone?

She made the same face when my first wife and Amie discussed tarot card readers. My first wife said, "I go for fun sometimes, and it's always just been no big thing, but recently this woman told me someone had put a curse on me in a past life. She kept calling me afterward, saying, 'I don't want money. I just want to help you.'"

Amie nodded solemnly. She said, "My tarot card reader told me I had a ghost living inside me!"

"What did she say?" my second wife asked, and Amie explained matter-of-factly about the imp who had become attached to her. Apparently it was harmless, and merely wanted to cause minor mischief.

Amie said, "I asked my guru about it, and he said, 'Amie. There is no ghost in you.'"

"Unless I'm the ghost," I said. They laughed. A little too enthusiastically.

"Fair's fair," I thought. Two ex-wives and my present wife all in our newly bought home; my divorce mediator, Ronnie Beach, had warned against it. I stood at the end of the table, amateurishly carved the chicken—this was the first chicken I'd roasted in a few years—and talked to my daughters.

But then dinner and dessert went very well. Every time I looked up to check on Amie she was smiling and chatting. When they left, all the hugs were natural. They took a pumpkin pie back home with them.

Good luck always makes me anxious. That night I woke at 3:00 a.m. in a sweat. Why had those once-married women stayed single? Did they understand something I didn't? Had Amie and I married too quickly? Was it because I need someone to love me? Did she love me? But if not, why marry a twice-divorced man with three children? I couldn't get back to sleep.

I went downstairs to the study, sat at our new partners desk, and made a list of all the reasons I'd married for a third time. I decided to be as rough on myself as I could. The first reason I wrote was: "I fell madly in love with Amie. She's the one." Wait, that's a copout. That was what I would say in a Nora Ephron movie. I started a new list. Tougher.

"Reason No. 1: I don't like to be alone. Reason No. 2: Life seems mostly sane when I am with the person who is my best friend." The list had eleven reasons. I could have kept going to fifteen or twenty.

After my second divorce, a friend and mentor said to me: "Give me this much: you'll wait as long as I did before trying it again." This friend had had an interval of about fifteen years between his two marriages. I reassured him there was no chance I was getting married again. Then, a few months after my promise, less than two weeks after the signing of my divorce decree, at the beginning of the monsoon season in a Tibetan colony in the Himalayas, I married for the third time. "For Christ's sake, why?" my married male friends asked me. My single male friends were quiet. My female friends laughed or shook their heads. My brothers were relieved. My ex-wives were emphatic: "Promise you won't have any more children."

"Marriage is like a cage," Montaigne wrote. "One sees the birds outside desperate to get in, and those inside equally desperate to get out." The metaphor is hardly value neutral; there is something noble, if frightening, about living outside the cage, secure but slavish within. (My father used to paraphrase Groucho Marx: "Marriage is a great institution, C.W., if you want to live in an institution.") For better or worse, Montaigne is right to point out that so many people who are married confess, after half a bottle of wine, that they would rather not be; catch a single person in a weak moment, and he will often admit his longing for a lover who is more than temporary. Divorce and the fortunate, growing trend toward real political, educational, and labor equality of women have made changes to the way we understand and practice marriage throughout the world, but most of us continue to value the ideal of dedicating one's erotic and affectionate attention to another human being for a lifetime.

Kierkegaard had the idea that there is both a first and a second immediacy to experience in life. The first immediacy is that of a child; it is the kind of freshness to experience that we enjoy when we are encountering the world for the first time. The smell of the snow in your first few winters (even as a teenager I could smell the snow in a way I no longer can), the first times you swim, what food tasted like then—all the newness that Proust is able to capture in *Swann's Way*, for example. The newness that Dylan Thomas writes about in that lyrical masterpiece of first immediacy "Fern Hill":

> Now as I was young and easy under the apple boughs
> About the lilting house and happy as the grass was green,
> The night above the dingle starry,
> Time let me hail and climb
> Golden in the heydays of his eyes . . .

We all remember what he is writing about. Then, Kierkegaard argues, comes life; familiarity and habit creep in, and the world loses its newness, its ease, its golden quality. And for many of us, perhaps, that's where it ends; we remember the immediacy of youth and never recapture it. But, Kierkegaard writes, there can be "a second immediacy," experienced perhaps through love (one way of reading him), perhaps only through faith (the Danish word is *tro*; it also means "belief"). In the state of second immediacy, we do not forget what the world was like before, when we were satiated with it; rather, we rediscover its newness. It is, as Alfred North Whitehead puts it, "reenchanted."

In the first months of our marriage, when my wife Amie told me she loved me, she often added, "I've never loved anyone like this since Hilary, my best friend in the third grade." Earlier we saw that first love will set the stage for the many frustrations of romantic love; best friendship in childhood may be something like marriage. One possibility is that the first love we looked at in chapter 2 is a kind of first immediacy, and marriage is the possibility of reenchantment. But in fact, I think that first love is already a stage of disenchantment with love, a necessary continuation of a disenchantment that begins as soon as we start to be aware of our separations from our mothers. As I argued in the first chapter, our understanding of our need for love (rather than our simple acceptance of the fact that we have it already) begins with the separation from our mothers and is a necessary stage for our development as beings who can choose to love. No one—certainly not Kierkegaard—would argue that we should remain in a first immediacy, even if it were possible to do so. But I do think that marriage may offer the possibility of a second immediacy, a reexperience of that childhood intimacy of love that nevertheless recognizes—and, indeed, requires—the many disappointments and heartbreaks love has offered along the way. It is not a return to the mother, nor is it the love of identification, but it is the re-creation of intimacy that makes Aristophanes's farce of the two halves of the whole's being reuniting more than just comedy and such an enduring metaphor.

AM I JUST ADDICTED TO MARRIAGE?

In the story I tell above about the vision I had while on an early date with my second wife I wasn't entirely honest. When I explained about the vision I had, I pretended not to understand why my future wife might have doubted me. But of course seduction is about much more than getting someone into bed.

My older brother and I used to talk sometimes about seducing women, and we would agree that the fun went out of it when they said, "I love you." Then you knew you had won. That was what my future wife was afraid of at The Spider House: that I was tricking her into giving me her heart, so that I could know that I'd won it and then could toss it away.

I am sure that men and women alike experience this desire and disappointment: to conquer the other person's soul and then experience the anticlimax of victory. No doubt there are as many man-eaters as there are players. But once I had married, the first time, that desire—to eat the victim's heart—went out of me. Or maybe it happened when my first daughter was born. I don't remember because I was faithful to my first wife until the affair that ended the marriage. And after that I never really dated in the same way again. I no longer believed in the enthusiasm of conquest. After that my lovers were friends of mine, or they weren't lovers for long.

I remember that the summer before I met my second wife I dated one woman after another, and at last, in despair, I called a friend.

"I think I've just gone through all of the real women I'm going to meet," I told her. "Everyone I date now, after two or three dates, I realize it's useless. I used up my good woman karma."

She laughed, and I laughed too, but I was miserable about it. I was sure that I wasn't going to meet another woman who could be a real partner. I was still clinging to that old Aristophanic myth, one that I may never escape, that there is an "ideal partner" for me, one from whom I've been cloven.

Now, when my third wife, Amie, and I are in bed together, sometimes when our hearts are beating at the same rate, one or the other of us will say, "Doesn't it feel like we are the same person?" When we finish each other's sentences, when one of us starts a thought and the other says: "That's exactly what I was just thinking." We both know the facts of the situation. We both hold out hope—sincere hope—that we will spend the rest of our lives together, that we will become only more intimate, that the trust between us and our level of commitment to each other is increasing with every passing day, week, month.

Are we just lunatics, fools, or worse? What kind of self-deception is this?

THE TRADITIONAL MODEL AND THE CURE

The contemporary philosopher Eric Schwitzgebel writes, in his short essay "Thoughts on Conjugal Love":

> There may be an appearance of paradox in the idea that conjugal love requires a lifelong commitment without contingency plans, yet at the same time is conditional in a way parental love is not. But there is no paradox. If one believes that something is permanent, one can make lifelong promises and commitments contingent upon it, because one believes the contingency will never come to pass. This then is the significance of the marriage ceremony: It is the expression of a mutual unshakeable commitment to build a joint life together, where each partner's commitment is possible, despite the contingency of conjugal love, because each partner trusts the other's commitment to be unshakeable.
>
> A deep faith and trust must therefore underlie true conjugal love. That trust is the most sacred and inviolable thing in a marriage, because it is the very foundation of its possibility. Deception and faithlessness destroy conjugal love because, and exactly to the extent that, they undermine the grounds of that trust. For the same reason, honest and open interchange about long-standing goals and attitudes stands at the heart of marriage.

This, it seems to me, is an excellent explication and defense of the traditional view of marriage and how it requires truthfulness for trust. Schwitzgebel recognizes that there appears to be what he calls a paradox in the marriage vow: to promise to love for a lifetime, while recognizing that life is a very unpredictable thing, looks like a risky act. It seems to involve predicting the future in a way that all of us acknowledge we cannot do (strange visions in coffee shops aside). To marry is to acknowledge that the future is unpredictable and to insist, "*But this part of life won't be: my commitment to you.*" Which is not to say that both partners in the marriage won't have changeable—and changing—feelings about the partnership along the way, but rather that given the fact that both partners expect that their feelings may and probably will be subject to change along the way, the commitment will not change.

There's a Cure song I've always loved that captures this unusually well. Monday is blue, Robert Smith tells us, and Tuesday and Wednesday still worse. He continues: "Thursday, I don't care about you / It's Friday, I'm in love."

The other verses are just as good. I remember when I told my second wife that I thought this was one of the best songs ever written about marriage, she looked at me with puzzlement and, a bit upset, said: "I don't get it." Later she explained to me that at the time she'd been hurt because she'd felt as if it should "always be Friday." But by the time we were talking about it she'd realized, as all married couples do, that it won't be Friday every day. Maybe months will go by, in some rough times in a marriage, before a Friday comes along. Nevertheless, Schwitzgebel argues, that's what makes a marriage vow such a unique, valuable—and slightly crazy?—promise: when I vow to be your partner for life, I am swearing to stand by you, I suppose, even if Friday never comes.

Now if that were true—that marriage means staying together

even after it's obvious that the relationship is no longer capable of providing either of us (or even only one of us) with happiness— then getting married really would be a bizarre thing to do. The nineteenth-century German philosopher Arthur Schopenhauer, a lifelong bachelor who seemed to love only his poodles, writes: "To marry means to do everything possible to become an object of disgust to each other." And there is a kind of marriage paradox shared by both Schwitzgebel and Schopenhauer: that transparency or openness—complete honesty, complete exposure—is the desirable goal of marriage.

Schopenhauer's idea is that insofar as we become more and more known to each other in the everydayness of living together as a married couple, the pleasantries, illusions, and charms—the social deceptions—that we all practice in order to get along with fellow human beings will be increasingly exposed, and so we will inevitably become repulsive to each other. His underlying idea here seems to be something like getting to know another person completely, in the marital sense, is like seeing one's spouse sitting on the toilet. But of course, as most married people will tell you, catching your spouse while he or she is peeing is an innocent, common, and often even charming event, as it happens, for a happily married couple. Schopenhauer seems to be afraid of intimacy.

But let's give Schopenhauer a bit more of a chance. In the 1989 movie *The War of the Roses*—one of the best satires of divorce— Oliver Rose demands an explanation for why his wife is leaving him:

OLIVER ROSE: I think you owe me a solid reason. I worked my ass off for you and the kids to have a nice life and you owe me a reason that makes sense. I want to hear it.

BARBARA ROSE: Because. When I watch you eat. When I see
you asleep. When I look at you lately, I just want to smash
your face in.

Anyone who has been married for several years probably
knows what Barbara Rose is talking about, and it is likely this
"Familiarity breeds contempt" view that Schopenhauer has in
mind. There will be times, in any marriage, if only because of the
sheer familiarity of the person you have elected to spend the
rest of your life with, that that person can seem, well, repulsive.
It's the same kind of repulsion we experience at times with
ourselves—think how unbearable, how inane your own inner
monologue can be at times, or even your own face in the mirror—
or with the thought, as Charles Bukowski once aptly put it, of
having to tie your shoes every day for the rest of your life, of
having to brush your teeth. (For Bukowski, the thought of having to tie his shoes and to brush his teeth every day for the rest
of his life was enough to drive a sane human being to commit
suicide.) And if marriage were nothing more than the pure
commitment to stick it out together, no matter what—if it were
the mere recognition of and insistence upon the bare marital
promise—then the many eighteenth- and nineteenth-century
attacks upon marriage would have the final word on the subject;
we could just admit, "Marriage is no good," and get rid of the
damned thing. In the nineteenth century in the West we elimi-
nated the laws that prevented people from ending their marriages for good reasons. And there is still a lively literature
attacking marriage—and even the very notion of enduring romantic love.

Schopenhauer and Barbara Rose have a point: if two people
are enduringly and irrecoverably repulsive to each other to-

gether, it's absurd for them to be married. Of course, Schopenhauer thinks that marriage will somehow increase their tendency to make each other miserable, and popular culture seems to support his idea. So many movies feature a scene like the wonderful one in *Out of Africa* where Meryl Streep and Robert Redford are lying at night in the sand, debating the virtues of marriage: he insists that his commitment to her is enduring, she demands that they marry, and he dares her to think of one example of a happy marriage. It certainly seems true that marriage encourages the kind of "taking for grantedness" that we all recognize as the death knell of a happy love life, and that many marriages suffer from the feeling, which tends to increase over time, that each spouse is the one really doing the hard work of keeping the love alive.

"There's nothing more scandalous than a happy marriage," Adam Phillips writes—scandalous in part, we suppose, because it is uncommon. My first wife has not remarried, and I don't expect she plans to; my second wife is a divorce attorney and insists she will not marry again. In a new trend, more and more couples are divorcing after the age of fifty, with many years of marriage behind them; there is even a formula, devised by John Tierney and Garth Sundem, that quite accurately predicts whether or not a celebrity marriage will survive. While gay couples fight for the deserved right to marry, the popularity of marriage is declining in the United States and has been declining for decades in Europe. Writers from Ibsen and John Stuart Mill to Betty Friedan, Andrea Dworkin, and Sheila Cronin have attacked marriage (especially of course in defense of the rights of women), and it is hard to find thinkers willing to defend marriage outside of conservative religious traditions.

"The marriage contract is unlike most contracts," writes L. J.

Weitzman. "Its provisions are unwritten, its penalties are un-specified, and the terms of the contract are typically unknown to the contracting parties . . . No one would sign it if they had read it first." Nevertheless, books like Patti Stanger's *Become Your Own Matchmaker* are bestsellers, and most of us think that a lifetime spent with a romantic partner is one of the most desir-able goods. As I hinted above, when I married for the third time, it was my married friends who most often asked, "But for God's sake, why?"

Eric Schwitzgebel presumably doesn't want everyone to stay married no matter how unhappy he or she has become. But I think he may have made the requirements for a successful mar-riage a bit less realistic than, say, Robert Smith of the Cure does. When we place unrealistically high demands upon love— demands like "deep faith and trust" in "true conjugal love"—we start to engage in practices that undermine, rather than support, the realistic hope that a marriage can flourish and prosper over many years. This is what I admire about Robert Smith's state-ment of the situation. Our feelings change from day to day, and yet if we don't expect too much from our feelings, if we don't re-act to those feelings too vigorously, if we are patient with our feelings, even a bit ironical about our feelings, we will remember that Friday will come around again, and we'll find ourselves once more in love. "Marital love fears nothing," Kierkegaard writes in the character of Judge William in volume 2 of *Either/Or*, "not even minor mistakes; it does not fear little infatuations—in fact these, too, only nourish the divine soundness of marital love."

Kierkegaard's Judge William and Robert Smith both recog-nize that part of the beauty and the virtue of marriage is its abil-ity to withstand the changing feelings that married partners will undergo through the course of their marriage. But it's going to take more than that. Our feelings aren't simply things we pas-sively suffer. We actively engage with them; we stimulate them; we create them. That's the real hope for marriage, I think. It's not that I will myself to be in love with my wife. But I am in love with her willingly, even willfully.

THE MARRIAGE PARADOX

If only the brain weren't so nimble, so practiced at partitioning itself! If self-deception were impossible or even rare—rather than, as is the case, the rule—perhaps there would be few af-fairs and many fewer failed marriages. How many of us have looked at our spouses and thought, How I love her, only to no-tice, fifteen, twenty minutes later, after she's left the room, an attractive woman glancing our way, and wondered, "Now, she's interesting . . ." When you're thinking about that other woman—probably (only?) to think, "How nice that she's attracted to me!" but maybe also: "Who is she? What makes her tick? I wonder what an affair with her would be like"—your love for, need of, and commitment to your wife have for that moment or minute flown entirely from your brain. The thought "Now, she's interest-ing . . ." is not a violation of your marriage vow. And the thought itself may not even be under your control. But most adulteries and destroyed marriages begin with precisely that thought. And whether or not you choose to act on it is certainly a decision you make.

I remember the night my second marriage ended. For hours that night I had told myself that the woman I was with—a friend was there too—was not interested in me and that I was not interested in her. She was drinking; I was not. By the end of the evening I knew what was going to happen. I knew that it could well end my marriage. I told the woman, once we were in bed, "I'm happily married. I love my wife." She said: "I know." And a month later my marriage was effectively over, and I was already sneaking shots of vodka. I never decided: Okay, my marriage is over now. But when I got into that bed, that's what I was deciding. And yet the whole time I was telling myself: "No, I won't let this happen; this is not what it is."

Remember the paradox of self-deception, introduced in the first chapter? To believe a proposition *p* and convince oneself that "not *p*." It ought to be impossible. And yet we do it with such fluency from such a young age. "This is not what it is": that belief is the core of self-deception. "What I know is true is not true." I both knew and did not know that I was ending my marriage that night. But somehow, also, as I was lying to myself, I knew I was lying to myself. I remember thinking: "You've done this before. You can't tell yourself this lie again."

The bad side of self-deception allows us to get ourselves into the kinds of love-destroying situations that I created when I destroyed my first two marriages. But there is also a good side to self-deception. And I think that the benevolent power of self-deception is in fact what makes long-term happy marriages possible, just as I think almost all successful relationships depend upon the benevolent power of self-deception. The crucial difference between bad self-deception and good self-deception, I think, is *knowing that you're doing it* and *knowing why you're doing it*.

Now, this is a bit complicated because it doesn't sound like self-deception if you understand what it is you're up to. But it is rarely the case that we simply "know the true belief" or "accept the false belief"; our belief processes are not like on/off switches. We are much more often in the domain of what Sartre called troubled belief, when truth and falsehood are blended together and multiple beliefs are combating each other, like waves tossing the boat of the mind on a troubled sea. When I claim that we should acknowledge that we are engaged in self-deception and why we are engaged in self-deception, I mean that we can play these sorts of truth and lie games less dangerously when we recognize that this is the sort of activity we are engaging in. If you refuse to recognize that you are playing the game, you are almost certainly going to lose. If you don't admit to yourself that the sea you are sailing is stormy, you are that much more likely to drown.

Here's an example that might be helpful: a child sees a rainbow and wants to go find it or sees a cloud from an airplane and wants to play in it. The rainbow and the cloud are no less real for the adult who sees them than they are for the child, but in better understanding the nature of those phenomena, the adult will not make the cognitive mistakes that the child might want to make. The naive lover believes his self-deceptions with the same naive earnestness that the child believes in the rainbow.

Here's another, cleverer example. It is Shakespeare's "Sonnet 138," one of the best meditations on love and deception in all of literature:

> When my love swears that she is made of truth
> I do believe her, though I know she lies,
> That she might think me some untutor'd youth,
> Unlearnèd in the world's false subtleties.
> Thus vainly thinking that she thinks me young,
> Although she knows my days are past the best,
> Simply I credit her false speaking tongue;
> On both sides thus is simple truth suppress'd.
> But wherefore says she not she is unjust?

> And wherefore say not I that I am old?
> O, love's best habit is in seeming trust,
> And age in love loves not to have years told.
> Therefore I lie with her and she with me,
> And in our faults by lies we flatter'd be.

Let's take the time to analyze this a bit. The first two lines are a delightful double paradox: lying, the lover swears she is made of truth, and he believes her, though he knows she's lying. But for him to believe her, he can't know she's lying: a lie works only when we don't believe it. Here we have self-deception illustrated as deception taking place between the couple. And better still, her lie is that she is made of truth: she lies about the fact that she is lying (she goes on to tell some other lies too that he also chooses to believe, knowing they are lies). Even ordinary self-deception—when we lie to ourselves about something—is, as we have seen, usually considered paradoxical by philosophers. But given that we are experts at the pretzel logic that enables us to believe the lies we tell ourselves, how does one believe a lie someone else is telling him, while knowing it's a lie? Here Shakespeare stacks up the paradoxes: next his narrator admits that he lets his lover believe that he believes her lies so that she will think he is young, which is also the lie she is telling him (that he is young), and he uses his acting as if he believes her lie to convince himself of the lie she is telling him ("Thus vainly thinking that she thinks me young"). This is so subtle, so convoluted, so hilarious, and yet so true to the phenomenology of how love actually works that suddenly we remember why, from just a few lines, Shakespeare was the greatest writer—the greatest thinker?—the English language has ever produced.

It gets better yet: "O, love's best habit is in seeming trust": not in trust, but in *seeming* trust, and not one of love's habits—

controversial enough—but love's *best* habit. That is, real trust in love comes in trusting even when we know there may be some grounds for distrust, when we recognize that complete trust is an illusion and should not even be a goal for the best lovers. To truly trust is to seem to trust, to trust with the acceptance of doubt, to be willing to extend the feigning of trust while hoping, even expecting, that the feint will be returned. It is a kind of "seeming trust," but Wallace Stevens gets it right when he writes, "Let be be finale of seem": sometimes the being is in the finale, the climax, of the seeming. Or, as Nietzsche teaches us, the profundity of the ancient Greeks was in the fact that at least prior to Plato, they were content to let appearances be enough; they didn't want truth's veils withdrawn; they understood that "the naked truth" was not what we lovers desire.

Of course, Shakespeare saves the best two lines for last: "Therefore I lie with her and she with me, / And in our faults by lies we flatter'd be."

There is the lovely pun on "lie," Shakespeare characteristically playful, and the introduction of "flattery," the most common and the most harmless form of lie. Flattery is crucial here because of course, we flatter one another all the time—even politeness is merely formalized flattery—but in flattery (as in politeness) we all recognize what is going on; the lie succeeds while being recognized as a lie. Language acts in many different ways, and so do lies: not every lie is of the bald-faced-I'm-trying-to-cruelly-manipulate-you-for-my-own-evil-ends variety, and the lies of love are rarely of this type. When we are falling in love, we tell one another and ourselves so many lies—who among us hasn't had the feeling, while falling in love, of "wait, but aren't I making this all up?"—and yet the lies are an essential part of the process. We are faulted by our lies, but our lies recover us from our faults, and the lies, flatteries. We see through all this, and yet we do it, and the lies work, and we love. The story of Beatrice and Benedick is a kind of illustration of how they come to recognize the necessity of this process and how it culminates in their marriage. We don't expect that the games they play with each other will end with the wedding, and we'd be sad if they did.

In marriage, I want to argue, this kind of activity of playful, open-eyed deception and self-deception—the willingness to engage in this kind of activity, even the necessity that one learn to engage in this kind of activity—is how love is fostered, nurtured, and maintained. "Couples last longer if they have a tendency to overrate each other compared to the other's self-evaluation," Robert Trivers tells us. If we tend to glamorize our partners, if we willfully encourage crystals to grow on them in the way that Stendhal describes, we will have stronger marriages. This comes as no surprise. If we take seriously the process by which we fall in love in the first place, it simply makes good sense strategically to encourage an ongoing falling in love.

Adam Phillips puts the same point from the negative perspective, but succinctly: "The point about trust is that it is impossible to establish. It is a risk masquerading as a promise." But we can take blind risks, foolish risks, ill-advised risks; we can also take practiced risks; we can enjoy risk; we can risk because to risk—what we have earlier called to gamble—is to live. A friend of mine, R. J. Hankinson, a great scholar of the ancient skeptic Sextus Empiricus and the ancient physician Galen, once raised the argument that being a skeptic might not be much fun because it threatens to take the risk out of life. If you aren't willing to be swayed by appearances, so this line goes, what's the fun of it all?

The lama Dzongsar Khyentse Rinpoche teaches that Bud-

dhism doesn't address erotic love—and certainly not marriage—
except as a problem.

> In relationships, we don't really have a choice. When it comes,
> it comes. What is important about relationships is not to have
> expectations. That always ruins the relationships. If you are a
> couple, your attitude should be that you have checked into
> a hotel for a few days together. I might never see her again
> tomorrow. This might be our last goodbye, our last kissing,
> together. Maybe it will help, it will bring the preciousness of
> the relationship. When the relationship comes, you should not
> be afraid.

When he married me and my third wife, in a shrine room in
a monastery in Bir, in the southern Himalayas, he warned us:
"You know, Buddhism doesn't have a marriage ceremony. We
don't really believe in marriage. But the best thing you can do is
live in the world. I would tell you from the day when you are
married, your practice is—let's forget about giving freedom to
the sentient beings—to start with giving freedom to your husband, and husband to the wife. By freedom what I mean is not
craving from your own ego's gratification, and you can start in
that way." What he meant in part is that we knew—that we should
acknowledge—that if life is impermanent (a core Buddhist belief), marriage is that much more so, but here we are, stuck in the
world, so why not risk it? Part of the risk is acknowledging that
the other human being, your spouse, is free; there's no telling
what she or he might do.

"Now, go run behind a tree or something," he added after the
ceremony was over, and everyone laughed.

Here a little more wisdom from Robert Trivers is helpful.

Reflecting with admirable candor on his own marriage, he writes: "I will never forget the sense of vulnerability I felt when I first realized my wife of eighteen months had been catching me in a series of lies without telling me. She was building up a library of my behavior for future use." He doesn't discuss the library he may have been building of her lies. He has the intuition, which I share, that women are more naturally honest than men and also perhaps more naturally inclined toward making inventories and catalogs of truths and falsehoods.

When Trivers had this very personal realization—and it is one of the more charming moments in his refreshingly frank, terrific book on lies and self-deception—he did not abandon his marriage, or confront his wife about it, or even, so far as we learn, significantly modify his behavior. What happened is that he realized that she was a more sophisticated lover than he was, that she understood what the narrator of "Sonnet 138" understands, and he, until that moment, did not. The lies he was telling to his wife were not being collected for use *against him*; on the contrary, they were being collected with the anticipation that they might be necessary in order to protect the marriage. His wife recognized his naiveté and was happy to work with it; she would introduce him slowly and gradually, as the *Kama Sutra* instructs wives to do, into the finer points of love, which are a mixture of truth and falsehood.

I remember when my own first wife admitted to me that I had a tell—as is said in poker for recognizing a bluff—that gave away when I was lying. "What is it?" I asked. "I'm not going to tell *you*," she said, laughing, and of course she was right not to. I would have tried to mask it. (Who knows if I would have been effective? These kinds of tells tend to be subconscious, and are notoriously hard to overcome. My little brother yawns every time before he tells a lie.)

THE VIOLENCE OF CREATING THE TRUTH

As I've mentioned more than once, my favorite philosopher on the subject of cultivating truthfulness in the context of intimate love relationships is Adrienne Rich. "An honorable human relationship—that is, one in which two people have the right to use the word 'love'—is a process, delicate, violent, often terrifying to both persons involved, a process of refining the truths they tell each other." The crucial notion here, the phrase on which the plausibility of her entire account depends, is "refining the truths they tell." *Refining the truth*: this is very much like Bonhoeffer's notion of the living truth. It is not an out-and-out lie, but it is a kind of creative approach to the truth that recognizes the frailty of love—and of the human psyche, of what we can bear to hear, especially from someone we love—and embraces the idea that what we are *really saying* is different from the actual words we are speaking. For Rich, to learn to love another human being is to learn how to speak to that person, to develop a language between the two of you, a language that ultimately captures the truth of your love for each other but need not expose "the naked truth" of what each individual lover may be happening to be feeling or thinking from one moment to the next.

The philosopher Irving Singer is useful here. In what he calls "appraisal" appraisal of another, in finding value, we do a kind of truth estimation (but also—though he only gestures toward this—a kind of projection, a kind of self-deception, a kind of illusion making), and this is a more individual process, a beginning, starting with me, something I do to you; in "bestowal" of value we are explicitly and necessarily creative, and this is ideally an interactive process. An artist can also interact with her novel, which reveals some of the possible dangers of bestowal; but real bestowal surely takes another human being, and that's where

creation is much richer and more demanding, where love becomes unique among human experiences. My wife can never really love her novel in the way she loves me or her mother or her
stepchildren or her friends. But she can love it, she does in fact
bestow her love upon it—as I try to bestow my love on my own
creative work—and we know the story about the creative act: at
the end of the day it has its roots in truth telling, but that truth
telling takes place almost entirely in fantasy worlds, possible
worlds, projections, fictions, dreams. For Rich, then, we might say
that love begins in appraisal and is cultivated through bestowal,
and the process of refining the truths we tell each other is a process of creating truths about our love for each other together.

Stanley Cavell argues that we should understand "the ability
to perceive distinctions as an intellectual and moral talent essential to the intimacy of marriage." Here he is thinking especially
of verbal distinctions (he uses the example of "I missed you," "I
missed you too," in Doug Liman's *Mr. & Mrs. Smith*). This is the
ability to understand what the partner is *really* saying. To understand the subtext. To become the good reader of another
person—which is also to recognize that as you are reading, you
are writing—and so is your partner.

MARRIAGE FOR GROWN-UPS

"I'm too romantic for marriage," one of Sandra Cisneros's characters remarks. One might also say, "I'm too childish for marriage." The view here—that romance is somehow importantly at
odds with marriage—is much like the view of a child who refuses to give up her belief in Santa Claus. Such a person is in fact
too romantic for love, unless she accepts that to love will mean
continual disappointment. To erotically love at all, once we are

no longer first lovers, means to accept that romance requires an active participation in the romantic activity: to accept that illusion, disillusionment, and reenchantment all are part of the process and that, particularly in marriage, both lovers have to commit to that process.

The opposite view—that, as unmarried friends of mine often say, "Marriage is an atavism"—is equally naive. But the activity of marriage isn't going anywhere. Whatever we call it, lifelong monogamous erotic commitment is with us to stay. If we want an "ism" for marriage, we'd more accurately say, "Marriage is a quixotism." It's a way of looking at erotic love that vigorously defies what superficially seems to be the obvious case: that it's very difficult to stay in love with another human being for years and years. It requires the kind of artistry of a Don Quixote. To enjoy a play or any work of art, Coleridge argues, we must adopt a certain attitude: the suspension of disbelief. What attitudes are the opposites of the suspension of disbelief? What do we express when we refuse to play the game of the artist? Cynicism. Boredom. Disappointment.

To lie to yourself—to be willing to lie to yourself and, when required, to be willing to lie to the ones you love—might not be, as Adrienne Rich thinks, an expression of unutterable loneliness, but on the contrary, an assertion of your love. How, when, and why we sort out the right kind of lying from the right kind of truth telling—and the wrong kind of lying from the wrong kind of truth telling—are a lifetime's pursuit.

When Aristotle discusses virtue in *Nicomachean Ethics*, he generally argues for what we often call the golden mean: the virtue of an activity lies between the deficiency and the excess. To be insufficiently brave is to be cowardly; to be excessively so is to be rash. To be insufficiently generous is to be cheap; to be excessively generous is to be a spendthrift. One exception he makes to this rule of moderation is truth telling: despite his generally good-natured tolerance for most kinds of lying as a relatively harmless vice, he insists that in the activities of truth seeking and truth telling there is no excess.

But perhaps here Aristotle's vocation as a philosopher and "lover of the truth" led him into an unhelpful inconsistency. I think that he would have done well to have stuck to his theory. Because in our everyday lives, and especially our love lives, moderation in truth seeking and truth telling is precisely what is needed. A deficiency in truth telling—being a bald-faced liar or always hiding the truth—is clearly a vice, but, and similarly, an excess of truth telling—always and only trying to confront the ones we love with the naked truth—also looks vicious. The territory we all are trying successfully to navigate, in both deception and self-deception, is the middle ground, the golden mean, where truthfulness and deception blend together, when communication, trust, love, and commitment require sensitivity and nuance.

When I think about my belief that the intimacy I've found and am continuing to develop in my marriage is a good thing, one of the best things in my life, one of my highest pursuits, I think about the joke that Alvy Singer tells at the end of *Annie Hall* and how he explains it to the audience:

> This guy goes to a psychiatrist and says, "Doc, my brother's crazy; he thinks he's a chicken." And the doctor says, "Well, why don't you turn him in?" The guy says, "I would, but I need the eggs." Well, I guess that's pretty much now how I feel about relationships; y'know, they're totally irrational, and crazy, and absurd. But I guess we keep going through it because most of us need the eggs.

I also think about the discussion at the breakfast table at the end of *Moonstruck*, when Cher's mother, who knows that her husband has been cheating on her, demands that he end the affair. He stands up, strikes the table, and then sits back down again. He's surrounded by his family, and his daughter is about to announce her own, equally crazy marriage. And he speaks these words of despair: "A man understands one day that his life is built on nothing, and that's a bad, crazy day." His wife looks back at him, knowing that he's had an affair and seeing that it means nothing, really, now that he's agreed to end it, says: "Your life is not built on nothing! *Ti amo.*" And he replies to her: *"Ti amo."* Yes, the truth is out, but what was at stake is so much more than the simple truth of the fact that he cheated on her. The point was that they loved each other, and their love was the real, fundamental truth. The "subjective truth." "The living truth," the "refined truth," the "most important truth."

Of course my account of my third marriage and the way it informs how I think about the truth is really just a philosopher stumbling awkwardly around the real story, which is that Amie called one afternoon to do a tarot card reading on me for a column she wrote for a magazine (the cards said I should work and avoid romance); I Google imaged her, and single at the time, I flirted with her; Facebook led to e-mails led to texts and then to long phone calls. I flew Amie to Kansas City, and one morning, coming upstairs from the basement of my apartment with laundry in my arms, I caught sight of her in the eastern sunlight making coffee in the kitchen, smiling with that half frown she makes when she's working, her long black hair in her face and on her shoulders; I flew back with her to Seattle, and walking through the jewelry department of Barney's, I saw a ring. That afternoon I proposed. That's the truth of it. We met; we fell in love; I asked her to spend the rest of her life with me; she said yes.

Yes, you might have your heart broken; yes, the whole thing might be an impossible joke, a game with outrageous odds; yes, you might have failed at it twice before, and there's no guarantee—just the opposite, really—that the third time's the charm. As I remarked above, life is risky; love, riskier still; marriage might be riskiest of all. But it's worth the risk. To choose to be married is, contra Montaigne, a paradoxical expression of one's freedom. When we marry, we proclaim: "I will love this person, come what may. I willingly, deliberately, actively participate in my erotic commitment." It's an insistence that whatever the odds are, to have the chance to spend the rest of our lives with the person we love most is worth defying the odds.

I know my wife does not always tell me the truth. She knows I do not always tell her the truth. Our intimacy is deeply involved with our ability to try to create some truth together, which always necessarily involves some lying to each other and lying to ourselves. I think we try to tell each other the most important truths. We willingly take the risk of love. We hope to succeed in loving each other. I think our eyes are mostly open. We both know we need the eggs.

And when I am with my wife, I do not feel alone.

Notes

Prologue: Why I Wrote This Book

4 *"in talking about the past"*: William Maxwell, *So Long, See You Tomorrow* (New York: Random House, 1999), p. 27.

5 *recent research on deception*: Great recent scientific work on deception and self-deception has been done by, among others, Dan Ariely, Kang Lee, V. S. Ramachandran, Victoria Talwar, and Robert Trivers. Their work has been of enormous help to me in this book.

19 *deception and self-deception have informed*: In *Swann's Way*, Marcel says of his love for his mother: "My sole consolation when I went upstairs for the night was that Mamma would come in and kiss me after I was in bed. But this good night lasted so short a time, she went down again so soon, that the moment in which I heard her climb the stairs . . . was for me a moment of the utmost pain; for it heralded the moment which was to follow it, when she would have left me and gone downstairs again"(15). Marcel Proust, *Swann's Way: In Search of Lost Time*, vol. 1, trans. Lydia Davis (New York: Penguin, 2004). I quote the passage at greater length in chapter 2 below. This becomes the model for all of Marcel's future attempts at and explications of love and indeed summarizes the narrator's pessimistic view of love. I do not agree with his view; I do agree, however, that how we will come to understand erotic love as adults is profoundly influenced by the kind of love we had with our parents. This seems perhaps uncontroversial, until we look at how few of our discussions of grown-up love and our failures and successes at erotic love include discussions of the kind of loving we did as children (even after Freud and Proust and the French psychoanalytical movement). Of course it can be an embarrassing project to undertake. In chapter 2, I try to look at how my own relationship with my mother influenced my later failures in love.

1. A Brief Introduction to the Morality of Deception

21 *The younger a child is when she starts to lie:* Richard Alleyne, "Lying Children Will Grow Up to Be Successful Citizens," *UK Telegraph*, May 16, 2010. See also A. D. Evans and K. Lee (2013), "Emergence of Lying in Very Young Children," *Developmental Psychology* 49: 1958–63.

21 *four-year-olds lied at least once:* Po Bronson and Ashley Merryman, *NurtureShock: New Thinking About Children* (New York: Twelve Publishers, 2011): "96 percent of all children lie. By six, kids lie once every hour, on average." See also K. Lee (2013), "Little Liars: Development of Verbal Deception in Children," *Child Development Perspectives* 7(2): 91–96. In another study, the evidence suggested that children who are born healthy are more likely to become liars later in life.

21 *the capacity to lie convincingly:* A. D. Evans and K. Lee (2011), "Verbal Deception from Late Childhood to Middle Adolescence and Its Relation to Executive Functioning Skills," *Developmental Psychology* 47: 1108–16.

22 *liars consistently have higher GPAs:* Benedict Carey, "I'm Not Lying, I'm Telling a Future Truth. Really," *New York Times*, May 6, 2008.

22 *told three lies in that much time:* Paul Ekman, *Telling Lies: Clues to Deceit in the Marketplace, Politics, and Marriage* (New York: Norton, 2009). While it's difficult to accept, many different studies have shown that "the average person" probably lies as much as three times every ten minutes if she or he is engaged in continuous conversation.

27 *doctors argue that the right:* Sandeep Jauhur, "When Doctors Need to Lie," *New York Times*, February 22, 2014. Jauhur helpfully reviews some of the literature on why and how physicians have defended the right to lie to their patients on therapeutic grounds.

41 *"extend the possibilities of truth":* Adrienne Rich, *Lies, Secrets and Silence* (New York: Norton, 2012), p. 195.

46 *life as literature:* The contemporary philosopher Alexander Nehamas championed this interpretation of Nietzsche's philosophy in his groundbreaking work *Nietzsche: Life as Literature* (New York: Harvard University Press, 1987).

48 *"life has not been devised by morality":* From section 1 of the preface to the 1886 edition of *Human-All-Too-Human*, first published in 1876. Friedrich Nietzsche, *Human-All-Too-Human,* trans. Walter A. Kaufmann (New York: Modern Library, 2000), p. 91.

2. Childhood

53   *the prettiest Lite-Brite:* Proust writes about the magic lantern he was given to make bedtime easier for Marcel: "Someone had had the happy idea of giving me, to distract me on evenings when I seemed abnormally wretched, a magic lantern . . . in the manner of the master-builders and glass-painters of gothic days it substituted for the opaqueness of my walls an impalpable iridescence, supernatural phenomena of many colors, in which legends were depicted, as on a shifting and transitory window." Marcel Proust, *In Search of Lost Time or Remembrance of Things Past,* vol. 1, trans. C. K. Scott Moncrieff (New York: Modern Library, 1998), p. 27. Unfortunately, like my Lite-Brite, the lantern in fact only makes matters worse for the young Marcel.

55   *"the feeling of being nothing":* Adam Phillips, *Monogamy* (New York: Vintage, 1999), p. 38.

58   *"we are brought close to formlessness":* Rich, 2012, p. 192.

61   *the more a child lies, the higher her IQ:* Alleyne, 2010: "Researchers have found that the ability to tell fibs at the age of two is a sign of fast developing brains and means [the children] are more likely to have successful lives. They found that the more plausible the lie, the more quick-witted [the children] will be in later years and the better their ability to think on their feet." The lead scientist in the study of twelve hundred children was Dr. Kang Lee at the Institute of Child Study at the University of Toronto.

61   *even as young children we can discern:* Robert Trivers, *The Folly of Fools: The Logic of Deceit and Self-Deception in Human Life* (New York: Basic Books, 2011): "Deception is an important part of the child's repertoire, pretending greater need than is actually being experienced and manipulating the parent psychologically, sometimes against the parent's better instincts"(80). Trivers goes on to argue that natural selection also favors self-deception in children, and this fact will be particularly important to us later, as we recognize the importance of self-deception in the development and cultivation of romantic love.

62   *lie to avoid hurting the feelings:* F. Xu, A. D. Evans, C. Li, Q. Li, G. Heyman, and K. Lee (2013), "The Role of Honesty and Benevolence in Children's Judgements of Trustworthiness," *International Journal of Behavioural Development* 37(3): 257–65.

62   *The best liars must also be mind readers:* Evans and Lee (2013).

63 *"Concealing the truth is often":* bell hooks, *All About Love: New Vision* (New York: HarperCollins, 2000), p. 35.

64 *"obedience is irksome":* Jean-Jacques Rousseau, *Emile*, trans. Alan Bloom (New York: Basic Books, 1979), p. 101. Recent scientific research confirms Rousseau's observation: V. Talwar and K. Lee (2011), "A Punitive Environment Fosters Children's Dishonesty: A Natural Experiment," *Child Development* 82: 1751–58.

64 *"Who from the terrour of this arm":* John Milton, *Paradise Lost* (New York: Modern Library Classics, 2008), book 1, stanzas 110–115.

65 *"Are you investing in a child":* Trivers, 2011, pp. 78–79. The reader will observe that I am deeply indebted to Trivers's work throughout my analysis.

66 *"punishment as punishment must":* Rousseau, 1979, p. 101.

66 *children lie because as parents:* A current leading book on child rearing, *Parenting with Love and Logic* (New York: Tyndale House Publishers, 2006), by Foster Cline and Jim Fay, gives an analysis of why children lie and how to correct the behavior almost identical to Rousseau's.

67 *"so they learn that lying is a way":* hooks, 2000, p. 34.

67 *"lies are all the work of masters":* Rousseau, 1979, pp. 102–03.

69 *"Zeus offered a solution":* Plato, *Symposium*, trans. Michael Joyce (London: Dent, 1935), p. 190 c–d.

71 *"the power to sleep":* Marcel Proust, *Remembrance of Things Past*, vol. 1, trans. C. K. Scott Moncrieff and Terence Kilmartin (New York: Random House, 1981), pp. 13–14.

73 *"the Wolf made a good meal":* Aesop, "The Boy Who Cried Wolf," *Aesop's Fables*, Lit2Go Edition (1867).

75 *he insults Geppetto:* Carlo Collodi, *Pinocchio* (London: Puffin, 1996), p. 32.

86 *"one is ignored for exaggerating":* Phillips, 1999, p. 25. Phillips seems also to be thinking of Aesop's "The Boy Who Cried Wolf."

87 *"learn from lying to ourselves":* Friedrich Nietzsche, *Human, All Too Human* (Cambridge: Cambridge University Press, 1997), p. 229.

87 *"at least double":* Marcel Proust, *La Prisonnière* [The Captive], trans. Anne Carson in *The Albertine Workout* (New York: New Directions, 2014), p. 21.

88 *we all lie easily:* Kim B. Serota, Timothy R. Levine, and Franklin J. Boster (2010), "The Prevalence of Lying in America: Three Studies of Self-Reported Lies," *Human Communication Research* 36: 2–25.

3. First Loves

92 *"doomed to end in disappointment"*: Sigmund Freud, "Female Sexuality," *On Sexuality* (London: Pelican Freud Library, 1931), p. 378.

92 *"a model of promiscuity"*: Phillips, 1999, p. 75.

93 *"every lover's question"*: Carol Gilligan, *The Birth of Pleasure: A New Map of Love* (New York: Random House, 2011), p. 61.

94 *"gratitude finds expression"*: Melanie Klein, "Early Stages of the Oedipus Complex," *The Selected Melanie Klein*, ed. Julie Mitchell (New York: Free Press, 1987), pp. 78–79.

102 *Discussions of first love*: Lisa Appignanesi, *All About Love* (New York: Norton, 2011).

103 *"force of speaking of love"*: Blaise Pascal, "Discourse on the Passion of Love," *Thoughts, Letters and Minor Works* (New York: Cosimo, 2007).

105 *tradition of troubadours*: Denis de Rougemont, *Love in the Western World* (Princeton, N.J.: Princeton University Press, 1983), p. 118.

106 *"I had no first love"*: Ivan Turgenev, *First Love*, trans. Isaiah Berlin (London: Penguin Classics, 1978), p. 28.

108 *"a hysterical desire"*: Thomas Mann, *Death in Venice* (New York: Vintage, 1989), p. 49.

108 *"closed my eyes"*: Turgenev, 1978, p. 39.

112 *"There must be self-deception"*: Nietzsche, 1997, p. 40.

115 *"the divorce of the body from the soul"*: Jean-Paul Sartre, *Being and Nothingness*, trans. Hazel Barnes (New York: Philosophical Library, 1956), pp. 97–98.

117 *"puts a bullet"*: J. M. Coetzee, "Storm over Young Goethe," *New York Review of Books*, April 26, 2012.

118 *the "real" Charlotte Buff*: Coetzee comments, ibid. "This synopsis is notable for the distance Goethe seems to be putting between himself and a hero whose story was in important respects his own. He too had gloomily asked himself whether a self-defeating compulsion did not underlie his practice of falling in love with unattainable women; he too had contemplated suicide, though he had lacked the courage to do the deed. The crucial difference between himself and Werther was that he could call on his art to diagnose and expel the malaise that afflicted him, whereas Werther could only suffer it. As Thomas Mann puts it, Werther is 'the young Goethe himself, minus the creative gift.'"

118 *"never wanted to date again"*: Nancy Kalish, "First Love, Lost Love: Is It Imprinting?" Sticky Bonds, *Psychology Today*, July 4, 2010.

120 *"take pleasure in deceiving ourselves"*: Pascal, 2007.

122 *"voluntarily focused:* José Ortega y Gasset, *On Love* (New York: Martino Fine Books, 2002), p. 76.

126 *"confused adoration"*: James Joyce, "Araby," *Dubliners* (London: Penguin Classics, 1993), pp. 345–46.

128 *"the disillusioned"*: Phillips, 1999, p. 22.

129 *"I know what love is!"*: Simone de Beauvoir, *Memoirs of a Dutiful Daughter* (New York: HarperCollins, 2005), p. 345.

131 *"Marcel's theory of desire"*: Carson, 2014, p. 18.

135 *"criterion of truthfulness"*: Adam Phillips, *The Beast in the Nursery: On Curiosity and Other Appetites* (New York: Vintage, 2010), p. 154.

136 *a fascination for the person:* Martin Heidegger, *Being and Time* (New York: HarperCollins, 2008), division I, ch. 6. Heidegger's relationship between caring and the possibility of truth disclosing itself is so closely aligned with Freud's that it is hard not to speculate that Heidegger may have found his famous, controversial account of truth and truthfulness in Freud's work.

139 *skills of the lover:* Despite what we usually think, only a very short part of the *Kama Sutra*, about twenty pages of a five-hundred-page treatise, is concerned with the actual practice of sexual intercourse. Its main subject is love. "This is why, in good society, women must secretly study the theory and practice of the *Kama Sutra*" (trans. Alain Danielou [New York, Inner Traditions, 1993], p. 51): not principally for the sexual pleasure of their partners but for the cultivation and maintenance of successful romantic relationships. It must be done in secret because part of the art of winning and keeping a husband is tricking him into thinking he's doing all the work. Among the sixty-four arts a woman must learn are such deceptive arts as No. 32, "the art of telling stories"; No. 56, "versification and literary forms"; No. 57, "the art of cheating"; and No. 58, "the art of disguise."

142 *"Now tell me the truth"*: Alberto Moravia, *Contempt*, trans. Angus Davidson (New York: New York Review of Books, 1999), p. 106.

4. Erotic Love

145 *"reciprocal torture"*: This is Marcel of *Remembrance of Things Past*, complaining about Albertine. Carson, 2014, p. 6, notes: from Marcel's point of view, the worst thing about Albertine is her lying. That

said, Carson adds: "Albertine lies so much and so badly that Marcel is drawn into the game. He lies too . . . Who is bluffing whom is hard to say" (2014, p. 15).

145 *Freud famously admitted:* I'm here paraphrasing Simon May in *Love: A History* (New Haven: Yale University Press, 2011), p. 202: "Freud himself came to admit nearly complete confusion about what exactly his theory of libido was trying to say."

151 *"the beautiful wound from a distance"*: Xenophon, *Conversations of Socrates*, trans. Hugh Tredennick (London: Penguin Classics, 1990), pp. 211–12.

153 *"He quite forgot"*: Anton Chekhov, *The Portable Chekhov* (New York: Penguin, 1977), pp. 159–60.

159 *Males are more likely to find sexual partners:* Trivers, 2011, p. 97.

159 *"sincerity, kindness and strength of feeling"*: Ibid., p. 99.

160 *"within our genomes, deception flourishes"*: Ibid., p. 7.

165 *"Delusional conceptions are necessary"*: See Hans Vaihinger, *The Philosophy of "As If"* (New York: Martino Fine Books, 2009), p. 343. For Vaihinger, all our cognitive and emotional experience is a kind of more or less deliberate acceptance of illusion as a condition for existence. The great virtue of Nietzsche, he thinks, is that Nietzsche is one of the few philosophers who recognize that we can embrace illusion while acknowledging it as such. This view, also championed by Shakespeare, will be crucial for my analysis of marriage.

166 *"one lies well when one loves"*: Friedrich Nietzsche, *The Will to Power*, trans. Walter Kaufmann (New York: Vintage, 1968), p. 427.

177 *"marriage is itself the mystery"*: Stanley Cavell, "Mr. and Mrs. Smith," *Film Comment*, September–October 2005.

180 *"Proust's chauffeur"*: Anne Carson, *The Albertine Workout*, p. 6.

180 *"probing for a bullet in one's heart"*: Proust, *Remembrance of Things Past*, vol. 1, trans. C. K. Moncrieff and Terence Kilmartin (New York: Random House, 1981), p. 507.

185 *"invisible as all night"*: Honor Moore, *Red Shoes* (New York: Norton, 2006), p. 32.

187 *Like Plato's* Symposium: This suggestion was first made to me by Michael Silverblatt, the fascinating host of the now legendary book radio show *Bookworm*.

188 *"There was love there, Mel"*: Raymond Carver, *What We Talk About When We Talk About Love* (New York: Vintage, 1989), p. 161. I have not noted the other quotations from the story, as my discussion of it ranges throughout the story.

197 *I tried the quiz:* Neither I nor my friend can recall precisely where he found this quiz. But in looking around the Internet, I've found that it seems to be a fairly typical list of questions for diagnosing sociopaths.

5. Marriage

209 *something unique happens:* M. Regev, U. Honey, and U. Hasson (2013), "Modality-selective and Modality-invariant Neural Responses to Spoken and Written Narratives," *Journal of Neuroscience* 33(40): 15978–88.

212 *"deceiving a husband":* C. S. Lewis, *The Four Loves* (London: Mariner Books, 1971), p. 92.

213 *"each lie is a brick in a wall":* Mary Karr, *Lit* (New York: HarperCollins, 2010), p. 174.

217 *"Addicts' impaired cognition":* David Sheff, *Clean* (New York: Mariner, 2014), p. 99.

217 *lying to my wife that I was sober:* The connection between love and booze and the similarities between the lover and the drunkard are venerable. Cf. Xenophon: "I see, too, that those who are given up to a fondness for drinking, and those who have fallen in love, are less able to attend to what they ought to do, and to refrain from what they ought not to do; for many, who can be frugal in their expenses before they fall in love, are, after falling in love, unable to continue so; and, when they have exhausted their resources, they no longer abstain from means of gain from which they previously shrunk as thinking them dishonorable" (1990, p. 22).

220 *"smash the vodka bottle":* Anton Chekhov, *Letters of Anton Chekhov to His Family and Friends* (London: Macmillan, 1920), p. 54.

229 *"Deception and faithlessness":* Eric Schwitzgebel, "Thoughts on Conjugal Love," *Fidelo Leonore* (Philadelphia: Philadelphia Opera Company, 2006).

232 *enduring romantic love:* I particularly enjoyed Laura Kipnis's *Against Love.* Cf., from her chapter "Domestic Gulags": "Love is both intoxicating and delusional, but in the end, toxic: an extended exercise in self-deception. It may not have started out that way, though usually it did . . . a naiveté to which any of us might fall prey and probably have. But still, how could you not see what was happening under your own roof?"(New York: Vintage, 2009), p. 99. Kipnis assumes that self-deception is always a bad thing, and that is what sends her account

astray: without self-deception, none of us could even get out of bed in the morning, much less fall in love, marry, have children, become writers. Truth has never been the point of all this: Where and how in being human are you ever going to enjoy a life that cultivates nothing but truth?

233 *the hard work of keeping:* Carol Tavris and Elliot Aronson, *Mistakes Were Made (But Not by Me)* (New York: Mariner, 2008). See chapter 6, "Love's Assassin: Self-justification in Marriage," p. 158 and following.

234 *"No one would sign it":* L. J. Weitzman, "The Economics of Divorce: Social and Economic Consequences of Property, Alimony, and Child Support Awards," *UCLA Law Review* 28, (1980–81): 1181–97.

234 *"divine soundness of marital love":* The great treatment of marriage in the philosophical literature is the second volume of Søren Kierkegaard's youthful masterpiece *Either/Or,* trans. Howard V. Hong and Edna H. Hong (Princeton: Princeton University Press, 1987). Here a married character named Judge William writes letters to a young "aesthete" about the aesthetic and ethical nature of marriage. The view articulated there is that in marriage the married person sees "the universal" in the spouse, so that the marriage can be "the absolute": marriage is an expression of ethical existence, and the love of one's spouse rests on the secure foundation of seeing "the good" (ethically speaking) in that person. The view is similar to what Diotima describes to Socrates when she speaks of the transition from loving one and then another person—the early stages of erotic love—to recognizing that all people one might love have something in common, what is lovable in them (which is how, on Diotima's account, we also come to eventually love law, justice, and, ultimately, truth). It is a familiar, traditional, albeit unusually clever and splendidly argued defense of marriage. Marriage "sees the relationship as the absolute and does not take the differences as guarantees but understands them as tasks" (*Either/Or,* vol. 2 [1987], p. 305). The fact that Kierkegaard puts the entire defense of marriage in the mouth of a judge should not go unnoticed; his defense of marriage contains within it the aroma of a critique: a judge is neither the most romantic nor the most loving character type. Kierkegaard himself never married. The passage I quote in the text is from *Either/Or,* vol. 2, p. 119.

237 *best meditations on love and deception:* First called to my attention—in this context—by Harry Frankfurt's short book *On Truth* (New York: Oxford University Press, 2006).

240 *"overrate each other"*: Trivers, 2011, p. 109. In words to the wise, he adds: "when the ratio of positive to negative acts toward the partner drops below 5:1, the marriage is in trouble."

240 *"masquerading as a promise"*: Phillips, 2011, p. 58.

241 *"When it comes, it comes"*: As taught by Dzongsar Rinpoche in Bir, India, on August 5, 2012.

242 *"catching me in a series of lies"*: Trivers, 2011, p. 98.

243 *"refining the truths"*: Rich, 2012, p. 194.

244 *"moral talent essential to the intimacy of marriage"*: Cavell, 2005, p. 111.

Acknowledgments

This book was begun at the University of Missouri in Kansas City, continued at the Kungri Monastery in the Pin Valley, India, mostly written in the Dey House Library at the University of Iowa, and completed at the Chateau Marmont in Los Angeles. My thanks to the people who helped me at those places and to the Guggenheim Foundation, which funded some of the work, and to the University of Missouri Research Board, which also funded some of the work.

In alphabetical order, the people who have helped me with this book include: Soumeya Bendimerad, Bruce Bubacz, Rocco Castoro, Peter Cooper, the late Arthur Danto, Gabriella Doob, Hank Frankel, Lars Gustafsson, R. J. Hankinson, Kathleen M. Higgins, Krista Ingebretson, Jameela Lang, the late Louis H. Mackey, C.D.C. Reeve, Daniel Reynoso, Peng Shepherd, Michael Silverblatt, the late Robert C. Solomon, Lorin Stein, Emily Stokes, Alan Strudler, Jean Tamarin, Karen Vorst, and Diane Williams. Special thanks go to my brothers, Darren and Patrick, to Wayne Vaught, to my patient and thoughtful editor, Eric Chinski, and to my generous and brilliant agent, Susan Golomb. My loving gratitude, above all, to my miraculous daughters, Zelly, Margaret, and Portia, and to the four kindest people I know: Victoria Moody, Alicia Martin, Rebecca Martin, and my wife, Amie Barrodale.

Clancy Martin is the author of the novel *How to Sell* (FSG, 2009) as well as many books on philosophy, and he has translated works by Friedrich Nietzsche, Søren Kierkegaard, and other philosophers. A Guggenheim Fellow, he is a contributing editor at *Harper's Magazine* and also writes for *The New York Times*, the *London Review of Books*, *The Wall Street Journal*, *The Atlantic*, and many other publications. He is a philosophy professor at the University of Missouri in Kansas City, where he lives with his wife, the writer Amie Barrodale, and three daughters.